WIDOWHOOD

The Death of a Spouse

Reflections on Death and Dying
Plus Nine Interviews
With People Who Lost a Spouse

Michael Rock, Ed.D.
with Janice Rock, M.A.

Cover picture of "Otter Lake" by Ross Rock, B.A.Sc., M.A.Sc., P.Eng.

Note for Librarians: a cataloguing record for this book that includes Dewey Decimal Classification and US Library of Congress numbers is available from the Library and Archives of Canada. The complete cataloguing record can be obtained from their online database at:
www.collectionscanada.ca/amicus/index-e.html
ISBN 1-4120-2452-8
Printed in Victoria, BC, Canada

TRAFFORD

Offices in Canada, USA, Ireland, UK and Spain
This book was published on-demand in cooperation with Trafford Publishing. On-demand publishing is a unique process and service of making a book available for retail sale to the public taking advantage of on-demand manufacturing and Internet marketing. On-demand publishing includes promotions, retail sales, manufacturing, order fulfilment, accounting and collecting royalties on behalf of the author.
Book sales for North America and international:
Trafford Publishing, 6E–2333 Government St.,
Victoria, BC v8t 4p4 CANADA
phone 250 383 6864 (toll-free 1 888 232 4444)
fax 250 383 6804; email to orders@trafford.com
Book sales in Europe:
Trafford Publishing (uk) Ltd., Enterprise House, Wistaston Road Business Centre,
Wistaston Road, Crewe, Cheshire cw2 7rp UNITED KINGDOM
phone 01270 251 396 (local rate 0845 230 9601)
facsimile 01270 254 983; orders.uk@trafford.com
Order online at:
www.trafford.com/robots/04-0280.html

10 9 8 7 6 5 4 3 2

TABLE OF CONTENTS

THE INTERVIEWS

Dedicated to

Marjorie Lait

and

Connie Fermo

Two very special women

"We are the only species whose fate is not simply a mute fact of our existence but a painful problem whose meaning we attempt to understand."

-- Michael Ignatieff. *The Needs Of Strangers.*
New York: Picador, 2001, 160 pages. ISBN: 0312281803

ACKNOWLEDGEMENTS

There are many people to thank for a book such as this. We are first of all indebted to the people in the chapters who gave of their time to recount their stories. In some cases, telling the story again was very painful. We have tried to capture some of this genuine feeling in the commentary at the end of each story. Telling our story is essential for healing. We all have a story to tell and, as you will read in this book, each story is unique and insightful.

Chapter 1 states: "Death contains me as my skin contains me. Without it, I am not what I am. Death is not a sinister door I walk towards; it is my walking towards." Every person 'walks towards' one day.

The stories you will read, therefore, are, in that sense, timeless. Grief, sorrow, sadness and mourning we have with us as earthly companions. That's not all, thank God. We also have hope, healing, and the possibility of happiness.

We thank also the many authors whom we have consulted. Your research and sensitivity to the dying was extremely uplifting. We trust that we have done you justice in referencing you.

We owe Sue and Gerry Mullin of Unionville, Ontario, a great deal because of their kind editorial comments and corrections, and to Betty McLintock (formerly of Seneca College, Toronto, Canada) who typed some of the manuscript.

We thank also our two colleagues, Bruce Bonaney and Mike Hopkins, for their constant encouragement and their generous sense of teamwork.

Janice: I am forever thankful to Michael for his encouragement of my work and creative development. He is a continuous catalyst for me in my efforts to write and to express my deepest thoughts and feelings. Thank you for honouring my work, Michael.

Michael: Janice, thank you for assisting me with the interviews, for your careful editing comments, but most especially for your kindness and encouragement to me throughout the project. You are wonderful at sensing "everything in its own time" — to everything there is a season. This was very helpful when I felt I "should" be doing more work to get the book completed than I had time. I learned a little more about patience, and waiting for birth to happen: of children, of ideas, of books, of life. Thank you, Janice.

Janice Rock, M.A.
Michael Rock, Ed.D.
September 1, 2004

"Our father was charming, self-educated and clever. As he struggled with his illness, we sought to give him the comfort, sense of security and dedication he had given us. As his sun was setting, he continued to educate us with his courageous battle. His legacy to use is a wellspring of fortitude, a hope with no boundaries, as we set out on a course without him."

— Theresa Tedesco, "He Was the Richest Man We Knew," *National Post*, Saturday, February 6, 2004, S7.

PREFACE

If you are widowed this book is for you. You know what it is like when a husband or wife dies. Death has occurred. Now there is no more. It is over; there is no more future with that spouse. Gone. Dead. Nothing, Stillness. Silence.

A death of a spouse confronts us with what we truly believe about ourselves and what is most fundamental about living and dying. A death of a spouse forces us to examine our attitude to fundamental issues.

Our attitude is like a navigational system. How we look at life — and death — is basic to how we feel about life and death. We become that which we love and we become that which we hate.

A death brings us face to face with that stark reality.

Experience shows that we die as we have lived. Stress, then, is a good barometer of how well we manage our feelings. We will probably live our dying and death in the same way we have lived other times of stress in our lives. We would do well now to examine how we do live and behave in times of stress.

What really matters, therefore, is our own personal maturity, our attitude to life, our acceptance of who we are and where we are in life.

What matters to a dying person is not the content of his/her faith or belief system, but rather the *comfort* that faith or philosophy gives him/her. In other words, the value of one's philosophy of life and death far outweighs any other factor.

When your spouse died all of these issues surfaced inside you. In a strange sort of way your spouse's death raised the question of the quality of life for you. You began to ask yourself questions, such as: what am I supposed to do now? what is my life all about? where is life taking me?

These are profound questions. These are the basic questions related to your wholeness, to your individuality. To be your unique self is your primary purpose in life. To fail that task is to fail it all. All other measuring sticks pale in comparison. The full development of yourself is the major goal in your life.

How you went about becoming yourself, as God meant you to be, is found in the details of each of our lives. We don't become ourselves irrespective of our relationship to God. We co-operate with this sacred intuition of a "Master Plan," as Marjorie would say in her story (chapter 6), but we must co-operate or we live out our destiny, as Dr. Carl Jung would say, "as pigs to the slaughter." Most of us, like the ancient Israelites, go that route at least once in our lifetimes. For the ancient Jews, it was the "fleshpots of Egypt" that imprisoned them; it was looking back, and even though it was a horrible vision of their experience in slavery, it seemed better than the unknown that lay ahead of them with Moses.

We are no different today. Today we have addictions and psychological disturbances. Just different 'fleshpots.'

Perhaps the greatest prayer of all is "Happy the person who follows in the way of the Lord and fulfills the mandate to become all that he/she was meant to be" because that is the way to health, wholeness, and happiness. It is for you; it is for me; it is for all of us.

INTRODUCTION

T his book is about those who are left after a spouse dies. Death has occurred. The one dead had been a living spouse: husband or wife. Now there is no more. It is over; there is no more future with that spouse. Gone. Dead. Nothing. Stillness. Silence.

PERSONAL REFLECTIONS

Like other people, each of us has thought of death, and like other people, each of us has thought specifically of our own death. Death, from all accounts, is part of life. Spiritual writer and contemplative, Kelly Nemeck, describes the process this way: *we live death* by going *into* death, going *through* death, and going *out of* death into the resurrection and eternity. We always see ourselves *in relation* to our dying; ego is involved. But we only live the dying process once — when it is our time to die.

Two ideas stuck out as we did the research for this book: (1) *We die as we have lived.* (2) What is important in the process of dying is *whether any belief system we have can comfort us*! A person can be agnostic, atheistic, or formally religious. The only thing that matters is the comfort one derives from their philosophy of life, religion or creed.[1] These two ideas gave us much to ponder.

Someone once said that before the age of 20 we have the face that God gave us; between 20 and 40 years of age, we have the face we choose to show to the world (i.e., our persona, or face mask, what we want the world to see and believe about us); and after 40, we have the face we deserve! We have never forgotten those words. One author puts it this way, "In older people, youth is more a matter of attitude than appearance."[2]

Our experience has also shown us that this metaphor (of the "face") could just as well be extended to one's whole body. In many ways our bodies tell us who we are. Have you ever noticed how a person walks, or holds him/herself? The body conveys powerful messages just as Freud pointed out in regards to when we are talking and our fingers are moving (unknown to us): our fingers do the talking even though we are not verbally saying anything.[3]

Researchers show the same analogy in dying: because death is a stressful event, we will probably live our dying and death as we have lived other "dark periods"[4] or times of stress in our lives. We would do well *now*, therefore, to examine how we *do* live and behave in times of stress. Perhaps we can, little by little, take a more positive or mature approach to our situations, and, in this way, learn to cope and manage the dark moments more effectively, so that when death approaches, we can live it fully and authentically.

"One dies as one has lived in the terrible moments of one's life," says Dr. Edwin Shneidman.[5] He says that this is so because "there are certain deep consistencies in all human beings. An individual lives characteristically as he or she has lived in the past; and dying is living."[6]

In other words, we are our history, especially our personal psychological and spiritual history. For those of you who may be saying, "Why bring up the idea of 'spiritual'?" You may be saying to yourself, "I'm not spiritual; I'm just me!" or, "I'm an atheist!" let us point out that you and I have no choice in being spiritual. *Spirituality is life*. In an interview Matthew Fox, Ph.D. said,

> I wish there weren't such a big difference between religion and spirituality, but people have to be very clear about the difference, and not simply settle for religion. Spirituality is about experience, and religion, unfortunately, ends up being about the sociology of the structures ... Spirituality is connecting to the source of things, to the source of wonder and awe and pain and suffering and creativity and justice and compassion. Religion ought to be about that but unfortunately it wanders off the path. (*Source:* http://www.levity.com/mavericks/fox.htm)

We all have a philosophy of life! In all fairness, of course, saying that "we die as we have lived" is more obvious in relation to those who are dying (over a period of time) with a disease such as cancer. Again, how one copes with life's demands and whether one avoids issues or confronts them surfaces in a heightened manner when one is in a crisis. The Chinese say that stress is both danger and opportunity. It brings out the best and/or the worst in each of us. How we cope, then,

> does appear to be influence(d) the most during the terminal illness. The uniform trend was for those who had previously coped well to be less depressed, anxious or irritable and to show less social withdrawal. This was one of the more consistent significant findings in the whole study ... Past difficulties in coping also increased the likelihood of current depression and anxiety ... There is support for the frequent impression that a patient's previous manner of living influences the way he dies.[7]

In the "short strokes," therefore, what really matters is our own personal maturity, our attitude towards life, our acceptance of who we are and where we are in life, and especially now, our acceptance of *how* we are on our human journey in our dying.

What matters is the comfort that our philosophy of life provides for us.

All of us have some kind of a philosophy of living, be it a formal religious creed, a belief system, a value system, or a way to live life. Each of us has some kind of a philosophy because not to have one is not to be alive! Even the insane have a philosophy. It may appear chaotic and counterproductive to us, but it is their way of making sense of their lives.

FUNAMENTALLY "SEEKERS OF MEANING"

Each of us has a philosophy of life, a belief system of some sorts, a conviction about life, one way or another; and this is what makes us intrinsically 'religious' and 'spiritual.' To have any meaning in life at all — and that's the one thing, xiv | Widowhood: The Death of a Spouse

reality, we all desperately look for — we must have some conviction or stance on life's fundamentals: where did we come from, where and what are we now, and where are we going? Not to wrestle with these questions is to become passive in the face of life; and even here, there is a choice -- or a stance, or a conviction -- to remain passive and allow life to happen to oneself.

DEATH: CONTENT AND COMFORT

In the process of dying, therefore, our convictions, our belief/value systems, our creeds, and our philosophies of living are tested, not for their *content*, but for their *comfort*. When the "11th hour" is upon us, will the convictions about life, loving, people, and ultimate value, that seemed so secure in the daylight of our living, give us comfort and reassurance now that we are facing what seems to be the darkest moment on life's journey — the journey into death? Will our noonday convictions uphold us, and give us a personal feeling of support now that midnight is approaching? *What* or *who* matters most to us will matter now! What lies deep in our hearts is 'the stuff of dying.' None of us escapes that reality. It's where our hearts are that matters most.[8]

What we value gives reassurance, comfort, and security. So, in spite of all the platitudes we may have mouthed during our lifetime, or the sermons we have given or heard, or the books we have read (or written!), it's what's in our hearts that counts, what we really and truly hold onto about life.

CRISIS EXPOSES OUR CORE. Who are we? Who do we believe in? Why do we believe the way we do? Is the universe personal? Will the universe ultimately support us? Are we totally all alone? Or are we held and sustained by a personal universe? These are important questions. As we live our dying, these are the *only* questions! Our comfort with them will be our comfort in dying.

LIVING: CALL TO INDIVIDUALITY

The meaning of life and a new lifestyle is the crux of the whole matter for the remaining spouse. When the death of a spouse occurs, the remaining spouse's personal skills and philosophy of life are dramatically called into question, and will be more so after the funeral despite the mourning, if he/she is to continue to live a productive and satisfying life in the years ahead. To grow and develop as a person is not now an option. Perhaps for the first time the remaining spouse is asked to "grow up," become the unique person he/she is meant to be, become an individual.

No matter how we view it, *individuation* — our calling to be our unique selves, our call to wholeness -- is the primary call for each of us in life. Each of us is called to be the individual he/she is meant to be. Each of us is called to wholeness. If we fail that, we have failed it all. All other measuring sticks pale in comparison. The full development of oneself is the **true** goal and if lived authentically brings us into adoration and union with the ultimate one, God.

Self-authenticity is its own measuring stick; it is the **only** one. The death of a spouse often brings this reality into sharp relief. If to love others is an integral part of the formula, it cannot be done without loving one's self as well.

It is amazing how many times a widow/ widower will, "I now have time for me, for my world, for some of the things I want to do!" Death has forced this person to search for his/her own vocation. Too often a spouse "lives out of the psychological pocket" of the other, will not dare to make a decision, take a stance, voice an opinion, do something, without checking with the other, nay, oftentimes, getting the other's approval! And now the person, because of the spouse's death, has to make that decision alone, take that stance alone, voice that opinion alone, take that action alone — and there is no one to check with!

And yet, the irony of it all is that the initial point for the journey together in marriage was so that each person would truly blossom into a full personality, not become an obedient mirror for the other! And the other ironic fact is that when there is a marriage where both people are "close, but not too close," to use Kahil Gibran's phrase, sometimes neighbours and friends -- who may often be "in-laws" as well as "outlaws" — complain bitterly because "he goes away and just leaves her all alone with the kids!" or "she's off 'doing her thing' once again!" when, in fact, one or both parties do(es) take alone time to rejuvenate, to write, to have some "soul-time," and both know how much better they are for it. Too many marriage relationships have too much of an unhealthy symbiosis — or dependency — of one spouse on to the other such that if one party goes away, or, in our case, dies, the other is left feeling totally helpless.

The immature person, in an "effort to overcompensate for feelings of personal inadequacy overinvests . . . emotions in supportive relationships with others, and is thus more vulnerable emotionally to the loss of his live object. More of his projected self is involved in the loss."[9] A massive, psychological regression to earlier, immature, ways of acting sets in. If this dependency problem is not managed by the remaining spouse, he/she will go out and find someone else to complement this dependency (as in the first marriage), or develop a personality that is withdrawn from the "living" of life.

Some spouses do recognize the unhealthy parts of their former dependency in the relationship (marriage) and seek ways now to develop themselves into more self-sustaining, assertive individuals. These same widowed spouses find that this is perhaps the first time that they can do what *they* want to do, come and go when *they* want to come and go.

In short, they feel as though they can finally breathe again. And for many this *is* the first time they are standing on their own feet and able to breathe on their own. It's a new feeling, and they feel great! This is so because they are experiencing themselves as alive, as growing human beings, often for the first time; they are experiencing themselves as mystery!

UNIQUENESS AND HUMANNESS

We are more than ever convinced that unless we truly live *our own* lives (and not only live as others, i.e., parents, spouses, society want us to live) we have failed at life's fundamental request: be and live yourself. If uniqueness is one of the traits which makes us human, then it behooves each of us to search our consciences every so often in order to make sure that we are in touch with ourselves, so that in the experience of dying, we may be most comfortably in touch with our deepest selves, and in the final moment, "most" in love with 'totally Other forever.'

CHAPTER ONE

THE EXPERIENCE OF LIVING

Each of us wants to live. The more absolute death becomes, the more intense life also becomes. Each of us yearns for more and more life, so much so that we have a built-in psychic defense, called denial, to guard us against total disintegration. We don't ever want to feel that we're falling into darkness, into nothingness, into that place of no return. Yet, we cannot avoid death. "Death contains me as my skin contains me. Without it, I am not what I am. Death is not a sinister door I walk towards; it is my walking towards."[1]

In this sense, then, "dying is living."[2] We live into our dying; dying is the final experience of our living. We live *into* death, *through* death, and *out of* death into eternity.[3] Some people, on a deep unconscious level, know that they are going to die, and set about getting their affairs in order. But

> no one can really ever 'know' that he/she is about to die. There is always the intermittent presence of denial. The recurrent denial of death during the dying process seems to be the manifestation of the therapeutic gyroscope of the psyche.[4]

In other words, we desperately search for life, even in our dying.

WOUNDED BONDS

The backdrop we have to the bereavement we experience in the death of a spouse is the tenaciousness of the human bonds we have made while in living relationship with the now deceased spouse. From this perspective this book could easily have been titled *Wounded Bonds*. All through our life with our spouse we have built up human bonds, human points of interaction, memories, meanings; and now with the death of our spouse, there is this dreadful feeling of emptiness! Now we are alone, 'the bonds' broken and wounded.

The word *wounded* is very deliberate. The bonds are also broken, broken to bits! But while the bonds are experienced as broken to bits on a personal level, on a far deeper level, the bonds are really only wounded. This wound of widowhood can serve to poison the living spouse, or it can be the catalyst for further growth. If the latter occurs, the deeply healing encounter with the wounded healer occurs. Like Parsifal, the wound can spur the living spouse on to deeper levels of meaning, to deeper currents of living where "the heart has reasons that the head knows nothing of" (Pascal). While very painful, the wound can also bring healing and hope ... eventually.

Dying is a *faith* experience. It calls forth in each of us the deepest act of faith/ belief in ourselves, in life, and in ultimate reality. We don't ask the questions in the experience of death; death asks us; and we realize that we had better have *some* answer to this reality of death, for we cannot withstand a vacuum for our personal meaning.

Henry Margenau, a Yale physicist, said that the difference between ourselves and the mystic is that "the mystic is able to peek through the keyhole of reality and see the truth."[5] The British philosopher, L.P. Jacks, puts this notion in a slightly different way: "Spirit is matter seen in a stronger light." Likewise, for the famous psychologist, J. B. Rhine, "it had become clear ... that the so-called audacious assumptions of spiritual beings throughout history were, in truth, based on valid assumptions about the nature of ultimate reality and man's relationship to it."[6]

For Rhine, therefore, ultimate reality undergirds a person's living. He believes that faith really is the most dynamic quality that will sustain us when we lose a spouse. In fact, he writes, "The life-perception of the God-conscious being far surpasses the biology of the death-event" and that the experience of death can be perceived "as incidental to the rest of life."[7]

The death of a spouse wounds deeply. No longer can the normal be upheld. A finality has set in; a rupture has occurred; human bonds have been shattered; loss is everywhere. Listen as we hear Peter, age 30, talk of his wife, Ellen, who died when she was only 28. He says that his whole being ached for her, that he wanted her back and could think of nothing else: "Every minute I thought she'd come through the door again -- that lilt in her walk. Again and again I'd hear her voice, see her in the crowd. Each time I thought of her it was like a knife in my heart."[8]

LIVING IN DYING AND DEATH

We live our dying *and* death because "death is my final act."[9] How many of us see dying and death in such a positive light? I think many of us see death as something that happens to us, and that it's off in time someplace, somewhere. But how many of us have really taken the time to see dying and death as part of the very experience of our living? As previously indicated, we live *into* death, we live *through* death, and we live *out of death* into eternity.

German existentialist philosopher, Martin Heidegger, has written that death confers upon each of us our own individuality. We die alone; we grace ourselves in our own dying and death. No one can die for us. There can be no substitute for our personal dying and death. All of life, in one way or another, seems lived with this unavoidable reality somewhere in the back of our minds. *No one can die for us; we do it alone.* Heidegger goes even further and says that to even shut out our awareness of death is to live inauthentically and to deny our own individuality! To be authentic means embracing our own death.[10]

THOUGHTS ON DYING

If most of us were honest with ourselves we would have to say we more or less fear death. We know what our experience of living is, but we don't know what death's encounter is because we haven't experienced it. All we know is that we are afraid, as one author puts it, "to lose consciousness permanently."[11]

In 42 B.C.E., Publicius Syrus said that "the fear of death is more to be dreaded than death itself."[12] For Seneca, the Stoic, death was a time to leave life's banquet and "retire gracefully at the appointed time."[13] However it is viewed though, our own personal deaths are the end of everything for ys or in our experience.[14]

Fear of death pushes us to try to escape death. In one of the English Francis Bacon's sayings, there is a rather apropos anecdote for us here:

> One was saying that his great-grandfather and grandfather, and father, died at sea. Said another, that had heard him, "And I were as you, I would never come at sea." "Why?'" saith he, "where did your great-grand-father, and grandfather, and father die?" He answered, "Where, but in their beds?" He answered, "And I were as you, I would never come to bed."[15]

OUR SHORT PERSONAL HISTORY

Our experience of living indicates to us that time passes very quickly: here today, gone tomorrow. Robert Francoeur, the philosopher, wrote about the history of mankind as consisting of one calendar year, in an introduction to Pierre Teilhard de Chardin's *The Appearance of Man*. Francoeur set up his calendar so that each day of the year consisted of 4,000 years.[16] (This history is found in Table 1 on page 5.)

IMPORTANCE OF ATTITUDE

We can see from the portrayal in Table 1 that our experience of living is very immediate to us, that is, it is very recent when seen through the perspective of 1 day = 4,000 years. Giventhat our development of consciousness or self-awareness really appears only on the last day of our hypothetical year, it is little wonder that we are reluctant to give it up to death. It seems as though humankind's hard won battle for consciousness is just only attained when it is snuffed out in death. Each of us is very close, when we come to think of it, to our ancestral heritage, using the metaphor of our hypothetical year. Indeed,

AGE	ACTIVITY
January 1	One and one-half million years ago, the first of our primitive anscestors
January	Evolution of tools, speech
Summer	Same progress as above, slow and tedious
November 1	First appearance of the Neanderthal person
December 17	First indication that our Neanderthal ancestors held any form of religious beliefs (as seen from their burial sites)
December 28	Beginning of farming and agriculture
December 29-30	The whole of our historical era, that is, our civilization
December 31	• 9:00 am, birth of Socrates, Plato, Aristotle • 12:00 noon, birth of Christ • 9:30 pm, birth of Christopher Columbus • 11:00 pm, all of the 19th and 20th centuries to midnight

Table 1: 4,000 Years of History in One Year

our experience of living and consciousness is tenacious, and our fear of death primal. We have fought too hard to lose it in death. But we cannot be so apprehensive about the fact of death that we decide not to love at all in case our love is taken from us with our spouse's death. We must also make room emotionally for love in the context of life that holds death as a certainty as well.

Bonds must be broken; wounds must be absorbed. We don't understand the mystery of death, but we know we must surely come to grips with it and our own annihilation. All philosophy, therefore, is really various positions people have in relation to death. All the theories are useless if they neglect death. Death will not bargain with us; death will not be camouflaged, as much as modern North America wants to do that.[17]

Death stands on its own and demands *everything* from us, especially our attitude. Our attitude to death is an extension of our attitude to life. All dying is living, and all living is gradually bringing us closer to our own personal deaths. Living and dying — they are inseparable.

PEOPLE AND RELATIONSHIPS

To view the experience of living, it is necessary to keep in mind two things:

- the presence of people, and
- the presence of relationships.

In short, we are *relational* people; we are the *people of relationships*. All of contemporary science is telling us that relationship is the basis for life and living. Nothing exists except in relationship to everything else. We are ecological in that sense. We cannot escape being in relationship.

When people die, relationships are lost; hence our experience of living becomes wounded. Relationships help us to establish human bonds. Death severely wounds these bonds. They're never destroyed; broken, yes, wounded, yes, but never destroyed. The more intimate the relationship, obviously, the more intense the grief when the relationship is lost through death.

Why is this so? We all yearn for positive relationships even though we know that one day a relationship, as it is experienced in this life with the person, will be over. Relationships help us to meet many needs, such as:[18]

- Our need for *attachment*, that is, for security and a sense of emotional place;
- Our need for social *relatedness*, that is, a way to share concerns, or, a way to belong (as Abraham Maslow's need hierarchy indicates);
- Our need for *friendship*;
- Our need for nurturing and to be *needed*;
- Our need for *reassurance* of our worth and our competence as a person;

- Our need for *interdependence*, that is, to experience a sense of dependable assistance when we need it; and
- Our need for *guidance*, that is, for direction and help when needed, especially in stressful situations.

With so much investment in relationships, is it any wonder that our experience of living is wounded when a deep and close relationship of ours is no more? In addition there are some additional key elements to bear in mind that emerge when one studies the research on relationships. Death impacts on them all.

RELATIONSHIPS ...

■ Operate on many different levels (and hence, the impact of losing a spouse affects not only selected dimensions of the relationship, but the whole relationship experience).

■ Occur over time (and so the focus of a spouse also occurs over time simply because of the threaded nature of relationships).

■ Store experiences as symbols conceptually and as inner images in people and are lived out in people's actions.

■ Are a matrix of present and past symbolic experiences since they hold many memories and shared moments.

■ Influence our inner image of what a relationship is and are influenced as well.

Table 2: What Relationships Do

PSYCHOLOGICAL PROJECTION

The most intimate human relationship is that of attachment. We can see this between the infant and the mother. In many ways, we can say that close human relationships have this quality of 'attachment' as well. There is a bonding effect, in other words, between two people in a very close relationship.

Dr. Carl Jung, the eminent Swiss medical psychologist, wrote about the reality of projection in relationships. Falling in love, for example, is an experience in projecting: each partner projects his/her idealized partner on to the other person. The experience of *falling in love* means that there has been an adequate 'hook' for the projection to 'catch' onto for each party.

Life, however, does not sanction people to live an idealized life of projected images; therefore, the journey in the relationship must involve self-discovery and discovery of the realness of the other person. For this to occur, projection has to decrease. Hence, reality enters the picture. This is often heartrending for most people; the feeling that 'the honeymoon's over' has taken place.

Yet, for maturity to occur, this heartrending, or taking back of projections must happen. But it should not be forgotten that it is precisely in the *initial* experience of projecting that we reach out to the *other*, and so learn about ourselves. After this, little by little, for the relationship to become real and acquire depth, there needs to be a *recollection of the projections*. This occurs with mutual feedback and often through the experience of disillusionment in the relationship. It is why marriage is 'for better or for worse.' We need commitment to weather the 'recollection of projection storms' throughout the years. In this way, each individual becomes more real to him/herself and to others. Each person, in a genuine relationship, escapes the fate of being an idealized version of a person, for this idealization will only lead to pain and disillusion. Why? Because no one can be as perfect as the idealized projection would indicate or want. St. Augustine said it well in his *Confessions* (I, 1): "Our hearts are restless until they rest in thee, O God."

DEATH AND PROJECTIONS

Ironically, death is *the* final determiner of the breakdown of the projections. Death breaks up projections. For one thing, the person on whom the projection was placed is now dead, no more. The projection comes flying back in the spouse's face. Incidentally, the projection can be a positive or a negative one. When you read Connie's story in this book, you will recognize her struggle, both with positive and with negative projections.

This is what causes a lot of the pain and anguish at the time of the death of a spouse: forced recollection of projections. If most of the relationship was locked into projections (e.g., he, as father-figure, strong figure; she, as daddy's little girl, quiet, pleasing, obedient), when death occurs, the 'hook' is totally gone! And the person goes into paroxysms of pain. That is why it is so very important over the years that both parties, little by little, begin to re-collect their projections. This means that they just first become aware of them, have the courage to accept them, and the fortitude to take the burden(s) off their spouse's shoulders. Both parties will win because both parties will become more themselves, and experience more freedom.

DEATH IN LIFE

This chapter is called "The Experience of Living" and yet it is about death. Death is in life; death is in living life. Death is not some 'thing' that happens 'outside' us, outside of our experience of living. Death happens in our living of life. The purpose of experiencing and living life is to come to one's fullest as a human being. It is to come to one's core, come to the centre of one's self and say, "I am!" In that act of self-authenticity, an individual recognizes his/her total dependence on the Ultimate Other, whom some have called God, and in an act of worship, declare, "You are!" or rather, because God is, therefore, I am.

Death will be the great clarifier of this mystery for us. Death will bring us to our naked truth. Death will bring us into ourselves in the unique way that life has finally destined us. The world's great religions have all tried to provide an answer to the kind of uniqueness that awaits us, and it is this anticipation — call it heaven, nirvana, etc. — that pulls each of us into our futures and gives us ultimate hope.

To quote Heidegger again, awareness of death confers upon us a sense of our own individuality.[19] To experience life is also to experience death; and to experience death is to experience the goal of our human journey in the first place: total, self-awareness and individuality opening to an unlimited eternal future.

THOUGHTS TO PONDER

1. We die as we live since dying is part of our living. It is a unique crisis point and will take on patterns of other crisis points we have had in our experience of living. If we have dealt with crisis in living, we probably will be able to cope with the crisis of dying and death.

2. What comforts us in our dying and death process is the quality of our philosophy of life, of our belief system, and whether it can emotionally sustain us in this, our death, and our crucial crisis in our human journey.

3. The task of the human journey is individuation, or wholeness, i.e., the innate vocation that each of us has to become the person life has chosen us to be.

4. Death is the final arbiter. Each of us will be forced to stand on our own two feet in death and speak for ourselves only. No one can speak for us; we are on our own.

5. If there is an ideal for human living, it is to be and live yourself, live *your* life.

6. Each of us craves to live. Death is the unique moment in this human journey to full life.

7. The death of a spouse leaves wounded bonds for the remaining spouse. On one level, the existential, practical level, the human bonds are broken, shattered, gone. But on a far deeper level, the bonds, while they may be severely wounded because of death, are spiritually eternal. The crucible of faith withstands the destruction and evil of death. The wounded spouse can also be the wounded healer.

8. Death gives us our unique opportunity to be ourselves.

9. The history of humankind is very short, and this explains, in part, the reason for the immediacy of our experience of living. We haven't, as human beings, been that self-conscious of ourselves for that long a period of time to see death other than a very direct threat.

10. Death fractures relationships, or human bonds. We often become very attached to our relationships. A marriage involves a particular bonding. Death shatters that.

11. The more intimate the bonding the more intense the grief when the relationship is no more. The reason for this is that relationships help us to fulfill many needs and because relationships are so central to the quality of our experience of living.

12. In our human journey, and in our experiences of living, maturity develops when each spouse, little by little, takes back projections, or images, of how the other person/spouse *ought* to be, and begins to see the other as he/she really is. Death is the final destroyer of projections. The total recollection of projections is literally forced back on to the remaining spouse. At this point what matters is the personal growth and development that the remaining spouse has for they alone provide the spiritual and interior anchors of meaning and stability.

"Every minute I thought she'd come through the door again -- that lilt in her walk. Again and again I'd hear her voice, see her in the crowd. Each time I thought of her it was like a knife in my heart."

CHAPTER 2

THE REALITY OF DEATH

We are not very old when we begin to become aware of the reality of death. When we are children, we see it when animals die, or perhaps when a brother, sister or friend dies. While it is hard for a small child to conceive of the total finality of death, the child does know that things are not the same. Little by little, as we grow older, we see that there is no escape valve from death.

Death is integral to living. "The knowledge of its inevitability is incorporated into the psychological structure of each person, and it is accommodated in many different ways."[1] A cursory glance of how people have coped with death over the centuries shows that people developed different kinds of rituals and myths and magical beliefs.[2] Much of this, of course, was to ward off evil spirits and to try to control death. In the middle of twentieth century America, for instance, according to a report by Parsons,[3] three distinct orientations to the reality of death were evolving:

- An orientation based on hell-fire damnation and on fundamentalism;
- An orientation based on existential despair; and
- An orientation based on a "saccharine sentimentality" of positive thinking.[4]

On the one hand, it seems that, as a society, we want to deny the reality of death. T.V. commercials and advertising about youth give every evidence to that. And yet, there is a strange fascination with death, what Geoffrey Gorer calls "the pornography of death."[5] Perhaps we have even romanticized death.[6] But for most people, there is a healthy fear of death. Fear may result from the fear of impending nothingness, or pain, or loss, of the unknown, of being alone.

To manage this fear, to try and control it, people will deny it, repress it, intellectualize it, displace it onto someone/something else or project it.[7] "Out of his fear man builds many futures for himself. And most of these include some symbolic concepts of immortality."[8] We know this to be true by going back to prehistoric people and their burial sites. The myth of immortality lives in each of us, and however many deaths there may be, and whatever our particular reactions to these deaths, we know deep down that our own death is very individual; it is very personal and inevitable.[9]

WIDOWHOOD: THE BIBLICAL TRADITION

Death in the Bible

When we look at the Bible, we must recognize both the Hebrew Scriptures and the Christian scriptures. It is interesting to note that biblical writers did not concern themselves *per se* with a theology of death or of an afterlife.[10] The Bible concentrates almost exclusively on God's presence at work in his people. It was a "here-and-now" focus, e.g., feed the hungry, take care of the sick. For the most part, the Jewish concern was "with the People and its historical destiny."[11] Death, for many centuries was basically regarded as the termination of the human being. What mattered was the posterity of the tribe. Everything was oriented to the future generations and the offspring. Abraham's dying act was to provide for the continuation of his offspring.[12]

There was no concept then (2,000 B.C.E) to think in individual terms in the Hebrew Scriptures. Abraham and the clan were one; so was his personality. "Thus, one can only speak anachronistically of his death as an end since, even dead, Abraham continues to be an important aspect of the corporate personality."[13] It was said in the bible of Abraham's death that "he was gathered to his kin."[14]

"Hebrew thought never developed a notion of soul or life-force which is separable from the historical man."[15] It was after the fall of the Israelite Kingdoms and the period of the exiles that a different formulation of how the Jew saw his relationship to God emerged. Hardship brought refinement and an inkling of the concept of individuality. At this point in their history, without a home or nation, the Jews sought to understand their dependence on God. The Wisdom literature, especially the book of Daniel, begin to talk about "the future inbreaking of the divine realm upon the sphere of human life in order to save men."[16] Daniel dreamed that a "Son of Man" would come to save the people. It is also at this time that the theme of resurrection begins to appear. Daniel says that righteousness or virtue belong to eternity.[17] It is still a corporate focus: it is the People who will be redeemed and live forever. [But it is still the resurrection theme.]

When we turn to the New Testament, or Christian scriptures, we realize immediately that they are grounded in Jewish wisdom and traditions. In relation to death, though, Jesus always kept "a careful tension between present and future"[18]: the coming of the Kingdom (the future) and the importance of his work (present).

Yet, Jesus' emphasis is a here-and-now one: concentrate on what he [Jesus] is doing, and then go, do likewise. Jesus does not talk explicitly of death; it never really occurred to him to do that. Jesus always tried to show that the God of Moses was concerned about people's lives and the quality of their lives *here-and-now*. Forget about death. Sure, it will happen. But what are you doing *now* to make sure you are developing as a human being (love of self) and what are you doing for others so that they too can have a quality life (love of neighbour)? As far as Jesus was concerned, these two commandments summarized the whole law![19]

Love of neighbour and love of self. In loving this way, people would automatically be loving God, which was his initial message in the first place. Jesus was not trying to be glib here in the face of death. Indeed, "at the time of his crucifixion, there is abundant evidence in the Synoptic Gospels that Jesus showed both fear and terror in the face of suffering. Unlike Socrates, who faced death with triumphant composure, he took death as a terrible and serious thing."[20] His final appeal was to God's will.

Thus, Jesus was concerned with life, and the quality of living. This was a radical idea in those Roman times, where life was not worth a lot. Jesus proclaimed a new age where everything could be made new, where the number one priority was an individual's *life*. Jesus concentrated on *life*, not death: *life* now, and *life* in the coming Kingdom of God. Jesus may have been vague (to our standards) on many things, but *life* and the *quality of life* were uppermost in his mind.

The questions of death and resurrection — which eventually could not be avoided — were left to the early Christian community (and subsequent ages) to sort out, specifically Paul's commentary on the life and work of Jesus.[21] As far as Paul was concerned, death was evil; death destroyed; but in the destruction of the individual self, the intervention of God in Christ Jesus occurs, and it is because of Jesus' own resurrection and glorification that people now have the only hope there is of victory over death.[22] There will be resurrection for the People of God.

Widowhood in the Bible

If the above remarks give us some views of how the Scriptures viewed death, how do the Scriptures view *widowhood*? In the Hebrew Scriptures, widows were seen as poor:[23] death before old age was considered punishment for sin. It was little wonder then that widows were scorned.[24] Upon the death of her husband, a widow had two choices: (1) go to her husband's family, or (2) go back to her parents![25] Mind you, the Hebrew Scriptures did say, "Don't mistreat widows."[26] However, that piece of advice did not stop them from being mistreated, and being seen as orphans and defenceless aliens.[27]

One can see attitudes of over 2,000 years ago vis-à-vis the feminine in life. Obviously such a patriarchal culture did not place much significance on the female, save as a helpmate and bearer of children for the man. O.J. Baab points out that "hers was an unfortunate state ... As an object of public concern she is often linked with the orphans or fatherless."[28] In fact, for the Hebrew, "it was ... a disgrace to be a widow." Even the Hebrew word for "widow" — 'almanah' — "resembles the word meaning 'be mute', ... suggesting the muteness induced by disgraceful widowhood."[29] Jamieson's comment that "in actual practice the lot of the widow seems to have been a very hard one in Biblical times"[30] is indeed an understatement!

There was no such thing as an independent woman in ancient society. As a member of a family she was dependent either upon her father or her husband. Again, in another understatement, this time by the scripture scholar John L. McKenzie, he states, "The position of a widow could therefore be difficult."[31] All the protection the widow had was public compassion and any acts of charity or justice.[32] From a contemporary's point of view, her situation was so awful that even though "the Law considered a widow's oath as binding (Num. 30:9)" when it came to the husband, "In contrast a husband could cancel out his wife's vow."[33] Even though the scriptures talked about care and concern for the widow, the law was still broken, however.[34] Eventually, because of the obvious disregard for the welfare of the widow, "sympathetic regard for them comes to be viewed as a mark of true religion."[35] The law of Israel tried to treat her as "a privileged person",[36] and by that means sought to redress the balance for her.

Even though the role of the feminine had not increased, in terms of its perception at least, by the time of the New Testament, Jesus was very supportive of widows, and angrily accused the Scribes and Pharisees for leeching off of them.[37] Jesus did not want them to be taken advantage of just because of their state and lot in life. But even with that, as in the Hebrew Scriptures, they were still seen as poor, as indigent and as orphans. The early Christian community, however, took it as their responsibility to make sure that widows were looked after.[38] As in the Hebrew Scriptures, this care and concern for widows was an act of religion and an integral part of the Christian community, the "ecclesia." Concern and care for widows were marks of one's commitment to God and the People of God.

DEATH AND MYTHOLOGY

We have alluded to the fact that death has captured the imagination of people from the earliest of times. Primitive people had a religion for themselves. In other words, their world was not explainable only in materialistic terms. Many people today see their lives and death only through materialistic lenses. They are at a disadvantage because they don't have the rich metaphors that religion provides to view the dynamics of living and dying.

Primitives wove their religion "around ideas of chthonian fertility and the cycle life-death post-existence."[39] Death was looked upon "not so much as an ending of life but as a mere interruption, which is followed either by a reincarnation or a form of existence in another world."[40] Interestingly enough, "… in most traditional cultures, the advent of death is presented as an unfortunate accident that took place in the beginning."[41] For instance, says Eliade, "… among Australian tribes and in the Central Asiatic, Siberian, and North American mythologies, … mortality is introduced into the world by an adversary of the Creator." In other archaic societies, death is seen "as an absurd accident and/or as the consequence of a stupid choice made by the first ancestors."[42] Eliade points out the Indonesian myth of the stone and the banana: since the people did not want the stone (as a gift) lowered down to them from the heavens, God then lowered a banana. This they liked and enjoyed; but, alas, it was perishable; death and corruption had entered the world. We can see it juxtaposed in the diagram (Figure 1, p. 19).

Life and death, therefore, become very complementary! This is so in many archaic cultures, according to Eliade.[43] Since there was this belief in the on-goingness of life, death became a chance for the primitive to become creative, i.e., to "'create' the new identity of the deceased."[44] Thus evolved the notion that death was a second birth, or a new spiritual existence, or an initiation. A new mode of being was envisaged. Eliade talks about this phenomenon as "fact."[45] This "passing over" insight that the early primitives had then became a model for all meaningful changes in life: the death-resurrection theme.[46]

All of these mythological references point to one incontrovertible fact for Eliade: death transforms one "into a form of spirit, be it soul, ghost, ethereal body, or whatever."[47] Another way to say this is that "death accomplishes the passage from the sphere of the meaningless to the sphere of the meaningful."[48] Finally, in case the reader still doubts the viability of talking about archaic cultures and primitives when it comes to death, let us conclude with these cryptic words of Eliade who says that the problem of life after death and its orientations is an extremely complex one. "In the last analysis, we have to do with mythologies and religious concepts that, if they are not always independent of material uses and practices, are nevertheless autonomous as spiritual structures."[49]

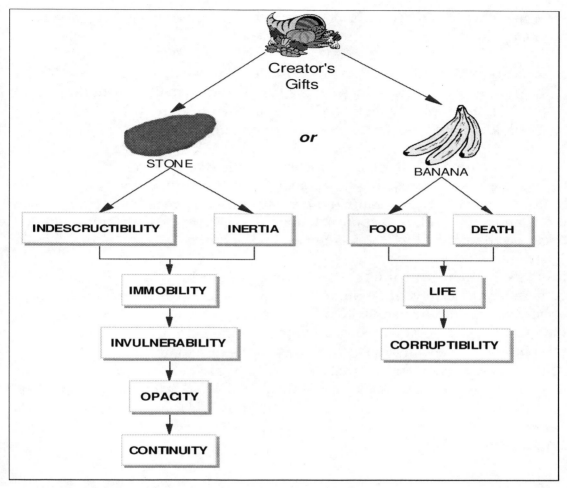

Figure 1: Creator's Gifts

PROBLEM OF DEATH IN THE MODERN WORLD

After the death of his wife, the English author, C.S. Lewis, wrote,

> I find it hard to take in what anyone says. Or perhaps, hard to
> want to take it in. It is so uninteresting. Yet I want the others to be
> about me. I dread the moments when the house is empty. If only
> they would talk to one another and not to me.[50]

How many widowed people have not felt what C.S. Lewis felt? Steve, a 58 year-old man, with no family, says it in his way:

> I went through a period of terrific loneliness when the doctors first told me — loneliness in the knowledge that all of a sudden you're completely dependent on your own resources. You're on that bottom line. It is no one else, just yourself.[51]

Much of the time our attention is focused on the dying person; but ironically, the widowed spouse also has a personal death: a finality to the human bonds built up over the years. Death, in other words, is very real, both to the person dying and to the widowed spouse. Rainer Maria Rilke, the poet, points out that "death is the side of life which is turned away from us."[52]

Rilke's comment brings us to the point at hand: how is death viewed by contemporary society? It is safe to say that generally speaking contemporary society wants nothing to do with talk or meditation on death. There is fear, fear that death "is the point where man in the most radical way becomes a question for himself."[53] Unconsciously, or consciously, in some circumstances, the contemporary person knows that death talks to us very "basically", i.e., at the root of who we are. Like the German theologian, Karl Rahner, we realize that "with death man's individual history finally ends."[54] Death concerns the whole person and is "an act which a [person] interiorly performs."[55] There is no avoiding this act.

Interiority deeply frightens contemporary people. It's always "go, go, go," and then some. Television, Bay Street (Toronto), and Fifth Avenue (New York) would have us believe that real living is "in the fast lane," "for people on the move," "for those who act now." The advent of the Internet and 'tech toys,' plus e-mail have more than speeded up life. The message is immediacy, action, speed, and alas, too often, superficiality. But death goes to the core. Someone once said, "You can't bluff death!"

If death, in general is difficult, it is doubly hard for the widowed because "unlike other cultures ... we in this nation refuse to anticipate widowhood as a normal transition in the life history of the family. Nor do we treat bereavement as part of our lot. We isolate the dying in hospitals and nursing homes and keep family members away from the event of death."[56]

In spite of the blessings of "scientific" medicine, it has also helped develop "the trend towards segregating the dying."[57] Robert Blauner talks about doctors suffering "psychic isolation"[58] because they shy away from the terminally ill. The biography of Elizabeth Kübler-Ross, the psychiatrist, is quite explicit on this matter when she was doing her seminars on death at the University of Chicago in the 1960s. Her doctor colleagues avoided her, were petrified of the topic, and put many roadblocks in her way.[59] The hospital becomes a "'mass reduction' system, undermining the subjecthood of its dying patients."[60] One physician, Dr. Melvin Krant, M.D., an internist, believes that the medical program needs to be turned around so that the physician learns to relate to patients of *all* ages and conditions, including the dying.[61] What we have in many hospitals is the result of a cultural climate from the late 19th century that stressed "rationalism, secularism, individualism, capitalism, and industrialization."[62] Scientific medicine grew out of this culture. Hence, today we have the values we experience when we visit or have to be in a hospital: "... innovation, bigness, success, efficiency, and productivity." Interestingly, says Manley,

> ... disease is defined in terms of physical and biomedical deviations from the norm; physicians are to be problem solvers skilled in ferreting out the causes and remedies of disease; patients are to be compliant raw materials for the enterprise of curing; and hospitals are to be places designed and organized for the specific purpose of controlling death.[63]

Earlier in her work, Dr. Anne Munley, a sociologist, makes a classic statement: "Technology cannot [however] substitute for love, tenderness, and compassion"[64] because it is beyond the power of technology to solve these essentially moral issues. People are not extensions of technology. And yet, by the same token, we know that too often individualism has replaced community, and science has replaced a sacred worldview. It is obvious that the more medical "breakthroughs" we experience, the more medicine may increase its "intense effort to cheat, delay, and conquer death,"[65] and the more also will dying people be segregated for they are evidence that death is always part of living.

In case the reader is asking how the "modern" way disregards the dignity of the dying, Dr. Munley points out at least four ways:[66]

- forcing a dying person's eyelids to close before death since it is more difficult to do so after!
- inserting dentures in a dying person's mouth (for the same reason as #1)!
- pre-wrapping portions of the body before death, so that there's just really "touch-ups" once the person has actually died!
- arranging for an autopsy or disposing of personal effects while the person is still living!

Speed. Efficiency. Assembly line! To take time with the dying would be to re-examine major assumptions about so-called "scientific medicine"! While we need to be grateful for the advances in modern technology, we must still keep in mind that technology was made for people, not people for technology! We have the Sabbath metaphor reversed in relation to the dying. Can you imagine how difficult it is for the spouse - who is already in deep pain for the dying partner - to see him/her be treated as an object, an extension of technology?

Dr. Munley's book, *The Hospice Alternative: A New Context for Death and Dying*,[67] is a beautiful book because she shows that dying does not have to be sterile or objectified. She points out that hospice "caregivers"[68] enhance the life of the dying patient during the remaining days according to "the body's dictates." This, for her, is dying within the moral order, and not for utility, expediency or efficiency. She points out that early people watched with the dying person and formed community to give protection and comfort. Up until the 20th century, and on up to World War II, death, at least in rural communities, was seen as natural, inevitable, and part of the community's experience. Today, however, people die in nursing homes or hospitals; a physician usually does not make house calls; the dying often die alone; old people are seen as burdens; children, now grown, wonder how to cope.

Dr. Munley also points out that dying, one of the crucial experiences of our life, is a social problem because individuals become alienated from society. If the dying are extensions of technology, they become objects, quantifiable, commodities. The quality of relationships is seriously jeopardized. If there was one thing that Jesus emphasized - as we saw earlier - it was the quality of our relationships. Physicians need to see themselves more as *healers* rather than as just *curers*. When someone is dying, both the patient *and* physician are partners in decision making. Munley points out a young dying nurse's comments: "Death may be routine to you, but it is new to me. You may not see me as unique, but I've never died before. To me, once is pretty unique."[69] We all need to face death more honestly and humanly.

At McMaster Medical School [Hamilton, Ontario, Canada], learning how to listen, how to deliver bad news and just be present in the room are a major part of "professional competency," a subject students study in their final year. One of the faculty members involved in teaching the new curriculum is Cathy Risdon, holder of the David Braley and Nancy Gordon chair in family medicine. "You can't just have a separate course in 'how to be a human being.' Those values have to permeate the whole curriculum. ... We want diligence, intelligence and knowledge, of course," said , "but we also want students with insight into themselves and a willingness to be self-aware and self-critical. It can't just be about stuffing people with information."

— *Slightly adapted from:* Marni Jackson, "Doctors + Patience," *Saturday Night*, September 2004, 34, 36.

THOUGHTS TO PONDER

1. People try to cope with the reality of death in many and various ways.

2. We are both afraid of death and attracted to it.

3. Death is not a major concern in the Bible. Rather, the emphasis, both in the Hebrew Scriptures and the New Testament, is on God's presence to people and God's works among people.

4. The big concern for the Jew in Hebrew times was for posterity, that life in the tribe and lineage in the clan would continue. Hence, there was a corporate focus.

5. Jesus, in the New Testament, was rather vague about death precisely because his main emphasis was on life, the quality of living, and the coming of the new order of living, i.e., the Kingdom of God.

6. Widows in the Hebrew Scriptures suffered a sorry lot, even though the Scriptures reminded people to care for widows.

7. It became a sign of religion in the Hebrew Scriptures to care for widows.

8. In the New Testament, care and concern for widows was an act of religion and an integral expression of the behaviour of people in the Community.

9. Different mythologies show us the interrelationship between life and death for primitives and people from archaic cultures.

10. For the primitive, death was a transformative experience.

11. Death in contemporary society is feared, ignored, and denied. The advent of modern scientific medicine, especially after the Second World War, only emphasized the atomized, materialistic aspects, such that a dying person became an object, and was seen as an extension of technology, much to the destruction of relationships and the dignity of the dying person.

12. Both the dying patient *and* the physician must be co-decision makers in the situation.

13. Death involves our deepest, most intense confrontation with our interiority. This frightens people today, because contemporary values are on speed, action, efficiency, and too often, superficiality.

14. The technological and clinical approach to the dying leaves out love, tenderness and compassion, essential moral issues and values.[70]

15. The hospice alternative offers the dying an environment to die within the moral order, and not for the sake of utility, expediency or efficiency.

16. Physicians must more and more see themselves as healers rather than just curers.

17. Each person's dying and death is unique. We need to honour that.

"I find it hard to take in what anyone says. Or perhaps to want to take it in. It is so uninteresting. Yet I want the others to be about me. I dread moments when the house is empty. If only they would talk to one another and not to me."

– C.S. Lewis

CHAPTER THREE

THE EXPERIENCE OF BEREAVEMENT

It is perfectly natural, then, to grieve at the losses that make one less than one used to be. And one is sometimes reduced to poignant wishes like: If only my stomach didn't hurt ... If only I could get up and walk across the room ... If only I could swallow ... If only...[1]

Although the above lines relate very directly to the dying person him/herself, the experience of pain and of loss bears just as directly on the remaining spouse. We could easily take the above lines as words spoken by any recent widow/widower. If we are to live any kind of a quality existence, we know that we must ponder two very important facts:

- a meaningful life is one that is crafted in relationship (and for many people this means having a spouse), and
- one day that relationship will cease because one of the spouses will die.

Hence, a major adult choice we must make in starting the grown-up part of our human journey is the decision to "become vulnerable to the exquisite agony of loss."[2] For the sake of the love of relationship, knowingly, lovingly, we deliberately choose life knowing that one day death and loss, pain and grief will also be our lot. We don't know the when or how for this, but one day we will experience this loss and grief; and we also know that the more we have loved, the more we have nurtured the relationship, the more poignant and "exquisite"[2] our agony of that loss will be. And yet we choose that path because it is better to have loved.

SENSE OF LOSS

The experience of loss is felt so personally, as we can see from one widower 's experience of it:

> The services were over. I was at the gravesite. I felt alone. Tears filled my eyes. I cried. For the second time I felt utter despair, and loneliness overwhelmed me. I was alone, surrounded by family, friends, loved ones. Each of us was alone in personal grief.[3]

Loss. Being alone in company, even with loved ones. One is alone with one's grief and abandonment. "Loss seems to produce not only deep and lasting sorrow but also disorientation, a failure of trusted meanings."[4] Researchers have astutely pointed out here that for the widow, in her time of loss, the real danger is not so much the loss, great and intense as that may be, "but rather an inability thereafter to summon her capacities to reorganize her life in a way she finds satisfactory."[5] We are back to the point referred to in an earlier chapter: that our true mettle is often tested when we're in a crisis and we either rise to the occasion or fail the test.

It is critical that throughout the years of the relationship, both spouses learn to be faithful to themselves individually, as well as to their partnership. Individual fidelity means that I'm in touch with how I feel about an issue, and make my truth appropriately present in the relationship. Individual fidelity means knowing what I want and don't want, and acting accordingly, appropriately and within the context and ambience of the relationship. This often means taking the risk of "disappointing" the other spouse; and it definitely means not living out of the psychological pocket of each other. There is closeness in the relationship, and there is also distance: to thine own self be true, and that's especially apropos in a spousal relationship. Otherwise, each spouse comes to neurotically depend upon the other, both living juxtaposed to each other instead of each standing tall, and coming to each other as two unique individuals, not just leaning posts!

Whether a couple chooses to live their truth in their relationship, or simply be a "yes-person" or mirror image for the other, is each couple's choice; however, in times of crisis — and the death of a spouse is a most severe crisis — the strength of one's own truth is what is going to carry the day, for one will be utterly alone, and comfort will not come from the fact that there was a relationship, but rather from the quality and strength of one's individual maturity in self-knowledge and truth that the spouse brought to the relationship. Otherwise, if one has not lived one's truth in the relationship over the years, there will be an enormous emotional vacuum at the moment of the death of one's spouse. "Deep emotional forces [will be] set at work. Old insecurities may be made manifest. Old patterns of solving problems, long since outgrown, that have been carefully hidden may burst to the surface of behavior."[6] It is when we give up being "creatively selfish" in our living that we hand over our psychological potency to another or others. At that moment we become extremely vulnerable. The task for each of us is to fight for our birthright: our unique self. In this way have we something to give in relationships, especially that most primary of relationships, that of spouse.

When one's spouse dies, a period of "life transition"[7] for the living spouse begins. When the death of a spouse occurs, the first effect to be felt is grief. The context for this grief is mourning; and the whole process is what is called bereavement. See the summary of the literature in image form in Figure 2 (p. 30).[8] As in any life transition a person starts out usually on an unknown path, with unknown markers, and with unknown and untested ways of how to cope. But start one must; this 'journey of a 1,000 miles' starts with the 'first step.' It's the willingness to start and the summoning of courage that will make the difference.

BEREAVEMENT: DEATH, GRIEF, MOURNING

Most widows mourn for the rest of their lives.[7] In the first two to three years, this mourning tends to be compartmentalized according to their individual personalities. The loss is still with them, though, and renewed feelings of grief do surface.

Walter Winchel said one time, "Nothing recedes like success."[9] This is especially true with the death of a spouse. The pain comes from not experiencing the

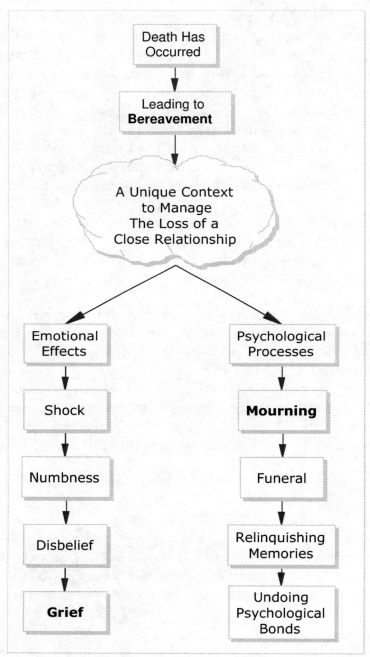

Figure 2: Bereavement Process

success of the relationship; there is no relationship; the person is dead. One is left with him/herself. It is as though everything has evaporated. May Sarton, of the *New York Times*, says that after a talk she will sometimes be lonely and have to come to grips with the feelings of loss that she is experiencing:

> I am lonely sometimes when I come back after a lecture trip ... when I have seen a lot of people and talked a lot and am full to the brim with experience that needs to be sorted out. Then for a little while the house feels huge and empty, and I wonder where my self is hiding.

> It takes a little while, as I watch the surf blowing up in fountains at the end of the field, but the moment comes when the world falls away, and the self emerges again from the deep unconscious, bringing back all I have recently experienced to be explored and slowly understood, when I can converse again with my own hidden powers, and so grow, and so be renewed.[10]

GRIEF: THE EMOTIONAL EFFECT

Death affects each and every one of us. As pointed out on the model shown previously, grief is the emotional reaction to death. For some, grieving has begun before the actual death; but it is not quite the same as when the person does in fact die. Dr. Phyllis Silverman refers to the three phases of grief.[11]

1.   THE INITIAL PHASE
2.   THE RECOIL PHASE
3.   THE PERIOD OF ACCOMMODATION

Grief is innate to us as human beings[12]; we are not socialized into grief; the reactions of grief are similar the world over. Freud, in his paper on the basis for a psychoanalytic theory of depression[13] points out that grief is the way whereby the energy that attached or bonded a person to the dead individual is progressively withdrawn.[14] In addition, while we can outline the different moments or phases of grieving, it is always personal and reflects an individual's strengths and weaknesses.[15] If grief is managed wisely, often one's limited perspectives and shortcomings about life and living can be transformed. The extent of one's grief is also proportional to the intensity of the relationship one had with the deceased. This is somewhat analogous to the idea that we talked about earlier in relation to the individual who clings dependently to the relationship only to suffer severe loss and separation when the spouse dies precisely because the person has never really learned to stand on his/her own two psychological feet.

The extent of grief is apparently proportional to the degree to which the object of love has been woven into the texture of living. Also, if it is lost without warning he/she seems to be caught off-guard. He/she has not had a chance to take a defensive stance, and this makes the impact more devastating. The implication, therefore, is that grief is apt to be most intense when the love relationship is most completely integrated into life and the loss comes without warning."[16]

Dr. Edgar Jackson calls grief "the illness that heals itself."[17] Normal grief deals with reality, is related to what is actually happening. Grief is abnormal when uncontrollable unconscious forces erupt at this time of death in the person's life, and these forces, in turn, throw the person back to unsolved fears and early experiences. The living spouse can get tangled up in this labyrinth and get very sidetracked. Shakespeare, in *Macbeth*, writes,[18] "So from that spring whence comfort seem'd to come discomfort swells," and "False face must hide what the false heart doth." Ironically, though, one of the salient features of abnormal grief is that it does reveal "conditions that might otherwise have been unobserved."[19] Hopefully, at this point though, the person has access to a therapeutic intervention.

If grief is an illness that heals itself, as Dr. Jackson so rightly points out, let us not forget though that

grief is a wound that needs attention in order to heal. To work through and complete grief means to face our feelings openly and honestly, to express or release our feelings fully, and to tolerate and accept our feelings for however long it takes for the wound to heal.[20]

Grief needs to be worked through "... in the emotional response to loss: the complex amalgam of painful effects including sadness, anger, helplessness, guilt, despair"[21] must be worked through if there is to be a healthy resolution. Tatelbaum uses the image of the tree to explain the pain: "When the shock wears off ... [it is] a time of the greatest suffering ... like having a tree that had been growing in one's heart suddenly yanked out by its roots, leaving a gaping hole or wound. The pain is intense but not constant."[22] Lewis and Berns have these wise words for us in this situation: "Do not tamper with a widow's grief. Let it flow freely so that she may be purged of guilt and remorse."[23]

A considerable length of time needs to be spent on the aspect of grief in the bereavement process. This is as it should be because of its stark obviousness and centrality to the situation. The widowed person has to go through shock, numbness, disbelief. In spite of these reactions, the psyche is allowing itself time to regroup in order to manage the future. The feelings of denial, of perhaps dread of the dead body, the pain of separation, the waves of distress, the intense yearnings for the deceased, the anger and the aggression — all these realities must find a home inside the widowed spouse. Reality is the best healer, and this usually takes time. Grief has lost its intensity when the bereaved is reconciled more and more to the loss of the spouse. Reality is the best medicine, but it is often the most painful. To see oneself and one's life situation as they actually are, now that the spouse is dead, is indeed painful. But that is reality. Reality pains; reality also heals.

MOURNING: THE PSYCHOLOGICAL PROCESS

At the time of death, the psychological process of mourning also began, specifically with the funeral arrangements. The funeral says publicly that the person has died. This death, in this funeral, cannot be denied. If grief is the emotional impact of the reality of the death of a loved one, mourning is the psychological process that initiates the undoing of the bonds of the relationship that the widowed person had with the deceased.[24] As stated in Chapter 1, the idea of "wounded bonds" in some wats is a misnomer, for the bonds are totally cut — death is final. Yet if we see life as all there is, and death as part of living, then the bonds have been deeply wounded, not irreparably lost or broken in a deeply spiritual way. The dead person is still a person from this perspective; and we have no idea of what this radically altered state of living (beyond death) is.[25]

The funeral, therefore, drives home the reality of death. When the body is placed into the ground, or cremated, a definite finality has occurred. It's often very difficult for the deceased's spouse to really recognize this event so great may be the grief. He/she is probably still in shock. A widow reports, "He was such a big man, I cannot imagine him in that small box of ashes".[26] When the funeral is over, the initial part of the psychological mourning process has only just begun. Many go through this period in such a state of intense grief that the funeral is only a "blur"! The shock of the death (grief) has interfered too radically with the reality of the death (mourning), at least initially, so that the deceased's spouse has really only gone through the motions.

However, once the loss has been accepted, the on-going process of mourning can proceed more evenly and organically. Freud suggests that undoing the relationship is to take each single moment that the person remembers about the deceased look at them, but then painfully relinquish them.[27] Another author, Bak,[28] suggest that it is perhaps the reverse of love. It is important during this period of mourning that the deceased's spouse confront issues as much as possible in order to avoid unhealthy depression, which is often inverted anger. Realistically though, sadness is the order of the day, for memories gone and for moments in the relationship that will never be again.

After the initial stages of mourning (early weeks and months), there is a lessening in intensity. The sadness, while still there, is not so total, not so overwhelming. There may even be moments of genuine happiness, new insights, opportunities, and affections. One of the most powerful helps during this period of mourning can be the immediate family and the social relationships the person has. The social network was very important for widows in reviewing their relationships with their deceased spouses.[29] Again, the measuring stick was reality: undoing the bonds, but first looking both at the good aspects and at the bad aspects of their relationships. Interaction with others, therefore, is critical to help resolve mourning caused through loss by death of a spouse.

Bereavement: a unique context to manage the loss of a close relationship. It includes the emotional impact -- grief — of the death of someone, and the psychological process — mourning — which initiates the reality of the death and hopefully, the effective resolution of undoing the bonds of the relationship to the deceased. To recover effectively, as can be imagined, takes courage, patience, resilience, perseverance, endurance, a capacity to distance oneself in order to stand on one's psychological feet, and a sense of humour. It's a tall order; but many have done it; and the hardest part, of course, is always the first step.

The University of Saskatchewan department of psychiatry is the first home to an American movement that encourages physicians to integrate the spiritual or world view of their patients into treatment. In 2001 Dr. Christina Pulchaski of the George Washington University Institute for Spiritual Care developed an approach based on the concept that "spirituality is a key dimension for achieving optimal health and coping with illness." She believes that health care practitioners have an "ethical obligation to treat the whole person and to respond to all their needs." She distinguishes between religion and spirituality. Spirituality includes a patient's world view and includes FICA: Faith, Importance, Community and Address in Care.

— Marvin Ross, "Teaching Physicians to Treat Body and Soul," *Toronto Star*, Sunday, September 5, 2004, F7.

THOUGHTS TO PONDER

1.   Grieving is a very natural response to the death of a close relationship.

2.   To mature in our human journey means to choose relationship, and that also means to choose to become vulnerable when the relationship is no longer.

3.   The death of a close relationship is a time of acute loss.

4.   Truthfulness to oneself in the relationship is the best antidote to a pathological reaction to the death of a close relationship.

5.   Bereavement is the unique context in which a person manages the loss of a close relationship.

6.   Grief is the emotional impact upon hearing of the death of a close relationship.

7.   Mourning is the psychological process of undoing the bonds that one had to that close relationship now that the person is dead.

8.   There is a sense in which mourning lasts a lifetime for one is always undoing and choosing to get on with one's present human journey.

9.   Grief affects one in the weakest and strongest aspects of their personality.

10.   Normal grief heals itself.

11.   Reality is the greatest healer: emotionally, physically, psychologically, and spiritually. Expect the unexpected. Envision newness for your human journey.

WIDOWHOOD
The Death of a Spouse

REFLECTIONS ON DEATH AND DYING
plus nine interviews with people who lost a spouse

Michael Rock, Ed.D.
with Janice Rock, M.A.

ISBN 1-4120-2452-8

TRAFFORD This book is available from Trafford Publishing

Suite 6E - 2333 Government Street, Victoria, BC, Canada V8T 4P4
Phone 1-250-383-6884 • Fax 1-250-383-6814 • Toll Free 1-866-638-6884
Email bookstore@trafford.com • Bookstore www.trafford.com

CHAPTER FOUR

THE DEATH OF A SPOUSE

T hus far in this book we have discussed the reality of death itself, and more specifically, the widowed state. In this chapter, we address the issue of the specific death of a spouse. Most of the discussion will concern itself with the widow because four of out five widowed people are women[1] and a great percentage of these are 65 years and older. Drs. Helena Lopata and Robert Fulton, in a 1972 report,[2] with 301 widows alone, found that 50 percent were 65 and older, and in the group they studied, only 10 percent had high school. They also point out that education-social status was the major difference with these women. This harkens back to some of the comments from the Hebrew Scriptures and New Testament: they were unfortunates and dependent on those around them after their husbands had died.

In the study by Lopata and Fulton, this reality of the 'dependent woman' was very much in evidence as well, although we also have to bear in mind that pre-1970, women pretty much let men run things. It was a mindset: in 1972, a woman, a widow of 65+, basically felt fixed, segregated, didn't know much concerning her husband's life away from home. We would think that the new women's movement would make a difference, but in a book published in 1975,[3] at least at that point in time, the women's liberation movement virtually ignored the widow. Tatelbaum[4] shows that in terms of support systems, self-support accounted for 25 percent of widows (i.e., they could work, earn income, etc.); 20 percent were supported by their spouses' monies; and 55 percent were environmentally supported, through welfare or public assistance of some kind. That is a terrible disadvantage to be in when left alone at age 65 after one's husband has died.

These facts are not at all helped by many of the prevailing attitudes that society has to the widow. In many ways, it feels as though not much has changed over the years from the time of the Hebrew Scriptures, 2000 B.C.E.! "The prevailing attitudes force a widow to feel like a displaced person. She has been tainted by the unmentionable. She is a leper, an outcast, a pariah."[5] It's interesting to note here that Drs. Lopata and Fulton found that the more highly educated widow, however, had been more emotionally involved, but at the same time, the loss of her husband meant the loss of *several* levels of experience with him.

COUPLE ORIENTATION

What makes the issue of losing a spouse more difficult also is that our society is a very "couple-oriented" one, which stresses the family, and having so many single women is a perceived threat to the male population.[6] How often it happens that two couples can be friends for years. The husband of one dies, and perhaps immediately, if not gradually, the "odd woman out" is perceived as a threat.[7] The threat can also come if it is a widower: other men will often feel threatened, because "you know what males are like![6]

DIFFERENCES BETWEEN WIDOWS AND WIDOWERS

Widowers experience loss similar to those of widows, but they don't experience the traumatic disruption of their lives in the same way as women. Kohn and Kohn[8] feel that widower's needs are:

1. to regain a comfortable place in society;
2. to satisfy their emotional and sexual needs;
3. to find some normal and natural way to re-enter the "paired world."

Hence, while men experience the loss of the affective bond (as do widows), they also react to the *disruption*, i.e., of the social roles, that the death of the wife has caused. If for the woman, the loss is one of **abandonment** (i.e., the husband who represented security, protection), for the man, the loss is one of **dismemberment** (i.e., the wife is the component, cut off from him now).[9] Men seem to be unwilling to display grief; they want to maintain greater control, but at the same time try to maintain a realistic outlook on their situation.

Men are not as successful in managing guilt as they are in managing anger, and there doesn't seem to be as much of an obsessional review of their spouse's death. There seems to be a lesser investment in the bereavement process and more concern around persona issues, i.e., how they will look to others around them. It's interesting to note also that more men (than women) had recovered at the end of the first year after their wife's death. This does not mean that their emotional recovery was any faster than widows. It is about the same, if not slower. But part of the difficulty here is that men do not show their depression as easily; there are fewer outward signs of grief. Given what was stated earlier about the poverty level of widows, it stands to reason to expect that widowers feel more secure concerning money, obviously since they are the ones who would have essentially earned it in the past.[10] Widowers also feel "less loyal" to their deceased spouse and move "more quickly toward re-establishing a stable life organization based on remarriage, and thus toward social recovery."[11] Widowers also wanted, generally speaking, to maintain the "highest level of functioning"[12] and needed to have someone in the home. Hence, the idea of remarriage was sooner for men because of the pressures of:

1. wanting to function optimally,
2. sex, and
3. overcoming loneliness.

It's interesting to note here a couple of other major differences between widows and widowers due to the loss of their spouse. Widows tended to have an obsessional review and search for meaning,[13] with self-recriminations, self-reproach, saying things like "... if only ...," or "maybe ..., " all of which, of course, compounds guilt. The other difference is that up until the latter part of the 20th century, widows tended to adopt the widow role. This would be more true of those, even today, who are 50 years and older. The widow's role meant being relatively independent of close relationships with other adults, organizing one's life around non-marital relationships with a man, and establishing a life pattern with kin around relationships.[14]

THE COMMON THREAD

Whether or not we look at the individual differences between widows and widowers, we still come back to the same common thread with the death of a spouse: "When the partner is lost, all the meanings of the marriage, all its memories, will be thrown into relief."[15] For either the man or woman, widower or widow, there are shock, numbness, disbelief, intense longing, waves and pangs of grief. In the beginning "behaviour is purposeless, despair overwhelming."[16] The future seems bleak, empty; life seems meaningless. Thus, they both experience intense grief: "His grief may be more hidden, and constrained; hers more open."[17]

Dysfunctional families at such a time of crisis will not weather these grief storms. Functional families that have flexible roles and the ability to express and share feelings are likely to get through the turmoil.[18] Many of us have a false idea of being "strong" in moments of crisis. What appears to be weakness (expressing and sharing feelings) is usually strength.

Little by little, as each person, widow or widower, confronts the issues and deals with reality, there will come progress. The person will be able to talk more and more about his/her deceased spouse. This shows that distancing is occurring; social tasks become important again. Others hear the widow or widower using more present and future verb tenses. The deceased has become a separate and more distinct part of the person's life. Friends begin to see smiles, and that the spouse is beginning to see the outside world again and its future, and finally, one day, the widow or widower realizes, "I haven't thought about him/her for a while now."

When one reads the literature on death and dying, and on widows and widowers, perhaps the part that strikes one the most is *the tremendous need for listening* that the widow or widower has when his/her spouse dies. A marvellous ending to this chapter and one that reinforces this critical dimension of listening, is the case of Mathilda H., a middle-aged widow, who's very talkative, and very eager to express her opinions. She's quite straightforward and forthright:

"A listener's the only medicine a widow really needs," she said. "And let me tell you from bitter experience, there aren't any. I'd call up people who were very close to me and try to tell them what I was feeling. I didn't get half a sentence out before they were breaking in with, 'Tillie, you're being morbid. You'll never get over it by dwelling on it. You can't live in the past. Think about the future.' Shows how much they knew... All I wanted was to find somebody who'd listen to what was going on in my mind and heart. Rarer than hen's teeth - that's what a good listener is."[19]

"Those who learned to know death, rather than to fear and fight it, become our teachers about life," she once wrote. And in later life she applied what she had learned from the dying to promote what she considered to be a more healthy approach to living. The expression of emotion was, she insisted, essential: "People must cry when they are sad, then they will not end up a bucketful of self-pity. Anger must be expressed, too."

— Obituary for Dr. Elizabeth Kûbler-Ross, in
"Changed People's Attitudes Toward Death and Dying,"
National Post, Friday, August 27, 2004, PM11.

THOUGHTS TO PONDER

1. Four out of every five widowed persons is a woman.

2. Widows generally average 53 years of age at the time of the death of their spouse.

3. Widows tend to be poorer than married women.

4. In many ways, the widow is still considered an outcast. There is a striking parallel here between contemporary society and ancient biblical society, 2,000 B.C.

5. Our society puts additional pressure on the widow-widower because it is "couple-oriented". Petty and perceived jealousies interfere with widows and widowers being fully accepted and integrated within our society.

6. Both widows and widowers experience, in their own ways, the intense feelings of grief through loss.

7. Widows experience loss as abandonment; widowers, as that of dismemberment.

8. Widowers tend to be "less loyal" to their deceased spouse and remarry earlier than widows (if they do at all). Widows spend a longer time reviewing and searching for meaning as a result of the death of the spouse.

9. The most important gift anyone can give a widow/widower is the gift of *listening*.

THE INTERVIEWS

The next nine chapters chapters are the stories of widows and widowers who graciously allowed us to interview them. Sometimes both both Michael and Janice interviewed the widowed spouse; at other times, it was Michael by himself. You will read about ordinary people, just like us, but people who have lost a spouse.

Chapters 12 and 13 are the same person, Connie. Her story consists of Part A (chapter 12) and Part B (chapter 13).

We are deeply honoured to have been able to listen to their stories. Some names have been changed on request.

The interviews were transcribed as they were on the dates, with the necessary editing required for the sake of clarification. Points of clarification in the interviews are enclosed in brackets [...].

At the end of each story is a commentary.

"The most powerful prayer ... is that which proceeds from an empty spirit. ,,, An empty spirit is one that is confused about nothing, attached to nothing, and has no concern whatever in anything for its own gain, for it is all sunk deep down into God's dearest will and has forsaken its own."

-- Meister Eckhart

CHAPTER FIVE

CLARION CALL TO NEW DEVELOPMENT:
THE STORY OF DEBORAH

We met with Deborah on a bright, sunny morning in her kitchen, enjoyed our coffee with her, and listened to her story. She was in her early 30s and had three small children.

MICHAEL: Deborah, the first question that I would like to ask here concerns statistics relating to your husband's death. In other words, how old was he? When did he die? What was going on at the time? How it happened? etc.

DEBORAH: OK. He was 34, and I was 34. We had three children.

MICHAEL: How old would the children have been then?

DEBORAH: Catherine was 9; Elizabeth was 7; and Geoffrey was 5.

MICHAEL: How did your husband die?

DEBORAH: OK. He had a job at that time with a company which sold veterinary supplies; and he flew out west to do some work there.

MICHAEL: What was his occupation?

DEBORAH: He was a veterinarian. [*Pause*] He did the work. On the weekend, he met an old college friend. I knew this guy because when we were married, he was still a student. They decided to go on this trip on the weekend to ride the rapids in one of these rafts. You see them on T.V., on the beer commercials. It was a weekend thing, where you rode down the river one day, camped overnight, and rode down the river the next day, and then you got bused back to where you started out. [*A company advertised and was in business to provide these kinds of outings*].

So they went on this ride; the current was very strong because it was the spring. Maybe the water was more difficult than usual, higher. There was a whole group of them, about 30 people or so. They went down the rapids, and somehow the raft hit a rock and pushed the front corner of the raft on to the rock. It lodged there. Because of that the bottom end got swept under the current, so that all the people on the back of the raft got swept right off.

MICHAEL: Sounds like a freak accident.

DEBORAH: Yes. It was very freaky because all the people who were at the front were able to actually step right out and get on this rock; and all the people at the back - who all had their life jackets on, and everything - were just swept right off; and depending on where you were, if they could get you out of the water, you were O.K. but if you got pulled under or swept too far away, too quickly, you were drowned, because the life jackets weren't buoyant enough to resist that kind of undertow. So my husband, Jim, was one of those who drowned.

MICHAEL: Incredible force of the water!

DEBORAH: It must have been! You know, I wasn't there. So, it was a huge blank! We just kept getting these phone calls from the RCMP [*Royal Canadian Mounted Police*]. So we didn't even witness it or anything; we had no idea what happened. I only heard about it [the accident] later because we actually had to go to court then, hear all the testimony against the company, or their lack of proper equipment, and that sort of thing. And I heard other people describing the story. That was the only way I got any idea at all of what had happened. You know, the company tried to play down what was going on, but the people -- a couple of women who were actually on the trip - came up to me after and said, "You hang in there. It wasn't like that! [*As the company described it*]. It was terrifying, it was horrible." You see, I wasn't there; so I didn't know; and they [*the company*] were really trying to underplay the whole thing.

MICHAEL: Those women said they didn't feel protected enough!

DEBORAH: Yes. They were scared to death. Really. They said, "We were just so lucky that we survived. It was the most scary thing. Don't let them [*company*] try and tell you that it was no big deal. You try and get something out of this!"

MICHAEL: Deborah, this was like a month or so after the funeral?

DEBORAH: No. This dragged [*emphasizing*] on for five years after he died! The court case itself, I think occurred, I would say about a year after it all began, because initially they tried to get settlements out of court and I said, No way!"

MICHAEL: Did you find that in fighting the court case, you were pulling yourself together as a person?

DEBORAH: I did. I found myself pulling together, sort of deep down within myself; but on the surface, I felt my self coming apart, because for one thing, I was just not that good at that sort of thing (i.e., dealing with lawyers). I knew nothing of law. You have to be sharp! There's no doubt about it. When the lawyer first threw me into this, the first thing I said to him was that we [*Deborah and the children*] had enough to survive, so I didn't want to throw good money after bad, chasing after something that I was not too likely to get. But he said [*and Deborah is animated here*], "Oh no! You're absolutely going to win!" Well, $30,000 later and two bosses later, we still didn't have a penny! By that time, I was having a mental breakdown (figuratively speaking), thinking I had made such a bad decision, that I was putting good money that the kids would need into something that was just, ah, a giant rip-off -- because lawyers think the whole thing is a big game. They couldn't care less! Litigation lawyers are ego-maniacs! That's apparently the first thing you need to know when you get involved in this sort of thing [*Deborah is able to laugh at this comment somewhat too. I think she enjoyed being able to say that! She was taking a stand*].

MICHAEL: In your vulnerability, you would see yourself as a pawn.

DEBORAH: You listen to them. You say, "What's your advice to me? I'm paying for your advice. What's your advice to me?" And they give you advice [*laughing*], but, of course, their Catch-22, or their little loop-hole, out of it is, "Well, ultimately the decision is yours!" [*Big laugh now at the table*] "Too bad, lady!" Basically, they play you that way all the way down the whole road. So, three years later (I'm putting myself through art college, and I'm raising the kids) I get a phone call, "You know, we've lost the appeal!" I almost died! That was $30,000, and we lost the appeal! I got pneumonia, was sick for two months. It was like "Game over! Forget it!"

This is where the story gets kind of interesting when you're talking about beliefs and, I don't know, destiny, or whatever you want to call it. In great despair, I turned to working that year on the P.T.A. I signed up because the school had been very good to the children, and I feel it was time for me to give something in return. Nobody else would take the job! So I said, "I'll do it just to get you on your feet. I need this like a hole in the head, but I'll do it!"

One night after one of the meetings, I was talking to one of the teachers [a woman]. Somehow this whole, long, horrendous story came out, because her husband was a lawyer, and she had relatives and connections who were also lawyers; and when she heard the story, she was just horrified and mortified, and said, "I'm going to tell my husband about this! His brother-in-law is 'high up' in politics and I'm going to call him up tonight! [*Deborah's voice has really gone high now, imitating the school teacher's*]

And lo and behold she did! The "political" relative phoned up this guy who was my lawyer. When that happened, the shit just hit the fan! [*She bursts out laughing*]. I'm telling you, it was almost funny. If I hadn't been feeling so absolutely terrible, it would have been absolutely hilarious! To watch them all fluttering around like crazy, like, "What's going on here?" All of a sudden, something from above coming down on them! Lo and behold, they got me a settlement!

MICHAEL: There was something "out there" helping you!

DEBORAH: I think so! You look at how those things connect, and you look at all the work you do on your own, and you try and make your life go well, and you see it fail before your eyes, and then you see something like that, just by some sort of fluke, to cause things to turn toward you.

MICHAEL: How many years after his death did you receive the settlement?

DEBORAH: Five years. It resolved itself five years after. Now, it is seven years since his death.

MICHAEL: Deborah, what's it like to have someone close to you die?

DEBORAH: Do you remember the movie 'Jaws'? Do you remember the young gal at the beginning who was sitting in the water? And all of a sudden, you hear this - "TSCH!" - she's just lying there as though nothing's happening, but the whole bottom half of her body has been bitten off, yet, on the "surface," nothing is showing! Do you remember?

MICHAEL: Oh yes! Now, when you say the "bottom" and the "surface", are you comparing yourself to her?

DEBORAH: Yes!

MICHAEL: You operated on the surface, but . . .,

DEBORAH: Yes, underneath I felt that a huge chunk had just been bitten right off. For me, it was all so sudden, that's a bit the way it was. You know when your body has been seriously damaged, you don't get any pain at first because there is so much shock. I feel more pain now than I did then. [*Pausing for a moment and realizing her words*] That's interesting! ... things come to take care of you. Yes.

MICHAEL: To get you through that period.

DEBORAH: Yes, what happens after, or what I metaphorically describe as: you feel yourself sort of quietly bleeding to death [*her voice lowers as she says these words*] in a way. You keep trying to plug up all the holes to keep yourself going, but it's really difficult.

MICHAEL: Deborah, short of having him back, how would some of the holes be plugged up in your fantasy?

DEBORAH: [Pause] I would think ... [*carefully examining her options and what she wants to say now, admitting these realities to herself*] ... building new friendships to get that kind of human support. Now, all the things in the world can't make up for that sort of a close bond [*with a husband*]. You can have a million friends, and it is not the same, right? So, starting maybe a new relationship would be a good way: eventually. In the meantime, you know, just have support from all the people you know in your world. What I found for me was my art. That was my cornerstone, for me; that might not be so for everyone.

MICHAEL: For anchoring yourself.

DEBORAH: Yes.

MICHAEL: Deborah, there's an expression that's used called "linkages with life". I'm hearing you say that once death happens, the linkages just evaporate.

DEBORAH: Yes.

MICHAEL: There are so many meanings wrapped up with an individual.

DEBORAH: Yes.

MICHAEL: And these are anchors for you.

DEBORAH: Oh, right! [*Deborah is understanding my observations/comments now*] Do you mean you feel so disoriented, as if everything is changed? all those links are broken?

MICHAEL: Actually they are shattered!

DEBORAH: Yes. I would say that's accurate.

MICHAEL: Did you find that you were violently thrown back on personal resources at that time?

DEBORAH: I would say so because I had another friend who also lost her husband. She lost her husband in a car accident. She lived in close to Toronto. I lived in Toronto at the time. She had a really good community support, you know. She told me all the things that were happening with her: her friend's husband was coming over on Friday night to help with things. I had none of that! I looked at her and thought, "Oh God! If I had that, would that ever be great!" So for me, I sort of really had to draw it up from within myself.

MICHAEL: The support system is what I'm hearing.

DEBORAH: Yes. I had seven brothers and sisters! My husband had seven brothers and sisters! But somehow those two families - I just didn't get the same kind of things that she [*woman friend above*] was getting. The message I got from my family was: things should go on as usual! There was a sort of complete denial.

MICHAEL: A "let's-pretend".

DEBORAH: Yes [*a little hesitantly*]. During the funeral the first thing my parents said to me was, "Well, you know, I don't think you should bring the kids to the funeral! I don't think you should show the kids the body!" I mean, the kind of stuff, so-called help they gave me -- I didn't listen to it. I realized they weren't doing very well, and I just had to choose not to listen to it. Even after that, like, a month later, they had a huge family party. I remember that to this day because I was sort of dismayed by the whole thing. They phoned me up and said, "Well, would you like to come?" I said, "Oh yes, I'd really like to come!" They said, "Well, we would like you to bring so many dozen sandwiches!" [*Incredulous laugh*]. I just thought, "Good grief! Bringing myself is going to be really hard, never mind the sandwiches!" There were days when just trying to keep milk in the fridge -- you were so depressed you could hardly go out to get the groceries! Here they were, like, lights should go on! They had no idea of the kind of shape

I was in, and they were making demands on me as if nothing had happened! It was incredible. I was so angry, and yet, I had to deal with it; I couldn't change their minds!

MICHAEL: They obviously really denied what was happening?

DEBORAH: Oh! God, yes! [*real emphasis here in tone of voice*] That made it about a hundred times as hard for me. It was incredible. I never forgave them for that. Things have never been the same with my family. You know, I'm really "shit-disturbing" now, and they're quite upset with me, but, my thing to them is, "Look, you deny my life the way it is now. You expect things of me. Obviously you don't understand. I'm not getting any support from you," and at the same time, there are often sort of implied criticisms about my behaviour, that sort of thing" [*Carolyn is trying here to sort out her feelings and what it is that is precisely happening. She feels she's getting it both ways. No support, yet criticism. A no-win situation*]

MICHAEL: You're not measuring up to their yardstick.

DEBORAH: Yeah! [*emphasis*]

MICHAEL: However that is or should be!

DEBORAH: Yeah! [*emphasis*] So, my basic response to that is to hell with your yardstick! Your yardstick just doesn't apply! [*Deborah feels very good about saying this and laughs. She's saying, "Stick it?"*] But it puts you in a crazy position: it alienate you from your family. Really! When you have to throw out that yardstick of theirs, you're alienated. There's no doubt about it.

MICHAEL: Deborah, however painful, what I'm hearing throughout all of this is that the death forced individuality on to you.

DEBORAH: Yes. [*admission of reality*] Definitely.

MICHAEL: You're not part of the collective, belonging to either side of the family.

DEBORAH: No. I'm definitely not! I'm standing out there all by myself! [*Laughs*]

JANICE: I think you look terrific!

DEBORAH: I think so too! But it's hard doing that when families feud, when none of them values what I've done, who I am.

MICHAEL: In the beginning of the first chapter of my book, *Reflections: The Human Journey*, that is what I am talking about. The goal of the human journey is individuation - wholeness - and a lot of times our society, especially in growing up, keeps that process shrouded in collective expectations. Then we get married, and we still have that "collective environment". All of a sudden, death happens, and we're forced back onto ourselves. If we have never wrestled with our own choices, it's very, very painful. I'm hearing that you took care of those choices, but now that you're standing for who you are, your family says, "We don't like it. We want you back under our umbrella." That's very alienating if you accept that. "Don't be you! Be what we want you to be!"

DEBORAH: That's it exactly! You've hit the nail on its head! I have been fighting with that for a long time [*low voice, then animated again*]. It's hard because the times when you need them the most is the time when you're alienated.

MICHAEL: That's interesting: at the same time that you experienced your crisis -- a crisis tells us how we can cope, our strengths and weaknesses -- your family also had its crisis, and the family's strengths and weaknesses were drawn upon. It seemed there was a collision [*lots of laughter here!*] of needs! Somehow you "came out" and took care of yourself, and they're still fumbling around with the collective. Deborah, a question: What do you want for yourself now?

DEBORAH: Well, I've got a lot of what I want for myself now, I must say. Winning that settlement [*court case*] has enabled me to buy this house, and I'm happy as a clam here. I am able, I have enough independent income to do some art work on my own and look after my kids without any sort of incredible poverty or stress - which, by the way, is another hassle with my family.

MICHAEL: Because ...

DEBORAH: They undervalue what I do in art. They think I should be out working and suffering. They're very ambivalent about it, and I resent that. I want them to feel happy for me after all I've been through, that things have sort of worked out.

MICHAEL: Rejoice in my successes!

DEBORAH: Yes! And they're not! They're sort of like, "Well, you should be out working and suffering!" [*At this point, Deborah laughs and laughs*]

MICHAEL: Deborah, in addition to your success, what do you want for you, just for you? You talk about art. Anything else come to mind?

DEBORAH: I want to be able to do my art. I would like to meet someone. So far nothing really has worked out. Because of all I've been through I'm sort of, I think, strong, and maybe a little bit too independent.

MICHAEL: Like frightening the men?

DEBORAH: I think so. I don't know, or maybe just the right one hasn't come along. Who knows? Eventually I would like to see myself re-established in a really nice relationship. I have to say I am terrified of it now. Whenever situations crop up, I notice how terrified I get. You get so used to sort of being on your own that you're sort of afraid to let go, fall into something almost. That's part of it. And part of it is that you're afraid to trust again. You're absolutely terrified to trust again because it's a bit like the difference between being a virgin and a non-virgin: nothing is ever the same. [self-consciously laughing at this point]. You know what I mean? Having had that experience, you always know that death is possible again; it's always there.

MICHAEL: Once bitten twice forewarned?

DEBORAH: Yes. I think so.

MICHAEL: Deborah, you talked about a bond. There's a reluctance now to take another possible wound.

DEBORAH: Yes, and maybe a reluctance to let go of the bond too. It's hard to describe. I sort of hold on to that. I can feel myself holding on to it. I can think now, "Gee, you know, if he could see me now, he'd be so happy. He'd think I'm doing such a good job?" I mean: that's still there. Who knows if I'm really truly thinking of myself as only myself? [*independent of him*]

MICHAEL: Or are just feeling in relation to him ...

DEBORAH: In a way, but maybe you do that almost like when you fantasize, out of desperation when you have so much deprivation, you fantasize in order to fill up the desert; and possibly, if something new came along immediately, that would just evaporate. Maybe it's only like a useful tool to get you through.

MICHAEL: What's the most difficult part of having lost your husband?

DEBORAH: I think it's that alienation: you're not a couple. Every single time people have parties - that is, couples parties -- they don't invite you.

MICHAEL: We don't realize how couple-oriented our society is until an event like this happens.

DEBORAH: Yes. When they have a ladies' luncheon they invite you. Whenever they have parties where gifts are required, they invite you! Whenever they have anything that is sort of "last minute" -- like, "Who can we get? who can we get?" -- they invite you. It's as though you're suddenly demoted! Bottom person on the totem pole! You try to understand it, how uncomfortable it must be for them, and yet, at the same time, you think to yourself, "God, why can't they invite me? I can go on my own; I'm sociable enough. I can sort of mix around" [*a bit sarcastically*]. But they all get horrified about that odd number, or that empty chair. Then I think if you had a boyfriend, or a male friend, you could just invite someone along, and you would solve the problem for yourself. But there aren't too many men around who are able to be just male friends. I mean, it sort of has to be all or nothing, and so, you're sort of locked out on that one too. It's really difficult.

MICHAEL: Deborah, how have you changed?

DEBORAH: Oh, I've changed a lot, I think. I'm much angrier now than I was before, sort of a "shit-disturber." I hate it when I see something going on that isn't just, or isn't right. I tend to confront things, cause problems [laughs] instead of just letting things go along as they are, whereas before I was very content, very easy going. If something went by that wasn't right, or that I didn't go along with, I hardly even noticed it. Now I tend to fight for everything. I don't know why that is.

MICHAEL: Becoming an individual means becoming aware.

DEBORAH: Yes. I see a lot. I see a lot now that I didn't even see at all. I see, maybe, too much now. It would be nice to be a little bit "blind" sometimes; it would be less painful.

MICHAEL: I know what you're saying, but that will settle down. You'll integrate that more and more as you go along. But there's a period when you feel you need to take care of everything, or you've got to get everything in its place, for time is short. Is this part of your thinking as well?

DEBORAH: Yes. You value life because you realize how precious it is. There's a bit of that. I find myself not able so well as other people to sort of take it for granted.

MICHAEL: Do you like yourself as an individual and as aware now?

DEBORAH: Sometimes I do much more and I feel full of - what would you call it - amazement and wonder and think, "Gee, isn't this great!" Some nights after supper, I'll make my coffee and go out and sit on the deck and say to the kids, "I think I'm going to go out and look at my land!" [Lots of laughter here] And I just think, "Life is great!" Oh, if I do a really nice painting or a piece of work, or something, ...

MICHAEL: Look at your land? [laughter]

DEBORAH: Oh, look at my land! [laughter] Other days I feel in a way that I must find something that is "acceptable" to do; that sounds funny. That's when the alienation business really gets to me and I hate who I am because I don't fit in with everybody else and it hurts.

MICHAEL: You have to struggle against accepting their evaluation of you.

DEBORAH: Yes! Yes! And those days are hard; those days I carry my burden. I try and do things to get rid of that. I find for me it can be a very self-destructive issue. I saw this show on T.V. I don't know whether you saw it. I think it was called "The Accident" where all those kids in a small town were in an arena at a hockey game, or something, and the roof caved in. Certain numbers of the kids were killed, others were wounded. It was sort of what you are doing, personal in-depth interviews of all the different families, how they were coping with that. Everyone was different; every family was different in how they handled it. There was this one woman who had an only boy child and lost that child. And she had a neighbour next door who had this fabulous greenhouse. He used to be out there all the time nurturing all these exotic plants of his; they were really healthy, and he had about a million kids! The mother who lost her child used to sit up at her window eating herself away with hatred: "Why did it have to happen to me?" He kept trying to be friendly with her, and get her to come around. But, I guess, she couldn't let it go; it hurt too much, or something. One night she went out and she unplugged his greenhouse; it was in the middle of winter! When he went out in the morning all his plants were frozen stiff! Then she said, "I wanted you to know how I feel!"

MICHAEL: Lot of anger there!

DEBORAH: You bet! Even her daughter said, "You can't let it be like that, let yourself self-destruct in that kind of way!" But, I have to say, I feel like that sometimes. I feel that when people do things that hurt you, they're just ignorant. I know they're not doing it on purpose; it's just because they don't know - you want to go and unplug their greenhouse! You really do!

MICHAEL: That's a good image!

DEBORAH: So that they can know how you feel and then they won't do that any more.

JANICE: For instance, when they leave you out of the dinner party!

DEBORAH: Yes. Or when they say something stupid, or when they ask you to bring sandwiches! I realize that that wasn't a positive thing to do [*i.e., pulling the plug*], but I understood it 100 percent! I thought, "Yeah! Yeah! You got it!" [*Lots of laughter*] "You've got it right, kid!"

MICHAEL: Deborah, what would you do differently, or over again?

DEBORAH: Starting from when? the very beginning? from the death?

MICHAEL: Let's say from the very beginning.

DEBORAH: Now that I have all this experience: if I had a complete fantasy, I would be born into a different family. I would change nothing that I've done in terms of art or the university, I'm very happy about that. I'm very happy about my kids; I'm very happy about this move [to new home]. I would be born into a different family that had values which were more in line with mine and were able to somehow bridge that area mentioned. I would hope maybe to have more of an extroverted personality, so that I could meet more men, or whatever, you know, to be a little better about starting a new relationship. I think that's an area where I'm not strong.

MICHAEL: When you experience that alienation, how do you feel?

DEBORAH: I feel [*pause*] I always blame myself. I think that's my mistake, instead of saying, "Well, they're wrong and I'm right!" I can say that to myself intellectually, but I can't feel like that inside. I hurt and become overwhelmed by it and I take the blame for it as though it all involved me!

MICHAEL: Psychologists make the difference in solving problems by saying that we handle the problem in either in flight or fight mode (unless we solve it, of course). With the flight mode, which is what you are talking about, you absorb the problem. You say, "There's something wrong with me; otherwise, the problem wouldn't be there!"

DEBORAH: Yes!

MICHAEL: The woman who took the plug out of the greenhouse took the fight mode!

DEBORAH: [*Laughter*] Right!

MICHAEL: And when you're saying that you're in a "shit-disturb" mode, what I'm hearing is that you're going from a flight mode and whipping over to a fight mode.

DEBORAH: Yes, yes!

MICHAEL: Eventually, that will balance itself. It seems that we have to hit the opposite in order to get in touch with it; and then you say, "Well, that doesn't deserve a 'flight' or "that doesn't deserve a 'fight'"! Do you feel any of that happening at all, or are you still in the transition?

DEBORAH: I think I'm still in a bit of a mix-up to be quite honest. I seem to really go from one extreme to another. I haven't somehow got that together that well yet.

JANICE: I've been listening to you, Deborah, and I'm wondering if standing for oneself is experienced by others as aggression, anger, frustration? Just taking a personal position that isn't fighting or fleeing, but a stance that says, "This is where it is; this is where I stand."

DEBORAH: Yes. My family thinks I'm being very aggressive and hostile, and unfeminine. They want to see my being completely crippled and helpless, and not having any fight, and then they can have complete control over me. That's the way I see them being.

JANICE: Do you experience a difference in yourself between when you're really fighting and when you're just taking a stand?

DEBORAH: [*Hesitating*] Um.

JANICE: Do you experience just taking a stand in the middle between the fight and the flight?

DEBORAH: Yes [*hesitatingly*]. I think I do, with them particularly. I see where you get that root, inner feeling, and I know this is right for me. Like, I know this has integrity, and I know that the things they're choosing for me aren't correct perceptions Yet, I can never get them to see what I'm seeing.

MICHAEL: Sometimes in order to get the standpoint that Janice is talking about, you have to go over to the "fight" mode and rattle their cages!

DEBORAH: Oh yeah!

MICHAEL: What you're learning is that it's important not to lock yourself in your own cage and rattle yours by yourself. That's the flight mode.

DEBORAH: Yes. It sort of goes nowhere when you do that, whereas with the other it can be a little more creative. Something new can happen.

MICHAEL: Did you know yourself in relation to this issue before the death?

DEBORAH: Yeah [*a little hesitant*], I would say so. I was already underway, to put it that way, because when Jim was a student I worked; he was still in school - and when he interned, I worked; and then when he started his clinic, I worked. Then we had these three kids. Once they were all born and around, and he was on his feet, I said, "I feel as though I'm climbing the walls here [*at home*]. I need a little something to do on my own! I want to go back to art school!" I knew I had to do it and I thought of it as being the right thing for me. I didn't see myself staying in the role [*of homemaker only*]. My parents laid a big guilt trip on me, about, "How could you leave those poor little children?" I knew they had a home. But what a huge guilt trip from them! a huge, big guilt trip from Jim's parents too, and Jim himself, who was a very Irish "women-should-be-pregnant-and-barefoot-in-the-kitchen" type just about took an absolute "hairy"! He used to go and take the distributor out of the car so that I couldn't go to school that day. That's how threatened everybody was! These are the same people who are turning around now, when I'm at home looking after my kids and painting and

I'm now tired out -- for this is as much as I can handle -- and saying, "You should be out working!" [*peals of laughter all around the table at that one*] You can't win. I tell you, they've done a complete about-face!

MICHAEL: So Jim would actually take the distributor cap off?

DEBORAH: Oh! He was awful!

MICHAEL: So, he was very much part of that whole script?

DEBORAH: He was [*emphasizing*], and, deep down in my heart, I know that he came to think that I would develop myself and leave; and deep down in my heart I knew that I would never leave! I knew I loved my kids and I knew I loved him, but I knew I also loved art, and I had to do this. So it was already in the works, that part of it [*self-assertion*]. I was reading Jung (Carl) at that time: constellate a clarion call to new development! That's what it was: right out of the book! [*Enjoying a good laugh at this point*]

MICHAEL: The death really forced you into your own individual journey.

DEBORAH: Yes! Much sooner than I anticipated. It would have [*before the death*] been a much slower process, more like a "tree" process before, whereas, when he died, I just got thrown out into the journey.

MICHAEL: What did you lose when Jim died?

DEBORAH: I lost the one person who, even though he couldn't see all of my vision or who I was, was still the closest person to me. I often think, "Oh, if you could see me now!" He would value what I have achieved, whereas the family can't.

MICHAEL: Sharing your success and affirming it with you! Rejoicing in you!

DEBORAH: Yeah! and not on a superficial level either but at a deeper level.

MICHAEL: Deborah, what do you believe in?

DEBORAH: Oh God! I don't know. No institutional religions for sure! Obviously I believe in something because of how I feel about that court case, of karma and destiny, and all that! I don't go to church. My kids say, "Look at your paintings!" There's always some sort of a theme in there. It would be hard to put it in a nutshell.

MICHAEL: If I could possibly help here, Deborah you talked about integrity, values, affirming individuals. You believe very strongly, from what I'm hearing, in relationships and their depth and quality. Am I correct in this?

DEBORAH: Yes. But I also believe in something else because I've seen that there are times when there are no relationships or those relationships are terrible. Human relationships are very limited. They can be as destructive as they can be helpful; and people won't even be doing that on purpose. It's just their own limits.

MICHAEL: What do you believe in at that point?

DEBORAH: At that point I believe in the individual. You have to somehow reach "above". You leap into whatever [*a chuckle here*].

MICHAEL: What kind of suggestions or recommendations would you have for someone else in your situation?

DEBORAH: I would have maybe practical ones, a lot of practical ones, like, when the person dies, you're not in a very good mental state to make certain practical decisions in terms of money, moving. I would say for one thing: do not move for a good number of years. Keep all your roots together as much as you can until things start to heal.

MICHAEL: Keep a foundation for yourself.

DEBORAH: Yes. Don't give anything to anyone! That's rule Number #1. I gave all sorts of things away, and both of the families came down like ghouls, like vultures! 'Can we have this? Can we have that?' You're in that euphoric state: the money is endless; the goods are endless, and you start giving everything away like one of those persons in the Bible [*laughter*]. Who gives away all his things because, after all, what are material goods? That is truly the way you feel at that time: "What are material goods? Material goods are nothing!" You give them all away and all these people take them. Then, five years later, you're living on a fixed income; your children are growing older; your costs increase, etc., etc. Certainly they are not going to come around and return them and be helpful to you. Now my situation may have been more negative. Maybe not all families are like that. But that was my experience. My experience is that they have never come across for us at all, and yet, I felt this need, guilt, to be giving all this staff to them. So, I would say to any widow: put somebody else in charge of everything and make sure you hang on to every penny and every piece of goods. If anything is going to be disposed of sell it, put the money in the bank for her for later, for the kids' college. Keep that attitude in mind. It sounds hard, but ...

MICHAEL: That's your experience.

DEBORAH: That's my experience. Oh, I don't know, this is going to sound awful: don't trust anyone because nobody has your well-being as much in mind as you do. They always have their own in mind first and yours second! There were a few situations where that occurred. It's sort of a sad thing, it's reality versus ideals. And if you're not protecting yourself [*you'll be taken advantage of*]... That's what I've learned. We owned a townhouse actually, and we had a friend who was a real estate agent. "Oh, gee, you know, I can rent this townhouse for you, blah, blah, blah!" She put these tenants in it who were -- the mother was never there, the kids were playing loud music, burning cigarette hole in the carpet, having drug parties -- God knows what! Eventually it had to be sold at a loss. If they had been good tenants, if this person had really come across for me, she would have found good tenants, and I could have held on to that property, and if I were selling it now, I could have made a profit. You know, that type of thing! There were some things that really could have worked better. People just didn't look out for me; they didn't do a good job.

MICHAEL: Deborah, in all of this it seems as though you've highlighted a couple of things. I'm summarizing here: (1) You really took charge of your life, and you're continuing to do that; (2) Yet, you were deeply wounded by the death, but also deeply wounded by those around who ...

DEBORAH: Failed to help!

MICHAEL: Failed to help!

DEBORAH: It's as though you're in the hospital in bed and you are doing as much as you can do, but you're sick, or something, you can only do a certain amount. You watch people around you handling your things. Then you find out later that when they came to visit you while you were in bed, they would say, 'We're looking after everything' [*ha, ha!*]; and oh, yeah, were they ever! [meaning that she was being taking advantage of] That kind of thing. Yet, you couldn't do it [*take care of things, details, etc.*] at that time; you weren't on your own feet. Maybe it's not fair; I don't know. But that is the worst feeling in the world: to know that you're "wounded -- to use your word -- and not able to look after yourself while you're in that state. It's a little bit like in the herd: when an animal gets wounded, it falls behind, and it gets hunted down for the kill. The others don't look after it to protect it in the meantime. It's that sort of thing.

MICHAEL: What you've done is you've said, "Even though the herd has left me, and I'm wounded, I'm still not going to let myself be destroyed."

DEBORAH: Yes. And the best thing you can you do is look after yourself. But you're still wounded and you can't look after yourself as you would in normal circumstances.

MICHAEL: And your deepest pain and your greatest joy?

DEBORAH: [*Pause*] I think my greatest pain is to feel so alone. That's a good question! because, also, my greatest joy [becoming animated here] is, or I feel my greatest joy is -- I'll just be walking along, and, "Ahh!" [*her breath is taken away*] - the stars are out! Isn't this great! So, they're sort of the same, because you are alone when you see all those things. I do it too with my kids, but somehow I seem to experience it more, maybe, when I'm alone. You can't drag them into it. For instance, Halley's Comet is coming. I would say, "C'mon gang, we have to go to the university!" They would respond, "And stand in line for two hours?" But I have to see this! I feel all pepped up about it; it's so wonderful.

MICHAEL: The irony of all this is that you were forced into aloneness, but also, you see the mystery there as well?

DEBORAH: I do. Yes.

MICHAEL: Thank you, Deborah.

During the funeral the first thing my parents said to me was, "Well, you know, we don't think you should bring the kids to the funeral! We don't think you should show the kids the body!" I mean, that kind of stuff they called "help," -- I didn't listen to it.

— Deborah, commenting on her parents

COMMENTARY

At the time of the interview, Deborah had been widowed for seven years. She was only 34 when her husband died accidentally, and a lot of the pain at that time came about because of (1) not knowing the details of how he died, for he died 2,000 miles from home, (2) the mishandling of the subsequent court case, and (3) the rapaciousness and lack of understanding of both families vis-a-vis her situation. But now, Deborah is on her way to mending. She has a new home, a forest at the end of her backyard, her art work around her home, her three beautiful children, and an individual focus gained through suffering and integrity. Deborah's story awakened in her, as she points out in reference to the Swiss medical psychiatrist, Dr. Carl Jung, the *clarion call to new development*. Deborah was yanked out of "the collective" and forced, by the death of her husband, onto the path of the search for personal, individual meaning, what Jung called wholeness, or individuation. Individuation is what it implies: one's own individual journey, not the collective journey.

In reading Deborah's story, you can see the journey from passivity to activity, from the collective to the individual, from outer-centred to inner-oriented, from "their" truth and perceptions to "my" truth and perceptions. Death sorts us all out, and death will only accept my (i.e., the individual's) answer to the question of my life and my meaning. Death and its reality forces individual consciousness. Deborah's journey is taking her from lack of self-confidence to personal standpoints, from tentatively stepping into life to making a mark on life, from being carried by the collective to walking tall as a woman. In doing and walking that journey -- our own human journey -- she finds, like the rest of us, that we are often alone; nay, the aloneness brings us into contact with mystery. In response to my comment that her husband's death forced her into aloneness and yet also opened up mystery as well, she said, "I do see the mystery. Yes!" What Deborah is experiencing is the only valid reason for living our human journey in the first place, and that is because we have a meaning to our lives; there is a purpose, unclear at times, but definitely there, and definitely oriented towards transcendence and mystery.

Deborah's experience of her journey over these past seven years has been encapsulated in her metaphor of "surface" and "bottom," in relation to the movie

"Jaws." In the beginning, when her husband first died, "surface" meant "superficial," "bottom" meant "emptiness," "hole." She felt she walked around with the "bottom" half of her just bitten off. As a matter of fact, in describing this metaphor, she unconsciously said, trying to explain herself more fully, "It was a bit like that!" [*i.e, "bit" and "bite"*] However, as wounds and time healed, and she started to come alive and in touch with her own personal resources the "surface" became "life lived fully" and the "bottom" became "authenticity" and "integrity." Both the height and the depths were experienced by Deborah. This is a Christic image -- that of the cross -- and we all must stretch out on that wooden beam in order to know who we are and to be called by name personally. The collective is never crucified, only individuals, and, by the same token, only individuals attain resurrection or new life. Deborah had to change from "the old life" to her "new life" — spiritually and psychologically. She had no choice; she was forced into it by the death of her husband. Her husband's death caused her personal "resurrection"! into life today as an individual, as Deborah, and not only as an appendage (to her husband) or role (for her children). Even the family feuds helped in the development of her intensity: her values were now different from theirs.

Of course, in her human journey over these past several years, she has gone through pain. There is a price for everything — costs and benefits — and individuation is no different. She experienced the pain psychologically of her ego-consciousness (that part of us which is aware, when we say "I") not having all the answers, and undergoing its own passion and death in being humiliated with that fact; of the illusion of its freedom, as well as its necessity of bowing to a far wider, deeper, richer experience of life, what Jung called the inner Self, the force at the centre of the psyche. Religions call this centre Christ, Buddha, God. The awesome power and direction of this self at first seemed to overwhelm Deborah, as it does anyone coming into contact with it suddenly. But little by little, while lying flat out on "a bed" (to use another of her metaphors), Deborah began to see the wisdom of this inner dynamism. She started to feel herself as a human being because the Self's purpose is to bring us to wholeness. In this sense, then, we learn to rely on "another" wisdom in us: the wisdom of the inner Self which unerringly guides us towards our destiny. Deborah has learned to listen more consciously (ego) to the pulse of this inner dynamism (Self) and is finding that she is becoming more healthy, whole, happy, and an individual.

She's becoming the woman that the Self has envisioned all along. That's the only true sort of peace: one's vocation to be oneself.

At the same time that all of this awareness has been developing, Deborah also has experienced more consciously the reality that is always seen more vividly when one leaves the collective: the reality of evil! The Garden of Eden was a "place" where "total bliss" (i.e., unconsciousness) prevailed. Because Adam and Eve ate of the tree of good and evil, they were, according to the Genesis myth, expelled from the Garden. Then they were aware! Deborah, through the death of her husband, was expelled from the Garden too, as we all must be if we are to attain consciousness. But, in being expelled, we leave that state of "innocence", "total bliss" and "unconsciousness", and we begin our human journey to individuation and wholeness. But, there is also a price: we now know about evil. Deborah knows about evil because death is real to her. Deborah knows about evil because she was manipulated by her lawyer; Deborah knows about evil because she met it in the waves of pain and depression she experienced; and Deborah knows about evil by the way the "vultures", including family, around her see her for what she has (to give away, to bring to a party) and not for who she is. Evil would kill individuality. But Deborah, although often alone on her walks, can still look up at the heavens, and in seeing the stars, exclaim, "Ahh! The stars are out!" And her breath is taken away once again.

Deborah is standing tall now, at times perhaps a bit wobbly; but she is standing, and she's doing it by herself; she's living her own human journey. She is taking credit for who she is. With courage, she is taking her personal insights, and putting them into action. She is living who she is and she is loving who she is. She is standing tall, as a woman.

CHAPTER SIX

ACCEPTING, TRUSTING THE MASTER PLAN:
THE STORY OF MARJORIE

Marjorie was 66 years-old at the time of this interview. Her husband, Charlie, had died seven years earlier. Michael conducted this interview by phone. At the time, she had moved back to her birthplace, Alberta, Canada. Two years later, she moved back to eastern Canada again, this time to a small community/trailer park for seniors just north of Toronto, Ontario, to be closer to her grown children. Marjorie has since died also.

MICHAEL: Marjorie, how old was your husband when he died?

MARJORIE: 61.

MICHAEL: How long had you been married at that point?

MARJORIE: We had been married 37 years and 8 months [being very definite and with a good feeling of pride about that memory].

MICHAEL: What's it like to lose a spouse?

MARJORIE: First of all, with me, it was sort of numbness when it happened; sadness; emptiness; and with Charlie, knowing how he had suffered [*i.e., pancreatic cancer*], there was thankfulness that there wasn't suffering any more.

It had been a strain because it [*dying*] had been happening for two or three months. [*starts to cry*] Then I had feelings of guilt because I hadn't been with him when it happened; then, anger [*starting to sob*]. Yet I knew in these circumstances that it was the best. I was angry at the hospital because they had not [sobbing] notified me so I could be there.

MICHAEL: The impersonality of it all.

MARJORIE: Yes.

MICHAEL: Marjorie, how long did you know about Charlie's situation?

MARJORIE: They had told us in March that he had three or four months to live.

MICHAEL: So the grieving process, in a way, began at that point.

MARJORIE: Then. That was from March, April, May, and he died on June 22.

MICHAEL: What did you lose when Charlie died?

MARJORIE: You feel as though you've lost a part of yourself. Also, I would say a friend, a person that I had a great deal of respect for, and [holding back tears now] a very trustworthy person. Mostly though, you lose a part of yourself.

MICHAEL: That's the biggest gap?

MARJORIE: Yes.

MICHAEL: I appreciate your taking time like this because I know the subject is very close to you.

MARJORIE: [*Sobbing*] Yes, it's a little difficult.

MICHAEL: Marjorie, what do you want to do now? In other words, after his death when you looked ahead, what did you want to do for yourself? and looking at it from where you are now, 7 years later? Back then, after six months or so, how did you see what you wanted to do?

MARJORIE: Gee, I don't know. I'm just trying to think back to that time.

MICHAEL: What about now, then?

MARJORIE: Well, now I would like to take some sort of a course, but I'm not close enough to anything to do it. I would like to travel. I hope I can keep active, you know, getting out, going places, doing things. I like meeting people. Basically what I would like to do is take some kind of course, I don't know what, but just to keep so I'm not getting stagnant — keep the old mind working and keep myself alert.

MICHAEL: Do you have access to that sort of thing in your little town or would you have to go into Calgary?

MARJORIE: Well, I'd have to go to Calgary or up to Olds; of course, not having a car, I don't have the transportation for getting up there. I don't know what kind of courses they would have at Olds; they would have quite a few.

MICHAEL: That's a community college?

MARJORIE: No. It's an agricultural college, actually, but they do have other courses. I haven't looked into it. [Getting very animated] I would love to take up swimming! But they don't have any swimming classes for seniors here.

MICHAEL: Really!

MARJORIE: Right!

MICHAEL: Another question, Marjorie: when you think about yourself over the years, do you see yourself as having changed much? Or, how have you changed?

MARJORIE: Well, basically, I don't think I've changed.

MICHAEL: The same kind of perspectives, philosophy?

MARJORIE: My outlook on life is really still the same.

MICHAEL: What is the 'core' of that outlook in what you believe?

MARJORIE: Well, death is a part of living. If you can't accept that it must be very difficult. But I can accept that, although I sort of think, "Well, gee, [cries] why do the good die so young?" You know! [crying now through her sentences]. It just doesn't seem fair: you see some of these real rotten guys ..."

MICHAEL: In an article, Marjorie, in *The Toronto Star* recently, a priest in the New York subway was reading the book *Why do Bad Things Happen To Good People*, when some fellow came up and stabbed him!

MARJORIE: Oh, no! You wonder! I believe God has a plan, but sometimes I can't understand it.

MICHAEL: Marjorie, when you say you have the same "outlook," you're saying you have a context within which to look at life's ups and downs.

MARJORIE: Yes. I think so. A philosophy, if you want to call it that. My feeling is that I do believe there is a master plan and these things will happen, but [*choking*] sometimes they're hard to accept.

MICHAEL: Would you do anything different or over again now having experienced your husband's death?

MARJORIE: I don't ... The only thing is ... if I had it again I'd try to talk Charlie into taking more holidays. Basically, no. I think we did our best so far as the family and that is concerned. No, I don't think I would do anything differently again.

MICHAEL: How about before Charlie died, would you do anything differently there at all?

MARJORIE: Well, no. [*Hesitant, holding back*] I did what I wanted to do, what I felt I had to do. They wanted Charlie to go into the hospital; even when they told me, I couldn't do that. If I were in the same situation again, I would do exactly as I did. It was difficult; it was very draining. But [weeping], when you love someone you do what you can!

MICHAEL: Any suggestions, recommendations for someone else going through your experience?

MARJORIE: Do you mean someone in my age group or do you mean overall?

MICHAEL: Let's take your age group first. When your husband dies after 35 or 40 years — he's still young, he's only 61 ...

MARJORIE: Well, the first thing, don't make any drastic changes immediately. Don't wallow in self-pity. That's the worst thing you could do. Take time to assess your financial situation. Get financial assistance and advice. And look at what options you have. I was 59. Another thing: don't let other people talk you into doing things. Do for yourself. Stop and consider the situation: check your financial situation, get advice, and decide what you want. I would also advise, but, of course, this is not true for everybody: don't move in with family! [*laughs*] Of course, Charlie and I always said that that was something we wouldn't do, even though it was offered. Thanks, but no thanks! Do sit down! You have to take time, and, as I say, forget the self-pity. That doesn't do you any good; it doesn't do anybody else any good. Just quietly assess. Weigh what you really want to do. Maybe you don't know, but take time. It will finally sort of fall into place. But take charge of your own life.

MICHAEL: Eventually you'll see some pattern emerging.

MARJORIE: That's right. It will work out! [*very deliberate here*] Take charge of your own life. Don't let others tell you or pull you this way or that way. And thank goodness none of my family did that. But I know of others who have had it happen. You have to take charge of your own life, be responsible for yourself.

MICHAEL: During that time, Marjorie, did you feel that struggle to be yourself more intensely than at any time before?

MARJORIE: Yes. I think so, because people do tend to pressure you.

MICHAEL: Deborah, another woman I interviewed recently, said she experienced that she didn't belong in a "couple" society any more.

MARJORIE: Well, I found that out to a certain degree. Of course, being older, I guess it wasn't quite as blatant as it would be with a younger person, because any of the young people, their friends, the wives right away are thinking, "Gee, she might be after my man!" But I did find that, even with our age group, there seemed to be just sort of a different feeling. I don't know if I can put my finger on it. I don't think it was really that sort of feeling, and yet, there might have been, you know, the wives might have felt threatened that maybe you might be looking at their husbands. I don't know. But let's look at that: this one couple never did come to visit me once after Charlie died, *not once*!

MICHAEL: Some people who were close to you just sort of "evaporated."

MARJORIE: That's it! And yet we always called the man [of the couple above] unofficially our "adopted brother." The kids called them "auntie and uncle." Another couple came and visited me, but the one thing that hurt was the first couple who avoided me after Charlie's death. I thought, "Well, golly, maybe they figured they just didn't know what to say, or just couldn't face it, or what." But it makes you feel badly. You figure, "Well, gee, you'd get some support." [*choking here*]

MICHAEL: As if there is something wrong with you!

MARJORIE: Well, that's it! You begin to wonder, "Golly, why? Do I give the wrong impression?"

MICHAEL: Deborah also had strong feelings here. She said you have to stick by what you want and not let others — "in-laws and outlaws" — interfere!

MARJORIE: Particularly the young people. People think they're helping you, but they aren't; and you just have to stand strong, and say, "Now, look! [*even to yourself or to them*] What do I want?" Just because somebody says you should do this, or you should do that — it could be absolutely the wrong thing for you. You have to stop and assess where you are at and what it is you want to do! Forget the rest of them. Of course, with children, you have your responsibility to them which changes some of your ideas. But when you're all by yourself, that's a different thing.

MICHAEL: Death, then, Marjorie, forced you into asking what you wanted for yourself and how you were going to take care of yourself so that you could have a future that was worthwhile. Is that correct?

MARJORIE: Right. You have to stop and think, "All right, now, I'm by myself. What do I want and how do I get it?"

MICHAEL: Looking back over the last seven years, what was your greatest joy and your hardest pain?

MARJORIE: Of course, the greatest pain is being without him.

MICHAEL: The loss.

MARJORIE: Yes. I don't know what I would say would be the greatest joy. One thing that did give me a good feeling was the way Dianne [*her youngest, 17 at the time*] — although she was so young [sobbing here, this is painful for Marjorie] — she took over and handled many things; she was such a kid! [*really crying now!*] This is difficult — if you can wait on me a moment [*to collect herself*].

MICHAEL: Marjorie, you mentioned one time that all of these feeling inside just "burst" one day on you, a few years after Charlie had died?

MARJORIE: That was when I was listening to the T.V. Frank Sinatra's daughter, Nancy — her husband had died — pretty much under the same circumstances as Charlie. That's when the floodgates opened! Now that was over six years afterwards. But I finally let go!

MICHAEL: Are there many moments like that when "reminders" occur?

MARJORIE: Yes. I sobbed, I guess for a good five minutes or more. [*Now crying again*] I have my tears at night! Well, ... other times ... Things come up, and ... [*crying a lot now*] ... can you hear me, I'm sorry! ...

MICHAEL: I used the expression "wounded bonds" in the book. Some people might say the bonds (after the death) are totally broken. What I am trying to get at is that they're broken, fractured, wounded, but we never lose the bond. It's radically different.

MARJORIE: That's right!

MICHAEL: So even though Charlie is dead, you still have that bond with him through God, through the force of life.

MARJORIE: Right. Right.

MICHAEL: Does that make sense to you?

MARJORIE: Yes, it does. [*sobbing*] He's still with me.

MICHAEL: So the bond is there, but it's been really wounded, in a really radical way.

MARJORIE: Yes. Right. But another thing: because he's with me, that's why [*crying*] I don't feel I should ever say "never," but, I just can't see myself doing that. He's gone, but he's with me!

MICHAEL: The bond ...

MARJORIE: Is there!

MICHAEL: The presence is there.

MARJORIE: Right! Always will be.

MICHAEL: For me, Marjorie, if I were in your situation, that would be a very intense "presence" of God all the time.

MARJORIE: Well, I believe in God. I believe in life everlasting. Maybe having that feeling proves I believe in God, although sometimes you wonder yourself. If you do, you have doubts. But I've always believed. I believe in God and I think I'm sincere in that belief. I know some people profess that they don't.

MICHAEL: You have a faith about life, about now, and about life after death.

MARJORIE: I do.

MICHAEL: For me, Marjorie, in this context, I would want a lot of "alone" time.

MARJORIE: Right.

MICHAEL: And I would want to pray quietly...

MARJORIE: That's like me. I'm alone, but I'm not lonesome. I'm alone in the physical sense, but I'm not lonesome. I suppose you could say in the spiritual sense, I'm not alone.

MICHAEL: Marjorie, you were really gracious to spend the time like this sharing your story.

MARJORIE: I'm sorry that I choked up on you.

MICHAEL: That's a very normal reaction; you're not alone.

MARJORIE: It must be harder for younger people. I know, as you get older, you get a little more philosophical. You are able [to cope] if you have faith. I feel sorry for anybody who doesn't have faith in God. You're able to accept that dying is part of living. I don't say it's easier, but I think if you can understand it, you can accept it better. It must be terrible if you don't have any faith and you're unable to accept it. That must be a terrible feeling.

MICHAEL: Real darkness.

MARJORIE: Right. I feel sorry for anyone in that position.

MICHAEL: Bruce, a widower I interviewed for this book, said that a certain time [3 *p.m.*] is the hardest for him, because he and his wife always phoned each other at that time.

MARJORIE: Well, for me, the longest time is lunch hour because I expect Charlie to come home. He doesn't any more; he's gone, but he's still with me.

MICHAEL: Marjorie, thank you very much for sharing your thoughts and feelings. You have been very generous with yourself and your time. Your story is very valuable.

"Hope
is the scaffolding
of our existence."

— Henryk Skolimowski,
Polish-American philosopher

COMMENTARY

Marjorie was 66 years old and had been a widow for seven years (1986). She was only 59 when her husband, Charlie, died (1979). She had four daughters, ranging in age at that time from 24-40; the youngest, Dianne — the one she refers to in her story who helped her so much right after Charlie died — was 24 years-old at the time of the interview. She was the "young kid," according to Marjorie who, by her still physically being present at home at the time when her father died, gave her a support that was invaluable.

After Charlie died, Marjorie continued to live in the same house for about four years in Toronto. She sold it and moved to western Canada. She was born in Nordegg, Alberta, in the Crow's Nest Pass of the Canadian Rockies, and had a number of relatives still there. She wanted to "go back home" again, but especially, "to see my mountains" (Rockies). Marjorie lived by herself in a little town outside of Calgary. In 1991, she moved back to Ontario to a senior citizens' trailer park north of Toronto.

Marjorie's story is like "her mountains": she is "solid" and "firm" in her belief in God and in a Master Plan, even if that is very painful and difficult to understand at times. Undergirding Marjorie's philosophical attitude to life is a conviction that God's presence is very much part of death, for "death is part of living," as she says. She is sustained in her convictions that "something good always comes out of everything," even if it doesn't make sense at the time. God, like the mountains is clearly, rock-solidly present. All she has to do is to look out and see.

You will notice that at the beginning of her story, she talks of death as "it." She had been under tremendous strain looking after Charlie the last few months at home, or, to quote Marjorie, "it [dying and death] had been happening for two or three months." Later on, in her story, as she talks about her conviction of the master plan, death becomes more personal; she cries; she weeps; she is making room inside of herself for the reality of death, especially her husband, Charlie's. Towards the end of her story, she says that one day the "floodgates opened. Now that was six years afterwards. But I finally let go!" Death was no longer "it," but accepted as death; and the pain of Charlie's death — her best friend, the one she so respected, loved, and who was so trustworthy — burst over her. She had entered into the passion of accepting her vision of the Master Plan, and she wept and wept.

Marjorie speaks of courage too: take charge of yourself. She was insistent in her story that self-pity gets a person nowhere. Because of her belief in herself and in her God's Master Plan, she was able to make contact with the personal resources within herself to keep body and soul together. As a matter of fact, she aches thinking about people who do not believe in God: how difficult it must be for them to go through the pain of the death of a loved one.

Marjorie did take charge of herself after her husband died. She continued to provide for Dianne who was still at home, and finishing high school, and she took the time to go within — her own inner sanctuary — to be alone with her thoughts and feelings. And while the "floodgates" perhaps didn't open for six years, she did weep and grieve in the solitude of her own heart each and every day. Noon hours were particularly difficult, for Charlie didn't come home any more; he was dead now. The presence that greeted her each day for lunch was no longer physically there any more. Charlie was gone; Charlie was dead; and Marjorie grieved.

Death is so final, irrevocable, absolute. Death stuns us with its finality. Before the mystery of death we are left with our own feelings, our own bodies, and our own hearts. But, for Marjorie, death is also part of life, and that greater Design and Wisdom, which is God, tells us that His ways are not our ways (Is.55:8), and conversely, our ways of seeing things do not necessarily coincide with God's ways. Faith in oneself, grounded in faith in God, became for Marjorie the cornerstone of her personal strength and vision; they still are. God, for Marjorie, will not depart, or leave her; neither will her mountains (Is.54:10). The mountains remind her, not only of her childhood home, but also of the steadfastness of God's love for her and His Presence in her life, especially in the dying and death of Charlie.

Charlie has died, yes; he is no longer physical. *but his presence*, according to Marjorie, "always will be." While the bond of their physical relationship is over, the spiritual bond still exists. This bond, or presence, occasions her to ponder God's presence. Charlie's death opens her to the presence of God. She feels alone, but she knows deep down that she is not alone. There is still for her, as the Nicene Creed says, "the communion of saints." Charlie is among them. So, while she is alone, she is not lonesome. But that faith still doesn't take away all the pain, for, being human, and being Marjorie, she has what she calls "my tears at night!" And in another place, she says, "He's gone, but he's with me!"

Marjorie thinks about Charlie and the suffering he went through. She aches for him because of that. Like many people, she doesn't understand how a "good man like that" can be cut down in the prime of life. Death plays no favourites; the "grim reaper" does its work regardless. Marjorie is aware of the truth that Webbe writes about: that there are "dozens" of ways to deal with evil and many ways to conquer it. All these ways show the many facets of truth, according to Webbe, but he says that the "only ultimate way to conquer evil is to let it be smothered within a willing, living human being." Only in this way does evil lose its power and stop because it has been "absorbed there like blood in a sponge or a spear into one's heart."[1]

I have written elsewhere concerning evil that perhaps the most vexing and troublesome part of our undergoing our human journey is the essential question of evil. Evil is so senseless, especially those evil acts and situations where there is nothing but apparent destruction. We must cry out against evil; we must fight it with all our strength.

But, we also know that in the end, evil (death) will beat us. We will be defeated. We will go under. But, if it is true that we receive quality in life more than we design it — and I believe that we do — then we have to see that in our moment of greatest need, dependency, and receptivity, we receive Infinite Quality through transforming union (death to self) precisely because of our infinite need and receptivity. In this sense, therefore, from a theological standpoint, we go to God through evil by going beyond evil. Nemeck writes,

> ... true victory over evil is situated in the realm of faith, beyond evil itself. Evil as such is not directly destroyed. It does not have to be. For, left to itself, as we transcend it by faith, evil self-destructs, falling back by its weight into the multiple (i.e., what

the Gospel called exterior darkness). This occurs in and through the personal death of each individual. It will happen collectively at the end of the world.[2]

Time and eternity. Marjorie knows there is that bridge, even if it becomes so acute with the awareness of death. She reaches out from time and touches eternity each and every day, for Charlie is now in eternity. But in the reaching out, she's also quite aware that she has taken the posture of the Cross; she is suspended as Christ was. Yet, she too hopes and believes in the transcendence of this suspension, which is resurrection.

I simply need only to quote Marjorie, "I believe in God and I believe in life everlasting."

She accepts, trusts, and lives the Master Plan. "I will go up to the mountains ..." [*Ps.72:3; Is.37:24*]

"My feeling is that I do believe there is a master plan and these things will happen, but sometimes they're hard to accept."

— Majorie, commenting on God's plan in our lives

CHAPTER SEVEN

MEMORIES OF THE PAST
ARE HOPES FOR TOMORROW:
THE STORY OF BRUCE

Bruce had been widowed for six months at the time of the interview. He was in grief; he felt it very deeply. He continued to work at his store, but there was an ache inside that was seemed overwhelming to him. His wife, Olive, was dead now. She was only 53.

MICHAEL: Bruce, how long ago did Olive die?

BRUCE: It is now six months and two Saturdays ago. She died on a Saturday — 6:00 o'clock today. Exactly.

MICHAEL: How many years were you married?

BRUCE: Twenty-four.

MICHAEL: [*Looking at a picture of Olive*] She looks quite young! Bruce, my first question is this: 'What's it like to have your wife die?'

BRUCE: It's like having a limb cut off. I didn't only lose Olive; I lost my very, very, very best friend. The only really true friend I had in my life was Olive [*cries*]. Gone [*weeps here*]. That has created ...

MICHAEL: You're left now with a vacuum.

BRUCE: Uh huh. [*weeping*]

MICHAEL: There was you and your friend.

BRUCE: Yup! [*weeping*]

MICHAEL: And now she's gone!

BRUCE: Yup! In the obituary — oh, the obituary in the paper caused a little bit of consternation with her family: "Loving wife and best friend." They're Presbyterians. Their ethics: one doesn't wear one's heart on one's sleeve. I did. I'm never ashamed to show it, to admit that.

MICHAEL: Bruce, what was the impact socially when she died?

BRUCE: Olive's sister had died of cancer before that and Olive's mother had died also before that. Olive only has one brother left. Olive left a bigger hole in my family than I think she did with any of her cousins, aunts. There's a void in my family.

MICHAEL: Her sister also died of ...?

BRUCE: Cancer.

MICHAEL: Is that a family, or genetic, disease?

BRUCE: I don't believe that it's genetic. I just believe that cancer is the luck of the draw. Personally. I don't know enough about it. Having seen the number of people I saw at the hospital and also at Sunnybrook Cancer Ward [*Toronto Canada*]— I believe that you and I are here because we didn't get cancer. And if I get it eventually, then that's my draw. That's how I believe in it. I also believe that there was nothing I could have done to prevent Olive's dying. I believe that our birth, life and death are preordained. That's how I see it. I don't think there's anything I could have done.

MICHAEL: You're not looking at that fatalistically though!

BRUCE: No! No! I'm not looking at it fatalistically. I believe that is true. My death is preordained and I will die on such and such a date. I don't think that's fatalistic at all. That's just the way things are.

MICHAEL: That's the way you see reality.

BRUCE: That's the way I see reality. Yeah. Olive's death left this great big hole, like a meteor, in Unionville [*Ontario, Canada*].

MICHAEL: The image of the meteor, Bruce, ...

BRUCE: Is *death*!

MICHAEL: The bang too (when it hits the earth)!

BRUCE: Yeah.

MICHAEL: Raised a whole lot of questions there!

BRUCE: Yeah. I was affected by Olive's death tremendously, but all through Olive's illness, the people; it was surprising. I don't know whether I have a good reputation in retail, or Olive's was greater than mine, but, you know, we had customers and people from — the three predominant churches in town: the United, the Presbyterian, and the Anglican churches — the ladies came here virtually every day with a hot meal or something. You have to take three hours to go from here to the shopping plaza, have lunch, have a beer, and come back. Olive's death also created a great big hole in town as well. Everyone who knew Olive was touched by her.

MICHAEL: Were you always a resident of this town?

BRUCE: No, only since '78.

MICHAEL: Was home back in Scotland? [*because of his accent*]

BRUCE: No, in Metro Toronto. I've been in Canada for 30 years and Olive was born in the west part of Toronto. Olive was a Torontonian.

MICHAEL: Bruce, when you put the notice in the newspaper, "To My Loving Wife and Best Friend", how did you experience the family around that? You mentioned that they didn't like it.

BRUCE: My sister's reaction was, "Well, that's not something you do. Why have you done that? Silly thing!"

MICHAEL: In other words, "It's not appropriate."

BRUCE: No. And "he's worn this great big heart on his sleeve, and he shouldn't do that. He should pull himself together and not show his feelings, or his emotions." I think that's a very Presbyterian, Scottish attitude: You don't show any emotion.

MICHAEL: Your accent, Bruce ...

BRUCE: Is from Scotland.

MICHAEL: In doing research for a chapter last night on men/women, the research is saying men don't show their emotions as much. You, obviously, are an exception to that.

BRUCE: If I had married a Scotch person, a Scotch woman, then I would have been a very staid, emotionally disciplined individual. Olive was a very emotional person, a very giving person. Consequently, when you live with someone for 24 years, then you become that giving person as well! I was very lucky: I was touched by Olive too.

MICHAEL: She transformed you!

BRUCE: [Emphatically] Yeah! I know that I'm quite open with my emotions. I enjoy showing emotion; I'm not ashamed to show emotion.

MICHAEL: In terms of the experience of grief and bereavement, how do you find that?

BRUCE: We're talking about a guy [himself] who can sit down in the family room, watch a movie, and cry, and quite openly cry. And I don't hesitate about crying.

MICHAEL: And after the death?

BRUCE: Oh yes, after the death and throughout Olive's illness. I did not go to bed for about a year, but sat in a chair, feet on the cedar box, covered with a comforter, just to be ready to give Olive her medication. I was dozing one day, and all of a sudden I woke up — I don't know whether this is a sign of being touched, or a sign of God — I woke up one night and said the 23rd Psalm from start to finish without a break. I think that means ... that answers the whole thing right there. The 23rd Psalm, "Though I walk through the valley of death [sic] ... "Whoever wrote these words they were the most appropriate words in death and dying.

MICHAEL: That whole context of the 23rd Psalm gave you the emotional ...

BRUCE: Emotional support ...

MICHAEL: Vision that you needed to carry on.

BRUCE: Yes. If it hadn't been that, if I hadn't remembered that, I think I would have had a much harder time. And the other thing — I know this is not answering your question, but — I find that I was privileged in my marriage: "For better, for worse, in sickness, and in health," and I was able to fulfill all of those pledges I made. I had all "for better, for worse, for richer, for poorer, in sickness and in health." I had it all. I'm probably one of the few who was privileged to live through those six vows.

MICHAEL: I have never considered this in this way before.

BRUCE: As I said earlier, I'm emotional, and I think of these things. I was at a wedding a week ago Saturday. The groom was a kid that Olive and I had been godparents to 25 years ago. I sat in the *same* pew that Olive and I sat in, the *same* church, the *same* time; only this was a Saturday, 4:00 o'clock, and the wedding service was Saturday, 4:00 o'clock. So, their wedding was, for me, just a replay of the whole thing. When they were giving those vows, I was thinking [about the groom], "Are you really, really man enough if you're called on?" I don't think I'm any better than any other man, but I think I was given the opportunity to play a part in those six vows. I did it. I think I did it. My biggest concern was that I knew Olive was dying, and I was concerned that I might not be there when she died. I was very fortunate. Olive would go into a coma, into apnoea, and then back into a coma. When she died, I was standing beside her; it was 6:00 o'clock Saturday, and her thumb pressed my hand [*palm*] right here. Then she died!

MICHAEL: What a moment!

BRUCE: Yes, that was my biggest concern: that I wouldn't be there [*crying now*].

MICHAEL: She knew also that she was dying.

BRUCE: Oh yes!

MICHAEL: Did you talk with her about death?

BRUCE: We were an odd couple. We had our funeral arrangements made on our honeymoon! We had discussed it on our honeymoon. I'm an accountant. I guess I like to have all the loose ends tied up, a contract signed, and everything done so that I can get on with the rest of the "job." The funeral arrangements were easy because I used the same funeral parlour we used for Olive's mum. I just referred them to the same day Olive's mum died, and exactly the same funeral. So I didn't have that big burden of indecision, of caskets, of flowers, and cars, etc. It was all done on a fairly rational basis. It may seem to be cold and calculated. It wasn't meant to be cold and calculated. It was meant to be done in a systematic, intelligent way.

MICHAEL: You have your own feelings and emotions to take care of. If those fundamentals are already being administered ...

BRUCE: Yeah. My emotions — I was down at the funeral parlour before anybody got there. During the day and in the evening, I always made a point of being there. I didn't want anyone to drive me anywhere, and I was there before anybody else. So I had that time with Olive. I had that time together, although what was there was her body, she had gone; I had those moments for myself, another thing important to me.

MICHAEL: Your privacy.

BRUCE: Yes.

MICHAEL: Bruce, what's the most difficult part of Olive dying?

BRUCE: Loneliness. [*crying now*] The sad ..., ah, I went to a movie last night — the first time I went to the show by myself. It was hard; it was a hard thing to do. It's just loneliness. The first time you do anything it's that way. It's a hard thing to do by yourself. First of all, you automatically think people are looking at you, like, "Why's he staring at you? Why is he by himself?" The first time by yourself is very, very difficult. You have to break that pattern; you have to break that mold. I haven't taken that mold of "togetherness" yet, and smashed it and cast it aside and said "Now, this is a new mold; this is now! This is now me!" I dust and vacuum. I'm dusting and vacuuming for me. I'm not dusting and vacuuming for Olive. I'm not helping her to do the work around the house that I'm doing. If I make dinner, it's because I have to eat, not as a token for Olive.

MICHAEL: Do you feel that comfortable with people asking you out?

BRUCE: I have discovered that it is a lot easier for a man to be single than a lady. I think — the women who are your friends automatically become mothers, and they want to mother you. They also want the adulation of another man saying that their roast beef is every bit as good, or their apple pie. This may sound cynical, but it is not meant to be: they want that man to say, "Geez, that's good!" I think for a man it is much easier.

MICHAEL: You're not a threat or competition [*to these other women*]

BRUCE: No. I don't threaten my friend's marriage by paying homage to his wife, or to her cooking! She wants me to be there and say, "That's a nice apple pie!" He, like every husband, just accepts it, her apple pie. But she needs the adulation. I think she needs my adulation, and my praise. That may sound very cynical, but it is not meant to be.

MICHAEL: For her, Bruce, your acknowledgment of her is a positive stroke!

BRUCE: Yes.

MICHAEL: Recognition.

BRUCE: Yes! And I think it's easier with my surviving than Olive surviving.

MICHAEL: How would she survive?

BRUCE: I had trouble, even with Olive's death, because I was thinking, "Poor Olive up there. She was never very good in directions; here's she off on her own" [*good laugh here*]. I'm not being funny. Our soul is up there, and I'm not there with her.

MICHAEL: She has to rely on herself?

BRUCE: Yeah. When I think of it, maybe I'm belittling Olive. Maybe over 24 years, I'm the one who's driven the car the most; I'm the one who said, "This is the way we go to Florida!" So, maybe in a way I'm belittling her. Olive probably would have survived wonderfully well if I had died. Well, for one thing she'd have a job; money wouldn't be a problem. I don't think other men would be a threat to her. I don't think Olive would be intimidated by another man.

MICHAEL: It's interesting, Bruce, that, as you talk, you refer so much to Olive as being the one who guided you. And now, upon another reflection, you see that you also guided her.

BRUCE: No. I think Olive guided me as a human being, but I guided her by taking her from here to there. I think Olive made — and this may sound trashy — me who I am today. She made me who I am and what I am. She made me a man; and then she made me a compassionate individual. But I think going to Florida — I took her to Florida, because her sense of direction was pretty awful.

MICHAEL: She humanized you; you operationalized her.

BRUCE: Right! Right! Does that sound bad?

MICHAEL: No!

BRUCE: I don't mean I manipulated her like a puppet on a string, that she didn't make any decisions.

MICHAEL: When Janice and I discuss the differences between the masculine and the feminine, we say the masculine [*energy*] is "focused energy," and the feminine [*energy*] is more of a "diffuse awareness."

BRUCE: That's right!

MICHAEL: "In psychological talk we say the masculine is "focused consciousness", the feminine is "diffuse awareness", like the difference we make between solar and lunar consciousness. At midnight the moon is out — which is the feminine symbol; you can't see things distinctly, but things blend, whereas during the day — high noon - the sun is very present. Too much sun and you burn up. And too much moon, you're just grasping through the darkness.

BRUCE: When I say Olive made me who I am today, I mean: we had a system in our marriage. When I was working in the town before we opened our store, Olive would get up in the morning first, and she'd "hit" the end of the bath where there's no taps. She went in one end and out the other end, dried, put half her make-up on, came out, went downstairs, made a cup of coffee, came upstairs; and I had a cup of coffee in bed, sat on the edge of the bed, had the coffee and a cigarette, and when I had finished the coffee, I went into the bathroom — showered and shaved — and when I came out, the bed was made and all of my clothes were lying on the bed. If somebody asked me, "What suit are you putting on tomorrow to go to that meeting?" I would have to say, "I don't know. Olive hasn't put it out yet!" When I came out of the bathroom, my suit would be there; my tie would be there, my shirt, my underwear; my socks were all turned properly. All I had to do was put my feet in them. My shoes were there. Everything was on the bed. That's what I mean when I say that

Olive made me who I am today. She was good to me, stuck her fingers up my nose and led me to what I had to do. I was a very lucky individual, very lucky person. There are very few men whose wife did as much for them as Olive did for me.

MICHAEL: Bruce, what would have happened if you had not had an Olive?

BRUCE: What would have happened if I had stayed a single person? I would have probably ended up like one of my uncles — bombastic little man working for some company in Britain as an accountant. I think probably I would have gone back to Britain had I not met Olive. I met Olive on my birthday, November 30, in 1961, flew to Britain for a friend's wedding, came back again December 17, and I was taking another girl out. This girl wanted me to go up and spend Christmas with her. However, once my feet were under the table, it was game over for me. I said, "No, I'm not going." We had a big argument. She went up north, and I was left in Toronto by myself over Christmas and New Year's. I then phoned up this girl I had met, an Olive Baker. I didn't particularly like her. However, I phoned her up. She said she was going out with somebody else. I said, "Well, break it!" [that date and go out with me] She did! We kissed at New Year's Eve in this friend's house, and I think by five after twelve we were engaged to get married! It was so crazy! The whole thing was so absolutely crazy! We were 24 years together and we *never* had an argument! Never! Never argued over money, never argued over the colour of carpet or any purchase we ever made. *Never, never*, argued! Explain it to me. I can't!

MICHAEL: What do you want for yourself now or is it too early?

BRUCE: I think in a way it is a bit early, but I still at times stop, and often hear Olive walking through the door! I think at this particular moment, to come out and say exactly what I want for the future is very difficult. Real estate companies make it very easy for you to change because the day after the funeral I had them knocking at the door here with offers to buy this townhouse!

MICHAEL: How would they get that information?

BRUCE: Olive was very well known in town, and with all the crowd ... The day after the funeral the real estate agent said he would write out a cheque and an offer! I don't know what I want to do! I really and truly don't know. Some days I come down and say, "To hell with it all," and disappear! Of course, I'm fortunate I have a dog and a cat that need looking after. I think that's the steady part.

MICHAEL: They root you.

BRUCE: Yes. I have two animals that have to be looked after. You just can't walk away from them. I think this is a good thing. You look around at the things you've accumulated over life. What do you do with them?

MICHAEL: What you're saying, Bruce, is that this is my home!

BRUCE: Yes. This is my home, and these are my ties to Olive. *My memories of the past are my hopes for tomorrow*. That's the way I've always said that. I firmly believe that that's true; what I remember of vacations and everything else are the things that are my hopes that will hold me together tomorrow. I have no desire to meet another person, no desire to become involved again.

MICHAEL: You just want to be you.

BRUCE: Yes, and get on with my life and try and retain my intelligence, my sanity. Try to stay a good member in the community, of good standing.

MICHAEL: Bruce, in what way, or ways, have you changed?

BRUCE: I think I'm more tolerant, much, much more tolerant, much more forgiving, and [*laughing*] — Olive would appreciate this — I don't think I'm quite as cynical as I used to be. I think I've mellowed. I think death, I think Olive's death — if any good has come out of it — has made me a better person, a more *understanding* one. Olive's death has also put me back in the Church again. That was something I never belonged to in my life. I believed everything I was taught, but I thought it was fine to sit at home in an armchair Sunday morning and watch T.V., and listen to a religious program and turn it off when it was time for the collection. I think you have to become a committed member of the community, and, I think, out of Olive's death, I've become a community member.

MICHAEL: What would you do differently or over again?

BRUCE: Regarding?

MICHAEL: The whole experience of Olive dying.

BRUCE: If I could go back to two years ago, I would go back through the whole experience all over again! And do it exactly again, look after her. I'd do all that again. My only regret is, I think, — although the oncologists down at Sunnybrook asked the oncologist looking after Olive, "When is her husband bringing her into the hospital? to put her in here?" — and even though her doctor said, "I think we should have Olive in the hospital," I kept Olive at home an extra four months. I looked after her in the home environment. In the long run, I think I put Olive into the hospital a bit too soon. I still say December 18 was too soon! I sometimes wonder if I had kept Olive here if she would have lived a little longer. I kicked up hell in the hospital: Olive was in bed from September to December, four months. When she entered hospital she did not have one bedsore. Not *one* abrasion to her body. She had only been in the hospital four days, and there was a bed sore! I kicked up so much hell in that hospital. When I walked in there the nurses all disappeared because they didn't want to have anything to do with me. But I think that was my *right* to do that because I was a person who wasn't trained in that type of care in the home. "Yet, I was able to keep bed sores away! Why couldn't they keep bed sores away?" [anger here] This infuriated me! I stood over them until they eventually cured it, and I made them turn Olive as often as they possibly could — which was every hour — and I was there all the time.

MICHAEL: You did that here!

BRUCE: Oh, yeah! I was the one who helped Olive up every time to take her to the bathroom. She did not need a bed pan; she would not use a bed pan. I helped her walk, took her to the bathroom, put her on the toilet, and then walked out, closed the door till she was finished. I allowed her to retain her dignity [*silence now for a moment*].

MICHAEL: What did you lose when Olive died?

BRUCE: I think, initially, I lost my sanity! I lost a place.

MICHAEL: Place?

BRUCE: It's like having a book; you drop it, and you can't find your place again. You become very frustrated, because it was a good book and you can't find where you left off. I think that happened too; but I think I've found a place. I'm slowly finding a place. As I said earlier, I lost my very best friend. I think I lost a reason for living at one point. I contemplated suicide; I'm not ashamed to admit that. Before I tossed all Olive's medication out, I mean I definitely contemplated suicide two or three times. But I think that is also a healthy, natural reaction; and the only thing that stopped me from suicide was that I wouldn't be any closer to Olive. I would be further away from her. I wouldn't be accepted into heaven if I had committed a cardinal sin like taking my own life. This is how I thought. I also called a crisis centre one night. I spoke to a young chap. His wife was killed in a car crash. Everything I said, he said he went through exactly the same thing.

MICHAEL: That was very fortuitous.

BRUCE: Yeah! I thought maybe I'm not stupid; maybe I haven't lost everything; maybe what I'm going through is a natural reaction under the circumstances. I believe that's what it was.

MICHAEL: You talked about your personal philosophy, Bruce, in different ways. What do you believe in? I don't mean that only in a religious or "churchy" way, but as far as you life is concerned, your life's philosophy?

BRUCE: Well, I believe that — I don't believe that he who turns the other cheek gets hit with the other hand. My attitude to that has changed. I certainly believe that you have to do unto others as you would expect them to do unto you. I believe that you have to help people. You only reap what you sow. But, then again, it's a hard thing to go out and help someone because at times people say, "Who the hell is this guy?" I think we all have to learn to live together, stop the bigoted, certain jokes about death. Sure, we're all guilty of it; we all have a good laugh. I'm sure black people laugh at white jokes But I think that is what we have to stop in this world. We've got to get back to basics. I really believe that. I used to say to Olive, "There are people keeping up with the Jones' and for God's sake, stop; I can't go any further!" I think we have to get back to basics. I live in Unionville. I don't have a yuppie syndrome. I don't own a Jaguar; and that is a yuppie symbol. The number of Jaguars that are driven in Unionville! Nowadays, people are saying, "I'm #1, and I don't care who's #2!" It's me, me, me! I think that's the sad thing; that's what got to change.

MICHAEL: Olive's death really highlighted the whole aspect of service for you.

BRUCE: Yes. I thought at one point to go back to the university in September and go into divinity (priest). I don't know. September is not too far away; I could still go back to university. I have thought about it. I have spoken to my minister. It might be a step in the direction. I might not go as far as becoming ordained as a priest. But I think that's what Olive's death has done for me is to make me ...

MICHAEL: Rethink.

BRUCE: Rethink. I wonder *why* these things happen this way. I'm also very scared in the last six months since Olive's death. I really think we're heading into a world conflict. That scares me. I think we need to stand up and take notice. Very few people realize what is going to happen today.

MICHAEL: What kinds of suggestions or recommendations would you have for someone else in your situation?

BRUCE: Don't be intimidated by anyone coming with suggestions to sell your house, move on, or do anything. *Definitely*, don't hit the bottle. It's a temptation, but, if you're not a drinker to start with, or a social drinker, you won't find any answers in alcohol. If you're a smoker, stop smoking. I did. I was smoking 200 cigarettes a day! A week after Olive died I stopped smoking.

MICHAEL: You were smoking 200 cigarettes? [*hardly able to believe the figure!*]

BRUCE: A day.

MICHAEL: A day? 200?

BRUCE: 8 x 25's or 10 x 20's! That was in the last two months before Olive's death. My cigarette intake had taken a ...

MICHAEL: And you just...

BRUCE: A week after Olive died I was sitting in the kitchen watching T.V. with the dog, and I had ten cigarettes. I said to my dog which is all of six months, "At midnight I am going to stop smoking. I'm going to smoke ten cigarettes ...," and I haven't had a cigarette since. I object to cigarette smoking. My brother and his wife were here last Thursday, and he smokes and smokes and smokes, and I can't stomach it! I told him, "Next time you come back you going to have to stop smoking!" So those are the things. People say, "How can you possibly stop smoking after your wife has died?" That was the easy part of mourning.

When somebody dies the things you have to get over are just shocking. You have to get over the fact that that person is no longer in your home; you're by yourself. All of these things are just like a big shock to you. So your bereavement takes over all these things. If you add your cigarette smoking on top and your drinking on top of that, it's just another thing that you have to get over. So you just get over everything at one time! I would say to people: don't be intimidated by people telling you what to do. Don't do anything! Just sit! The biggest decision I made was opening the store. And I haven't made a decision other than that. This place [*home*] has to be painted. Olive said, "What colour are you going to paint it?" I said, "White!" and that was it! That was an easy decision. That's it! I won't make any decisions until next year. Decisions now are mainly emotional. You think you're making a decision to sell your house. You have to be cold, calculating; you sit down and discuss it. That's why I say to people:

don't make any decisions, and don't be upset to talk about your loss. Don't be afraid to go and talk to somebody that you know — like my brother. My eldest brother is great. I can talk to him, put my hand on his shoulder. A wonderful guy. He doesn't say much, but when you walk away after you've spoken to him, you've left your worries behind. Maybe he was sleeping all the way through them [*chuckle*]. But I feel good about him. He's a listener. And I think the most important part of the conversation is a listener.

MICHAEL: In preparing a chapter last night, Bruce, I marked down that probably the most important thing is to have a listener.

BRUCE: Uh hum!

MICHAEL: This is what a lot of people I've talked to and read about are saying.

BRUCE: You need someone to listen to you. It's surprising: the survivor needs a cadre. We need a cadre of people where we can get together. I know a young lady — a young mother — whose husband committed suicide. She says, "I don't have support." But there has to be that type of support. I don't mean you go out and sleep together, but a place where people can meet and say, "My kid is giving me a hard time. Does anyone have this kind of problem?" Some guy might say, "Yeah, when I had a kid that age, I thumped him!" And that's the answer. I really believe that. I was looking at Ted; his wife died two years ago. He has three sons. But I know one of the sons needs a good slapping. Two years after his mother died, he's still laying everything on the fact that it's his mother's fault. I think it's time to take him aside, take him behind the garage, and give him a good thumping! I said, "It's *not* your mum's fault."

MICHAEL: Quit blaming others!

BRUCE: Yeah! Quit blaming others! That's something we often attempt to do. Sometimes I come in the house and look at that photograph and say, "Olive, I'm mad as hell at you, for you've no bloody right dying!" I tell her she's had no bloody right doing that because it screwed up my whole life.

MICHAEL: Olive "up and died on you"!

BRUCE: Yeah! And at times I get really angry. Other times I say, "OK, sit down!"

MICHAEL: Bruce, what was the deepest pain and what was the deepest joy?

BRUCE: The deepest pain was knowing that Olive was going to die. Knowing that day in November, [*that she was soon going to die*] ... knowing for months, that was the biggest pain. The biggest joy? I got Olive into the car one day when she was feeling kind of good [*and left the dog and cat at home*] and we drove all the way along Highway #2 to Belleville [*Ontario*]. We had a nice lunch, and then drove home. She was in a good mood; she was happy. I think that's one of the things I will remember most of all. She was so happy. When Olive was going to the hospital — the first time she had to go to the hospital [for treatment] — I wrote letters to her. I wrote every day. About 2,000 in total eventually. They will probably never ever be published; they'll probably never ever be read by anyone else. But they were letters to Olive telling her what was happening to her and what was happening to us. They're very emotional. I get a lot of joy in reading them. I should take them out again. That was a good day.

MICHAEL: There's a lot of therapy there!

BRUCE: Yes. It also made me understand more of her cancer. Someone asked me if cancer is a great enemy. I said, "Yes, cancer is my enemy; there's no doubt about it. You can't turn your back on your enemy; you have to fight by helping other people with the disease.

MICHAEL: Know thine enemy.

BRUCE: Yes.

MICHAEL: Bruce, thanks for your time. I know it was difficult talking about certain parts of the story again for you; but, as you say, "I'm not afraid to cry; I can show my feelings." You have been most gracious, and I wish you the very best.
continue living; he chose life; he heard a deeper call to *live*, after Olive died, than to go to the "land of the dead" where she was. He thought of it, but he chose life; he chose "the land of the living," and in that choice, he chose himself:

COMMENTARY

At the time of this interview Bruce was now 55 years old. His wife, Olive, had been dead only six months. He was still deeply grieving. He missed her very much. She was his "loving wife and best friend," in spite of how all the relatives felt about that!

As Bruce describes his marriage of 24 years, in some ways it is so inexplicable. How do you meet a person on New Year's Eve, kiss her at midnight in your friend's house, propose to her five minutes later, and then live happily together for the next 24 years? How do you account for the loving attention, the tender sensitivity to each other that was theirs in their relationship? How do you account for the deep devotion and selfless dedication in looking after his wife that Bruce had for the last number of months as he watched her slowly die, and then, at the last moment to have Olive press her thumb into his palm and die?

Listening to Bruce is listening to a man who deeply loved his wife, Olive. More than ever, he sees now how she transformed him from possibly going the way of "the bombastic little man" to becoming a real lover, a man who could feel deeply, a man who could love her, and a man now who can love others. His relationship took him from himself to Olive to others. Being an accountant, he liked things "all neat and tidy," and he used this talent where appropriate in his marriage. But Olive, "who had a terrible sense of direction," somehow knew that love has its own direction; and Bruce was loved.

The great Church Father, St. Augustine, talked about the importance of memory. Memory is what links past and present. Memory makes us human. With Bruce, memory links him to his past with Olive; and in that experience, he draws hope for tomorrow. The memories of his past are the hopes for his tomorrows. Nothing is wasted, not even death. Life transforms and life redeems. The hopes of tomorrow find their roots in the seeds of today. And in Bruce' life, the parable by Christ of the seed that must die to bring forth new life is literally true. He has lived the dying and death of Olive; he now lives for the hopes felt and the promise of the tomorrows.

It wasn't always easy, of course. He thought of dying too, but that would not solve the problem of living for today, which is the main task. Bruce chose to continue living; he chose life; he heard a deeper call to live, after Olive died, than to go to the "land of the dead" where she was. He thought of it, but he chose life; he chose "the land of the living," and in that choice, he chose himself: he chose to be himself. He chose to go on loving as Olive had taught him. He chose to love life.

Bruce also talks about the critical necessity of *listening*. It is especially at a time of grief, bereavement, that one needs listeners. To listen is a very important aspect of loving, for it says that I am open to you — to your world — as you are and that I will accept you as you are. When we are accepted by others we learn to accept ourselves. We learn this in childhood. We learn this in our experience of God. It is because God loved and accepted us first that we can now love God and others (John 16:20). True listening is being open to another's thoughts and feelings. So often we listen to ideas. Many times it is difficult to listen to others' feelings, especially if these feelings are negative ones or arouse in us discomfort and unease. Feelings in bereavement are "difficult" feelings, and are "discomforting." Many of us do not want to think about death. Perhaps this is why then so few of us listen to those who have experienced the death of a loved one. To listen would mean to be open to the reality of death, especially my death, and that is much too "uncomfortable" for many of us!

Bruce could listen to Olive. He opened himself up to her living and dying completely. He closed his store for the last number of months to look after Olive at home. As a matter of fact, during those last months, he never went to bed at all, preferring to stay in a chair, with his feet up, and a blanket over him, "in case Olive should need me." His biggest concern was not being there when she died. But he was there and she knew it. She acknowledged his loving and attentive presence in the moment before she "slipped the surly bonds of earth"[1] by pressing her thumb in his palm. Contact listening. Presence.

Bruce listened also to his marriage vows. He remembered the six of them: better or worse, richer or poorer, sickness or health. He feels "privileged" to have lived all those pledges he had made. "I had it all!" He was able to fulfill those vows, however difficult the one — sickness — was at the end. They make him think of the meaning of them for young people today, and without sounding supercilious or inflated, asks if they really know what they are committing themselves to. Perhaps life is good to us that way: if we knew the details of our futures, many of us would give up and not remain faithful. Ignorance in this situation allows us to live into our futures and into the commingling of suffering and joy that is part of our every journey.

Bruce was ready when life asked him to listen most intensely; he did not fail life here. Cancer is still his enemy because his loving wife, and best friend was killed by it.

Yet, he also knows that a cleansing deeper than superficialities and a clarity more poignant than pain have tested his mettle, and he has survived.

All the theories come crashing down into the crucible of experience, and when life asked Bruce to live the dying and death of his loving wife and best friend, he said "yes" and lived it thoroughly. He listened to the depths of pain, of despair, of agony, and he found hope: in the memories of the past that become his hopes for tomorrow.

"We were an odd couple. We had our funeral arrangements made on our honeymoon! We had discussed it on our honeymoon. I'm an accountant. I guess I like to have all the loose ends tied up, a contract signed, and everything done so that I can get on with the rest of the 'job'."

— Bruce, commenting on his funeral arrangements

CHAPTER EIGHT

FACE THE WORST, TAKE UP THE BEST:
THE STORY OF ALLAN

> Allan was a professor of philosophy in a large mid-western university. His wife, Meg, was 40 years old when she died. Allan and Meg had been married for 19 years. For the last nine years of her life she had leukemia, and she knew it. They had two small girls at the time. Today they are both adults. Both Janice and I interviewed Allan.

MICHAEL: Allan, would you kindly provide us first with some details around family statistics?

ALLAN: Meg was 40. We had been married for 19 years, the last nine of which we both knew she had leukemia. We had married fairly young and had our children early. The leukemia diagnosis came when our kids were just around 10 years of age. We had two girls. We had picked the leukemia up because we were going to have another baby. So, she had a health check-up; and that's when they found the white cell count at 65,000! I think probably, of the hard things in it all, *the very hardest was not having a baby*! and it's been hard since. Two close friends have had babies; and we had very difficult pregnancies both times. One friend I haven't re-established contact with, partly because they have had illness as well, and have just been too tired really to entertain, but the other couple have let me play with the baby quite a bit, and I found through that that the whole pain of not having a baby has eased. This was just in the last month.

MICHAEL: What is it like to have a spouse die?

ALLAN: Well, there are two parts to that: (1) What's it like to find out she's *going* to die? There's a great deal of anger. I think more than anger, there's dismay.

Our most painful and long-lasting dismay was about not having another baby. In fact, two more, because we wanted a second pair to complement the first two. But there was also, for the first few years, a great deal of anxiety about the girls that we did have because we were worried that it [death] was going to come at just the very *worst* possible time, not that there is ever a good time to lose a parent, but that it was going to hit them just as they were starting into puberty.

MICHAEL: They knew at the beginning about . . . ?

ALLAN: No, they didn't know at all. I'll back up and come to that in a minute. We were anxious that, as much as possible, they have a normal childhood and a normal adolescence. We didn't want them forced too early into being too old.

JANICE: How old were they when you discovered this? [*leukemia*]?

ALLAN: Well, you can do the dates more carefully if you back up ... well, it was '67 and '68 that they were born ... and '76 that we knew.

MICHAEL: And they would have been older, then, when you decided to talk to them about their mom's situation?

ALLAN: Yes. So we went actually seven years before we told them. One of the reasons was that Meg didn't want *anybody* to know. She, at first, didn't see much point to going on. The despair was quite generalized. "What's the point, I mean, in any event?"

MICHAEL: Did you know that she could live that long when you first knew about her illness?

ALLAN: No. The reasonable estimate for chronic mylogenous leukemia then, and still now, is between 2½ and 4 years from diagnosis.

MICHAEL: And she lived?

ALLAN: She lived nine years. Certainly after the first year or two we realized that our main problem was to live richly and well with as much time as we had. By then, I think, the adjustment to death had been made and the hard thing was adjusting to going on living. They are two very different sorts of things in a way. One is sort of being able *to face the worst; the other is being able to take up the best*! and to take it up wholeheartedly. I think we learned to do that. The years got happier and happier. We felt more and more lucky. It sounds strange to say it, but I think the very best of all our months was the last one. You asked for some particulars of the death experience: we got to be very good judges of the condition. We knew when she would likely need a transfusion, or when things were enough out of control that she was likely to go into hospital, and so on, because she was a trained nurse as well.

MICHAEL: She was aware of a lot, then?

ALLAN: She knew. I did as much reading [*on the illness*] as I could. So we had far better than average lay knowledge of her condition. But she also had a very good physician who kept her well informed, let her know how he thought things were progressing because he was usually very realistic about this. He pointed out the general uncertainty of applying statistics to an individual case. So, we knew that our time was running out, but Meg knew better than just in general that one day she'd be ill. I think that for the last few months she realized that the changes that were taking place were ones that probably were not quantifiable in the blood or enlarged spleen, or whatever. She could just feel her body losing strength and not regaining it, and in a strange way felt relieved. It was an end to some of the uncertainties. It forced home *just* what that nine years had meant. It had meant that small children had become young women. Indeed, they had. They were both exceptionally good, with themselves. They went on and did their school things, went out with friends, and had a lot of fun. And they found time to talk and to do some practical nursing. They didn't do a lot; there wasn't a lot that needed doing. But most of all, what they did was show her [*Meg*] what she had done, how far she'd gone with them. And, I think by this time the uncertainty and the gradual weakening brought about knowing that.

MICHAEL: There was a definiteness.

ALLAN: Yes. So, when it looked pretty dangerous and pretty sure that she would go into hospital and not come out, she persuaded me to go up to the cottage. When we first went down and saw the hematologist, he said, "Well, it's pretty critical. Even going into the ditch [with the car] is enough to rupture the spleen, and you're too far away there for anything to be done, not that, with a ruptured spleen, you'd even be able to do anything in the city, but you would be less likely to get injured. So, it's a risk. I think you should go!" He was that kind of hematologist [*laughs, pleased that the doctor had taken that attitude*].

We went and we drove carefully. We spent a wonderful week up there. It was just this time of year [*March*]: cold and raw when you get up there, and in the course of the week, the leaves come out. We had some *stupendous* [*really emphasizing this*] sunrises and sunsets over the lake. The cottage has bay windows and is up on a cliff so that when you sit up in the living room day bed and look out, all you see is the water between the toes and the trees. It's really marvellous! Anyway, this too is part of the overall thing, the realization that the world is good and what makes it worth it is the beauty of things. When they're spoken [these kinds of thoughts and feelings] they sound like abstractions, but they're truths. They're more important than truths, maybe.

There was one night like that just in the last few weeks. We went back in to town; she was admitted and three weeks later she was dead. One night, in the last three weeks, I was out in front of the hospital and I think it was the happiest moment of my life. I knew that it was only matter of a few days, but I was *so* happy! And near that time, in the hospital, we had some strange experiences. [*Pauses*] I don't remember if I told you about the time we were making love. Did I? I was fiddling with the bandages. Actually, I got pretty good at changing the dressings. Meg started running all kinds of infections, and she always had a little tendency toward a sore toenail; it was just the way they grew. So, sure enough, those sorts of things, which are minor irritations in ordinary life become medical problems once your immune system starts to get infected. She got an infection. I kept it cleaned, and so forth. The nurses would have done it, but I liked doing it. It feels good to do *real* things! to show you care. Anyway, I was changing it. Meg was also shifting a lot of fluids because the salts balance would upset her tissues. And so her skin got kind of puffy and stretched like a water blister. So, with the hand cream I was massaging her ankles and changing dressings and things like that; and she suddenly just got aroused, looked at me, and said, "I really wish we could make love now!" I said, "We can!" We just looked at each other; and I was rubbing her feet and looking at her, and it really was lovemaking! It was very close. And the nurse walked in. She saw us. Now, she had seen me a hundred times, changing dressings, an so on. So, it must have been something in the room, rather than the situation [*laughs*]. She was shocked! and backed out and, Meg said, "Go find her." I went down the hallway, and there she [nurse] was crying, and I told her that Meg wanted to see her. She went in, but before she went in, she said, "But, don't you people realize how serious it is?" I said, "Yes, I know but there is only a little while left."

MICHAEL: Yes, precisely.

ALLAN: So, she went in and they talked for about half an hour, and the nurse came out, came up to me, put her arms around me, kissed me and said, "You are the luckiest man alive!" and just walked on down the hall [*Allan laughs*]. I went in and said to Meg, "What did you two talk about?" She said, "I think you know; I don't want to say." So, it stayed at that. But I, I *think* I know. I don't know the words. I know the sense of it. I know because it's what she said to *me all that time* [starts to weep at this point], all the many years. So...

MICHAEL: You said before in an earlier conversation that you have experienced different perceptions and feelings about your experiences.

ALLAN: I've never had a great visual memory. For instance, if someone said, "What does Michael look like?" Of course, I'd recognize you on the street. But, if someone had said to me, "Describe him," I couldn't have come within six inches of your height or fifty pounds of your weight! [*laughs*] I wouldn't have remembered your hair, your face shape or your build or anything. Just wouldn't! But, I would remember your *voice*, and if I had read anything you wrote, I would remember it. It's a funny thing, when I mark papers [*at the university*] I can go through a pile of sixty essays, and if it's their second essay for me I know every single student. I could open the paper in the middle and read a paragraph and I would know whose paper it was. It's something in the way people put words together and the sound of things. Most of my dreams are like listening to the radio rather than watching TV [*laughs*]. So, Meg's face was something that just rarely would come to me; if I'd sit and look at a photograph of her, then memories would come. But not much otherwise. But the *voice* was always there. I could stop and hear her voice. I could think how she could say something and it was as though she was speaking. About a month ago, the voice stopped.

MICHAEL: The voice stopped a month ago.

ALLAN: Yes. It was just *really* ..., I mean, I hadn't even realized how much it was present! Like how often, I would think of her saying something, and it wouldn't be just "I" in my own idiom and in my own voice-tone. My mind would say it to myself and say it was actually she who said that. It was rather as though I could hear her voice. But it's gone. Now it's shifted over to the other side, "I know *that* she said..." Even if I read something she wrote, the voice is gone. The hand notes evoked a response just the way a picture would. But the sound of the voice is gone.

MICHAEL: Is that a sense of objectivity now, or...?

ALLAN: I haven't a clue!

JANICE: I do know that people who go blind forget what objects look like and forget the colours.

ALLAN: It could be something as marked as that. I am just not sure how to describe it because in a way it is like describing an absence; it's describing something gone.

MICHAEL: Now you're moving into the realm of poetry, perhaps.

ALLAN: Yes. What it describes is the sense of something like that. I had a girlfriend in high school who had her leg amputated. It took a while before she knew, of course, she knew that it was going to be taken and woke up knowing that the operation was over. But there is another kind of knowing...,

MICHAEL: Acceptance knowing.

ALLAN: I guess so. But it is more. It isn't just a sense of acceptance that you're ready to really believe...

MICHAEL: That it happened.

ALLAN: I understand what you mean by that. This is another thing. This is to feel the loss. You feel for the first time what you had before you lost it. You and I don't know what it is to have legs as completely as Mona did [*girlfriend in high school*] because we've *always* had them. Now I can say this, yet I don't know: if you know what it's like to have children in the house all the time. As they grow up, every way your day tempers itself toward you having these children. I get up early for work; I'm looking at my watch, about 7:30 or 8:00 AM, to call the girls for school. Well, one of them has moved out, and the other is a big girl who gets up when she pleases. 4:00 in the afternoon, I am ready to put the kettle on because they will soon be home. Of course, they're not [*coming, because they have their own lives to live now*]. Things become so deeply ingrained in us and then they're shaken up! All the little things — not having to do them now — shape themselves around us, and are now shapeless. Now they fall over. *I don't know when to make tea any more*!

MICHAEL: I subtitled my book *Grippings* with the expression "trusted meanings." I got that subtitle from the research on this book on widowhood. Researchers talked about people experiencing a "loss of trusted meanings" which they would express by saying something like, "I don't know when to make tea!" When Janice and I lost our *in utero* baby at six months, we lost some trusted meanings. We now look out and babies are alive for us... not that we haven't had children before. Babies are miracles in the most profound sense!

ALLAN: Yes! That is *exactly* what I mean. It's because you have *had* a baby, you know the wonder and the joy of having a baby. But I don't think I knew the whole of having a baby until my two [*girls*] stopped being [*babies*] by growing up! That completes the experience. I'll always be their father. Well, you ask what's the hardest thing... I don't know if I told you, but I went back last fall to visit my mother. My father died when I was 15. My mum at the time went through two very, very difficult years. I sort of had to "be her husband"! She'd often stop and call me "Paul" [*husband's name, Allan's father*]. I have never actually called the girls "Meg," but, I've certainly turned to them. I hear them walk in, or they make some gesture, and suddenly, I catch myself [*because the noise reminds me of Meg coming in*].

My mother went through two very hard years, and then she buttoned everything down emotionally, and went twenty-five years without. But last fall was the first time we ever *really* talked about it all, after twenty-five years! We talked an enormous amount. And one of the things she said — she said it in response to what I'd done — a cousin was showing us some amber jewelry from the Baltic. It's one of the family treasures... lovely pieces of amber! Anyway, I like amber because it's irregular and pretty. I said, "O Meg!" I said it very softly, and just looked up, of course. I think everyone... or I didn't know if people had noticed, or had "politely" not noticed because there was another conversation going on sort of over our heads. But mum had noticed. On the way home she said, "That's the one that's the hardest of all!" She went on. "I do that." There'll be a beautiful sunrise, and I'll say, "Oh, Paul, come and look!" The greatest thing is when you know what they're missing. It's not missing them, because in a way you don't miss them. Either they're out of your mind, and you're not thinking of them for awhile, or you miss them very acutely because you're really experiencing their absence. Suppose you're deeply in love, but separated by a few miles. Well then, you're longing for the loved one; the loved one is still in your thoughts; you feel sort of lonely, but excited, and closed up and far away, and all this. So when there's this poignant recollection, in a way it's sweet; it's a memory of the good times. Certainly after twenty years of living with her, I couldn't feel cheated that life hadn't given me enough, not that I wouldn't have wanted another forty! But the twenty were already pressed full, heaped up, and running over! [*laughter all around*].

JANICE: That's really wonderful!

ALLAN: It *was*! I honestly don't feel sorry for myself.

MICHAEL: Your life was so rich as it was.

ALLAN: Yes. But I can feel sorry that there are these things: the amber jewelry, the sunrise, babies...

MICHAEL: How wonderful it would be to experience that together.

ALLAN: Yes, or for her to experience it. This is what death means to the dead: no more of this; it means not being here for this. And the loss of it all is very hard. I do remember it — this is weird! — *I just heard her!* [*weeps at this point. Allan has been telling us that Meg's voice is gone, but now, as he tells his story, it is back once more. It surprises him, and he weeps!*] I just remember her saying that the hardest thing is to say goodbye to you! and that's what that [weeping] meant. I mean, she had worried, "Will you cope?" "Will you crack up?", "How will the girls do?", "Will you try and change too much too quickly?" All the practical and intelligent things that people help each other sort out. But I think it was the leaves coming out, and the thing we learned that last week at the cottage was that death means giving up the world and that the world is beautiful. That's the real tragedy of the whole thing. I mean, so far as one has projects that one wants to complete, that's very frustrating to an active person. If you are suddenly sacked from your job, how will you cope? What one has to work out of it all is that our achievements are small, and really, part of maturation is realizing how small they are. So, not to do everything that one dreams of doing is, in a way, a relief, and a good thing. It's a bit of realism; it's sometimes painful, but at the same time, there is gain. But the thing that there is no compensation for - I don't want to say the enjoyment of life -is the appreciation of the world. Being able to see: this is what's cut off. Death is a kind of barbarian that comes in and ends the glory of the world for the person who dies. It's all over for them; that side of it is over.

JANICE: Allan, what you are saying is very beautiful!

ALLAN: In another sense, that I've already mentioned, there comes a moment of peace. I remember having a very, very vivid dream. I can't remember the dream at all vividly now, but I remember that I had this dream. I held her [*Meg*] in my arms and was going to make love and gradually her body turned to a corpse and disintegrated! But she spoke to me, and it was, "Let me rest now." It sounds obscene, but it wasn't; it was beautiful! It was an erotic dream, fundamentally a dream about love, and about letting go, and it was really good.

MICHAEL: Did you have this dream last fall?

ALLAN: Yes. This was in the fall, probably three or four months ago. But it was powerfully erotic and very, very vivid. This one was like an actual bodily experience, including the experience of the dead body, and of the decay. I mean, it was veiled, but it was not ugly. *It*, too, is beautiful. This was the peace that we found at the end, that there was a time to die. We had talked about going into intensive care, and earlier on we had talked about bone marrow transplants, and so on. She had, and her hematologist supported her in this, a very naturalistic attitude toward health. But medicine doesn't save us. Basically, it isn't something that comes and *does*! You do it for yourself. Either your system reacts and uses the medications it's given, and heals itself, with their help, or it doesn't. So there was this attitude to it, and that seemed right. And toward the end it seemed very right that we wouldn't just prolong things at all costs, squeeze another five days out of it if we could. That's part of the affirmation of the beauty of natural processes and the beauty hasn't stopped! But, she's not here to share it! I think I'm [*taking a pause now*]...

MICHAEL: Doing fine. Allan, Janice keeps saying, "You've got to have Allan tell about..."

JANICE: Oh yes! Allan, one time, in a conversation with us, you went down the scale about raisng young women, and you went all the way down, and you had little metaphors all about how you reacted to raising your daughters, and dealing with them all the way down [*the years*]. It was so beautiful. You said, "I'm not bad in dealing with young women; I'm pretty good with teenagers. You then went on back down, and worked your way down to saying that you were a "Michelangelo of babies!" [*everybody laughs a lot*]. Allan, are you finding it difficult with the girls' leaving home? Are you experiencing a sort of empty nest syndrome?

ALLAN: Yes, very much.

JANICE: Would Meg have experienced it too?

ALLAN: Oh, yes!

JANICE: But you would have worked it out between you in a nice way, because you would have had each other to bounce ideas off?

ALLAN: I don't know. We would also have had each other to intensify it [*the girls leaving home*]. In part, I turned away from it; there's only so much pain you can carry alone. We really didn't fear pain that much. I had been a commercial bee keeper for four years. She had needles stuck in her all the time. And with the leukemia, sometimes the bones would really hurt. The bone marrow would produce really deep aches. But, as cancers go, it was by no means a bad one. In fact, probably of all the ways to die, it was gentle and as dignified as could be. Most cancer is associated with a great lot of pain, and this was "bearable"! That's because she controlled her own medications, being able still to be active rather than a patient. I think the dependency is what hurts, or makes the hurting hurt in a way that makes it abusive of the self. If the hurting is something you can manage, and try to do the best you can with it, then hurt just becomes, I guess, like the sore muscles one gets from working in the garden. If you sit at a desk all day, it feels good to have blisters on your hands [laughs]. In somewhat the same way, if you have bodily pains, you can cope with things. Now, I think we would have hurt a lot more about Sarah's leaving home [daughter] and Jennifer getting ready to if we'd been together, because we could have hurt more. We could have done more about it.

No, I'm almost a remote spectator. In a way, it is like Augustine's matter about the mother blackening her breast so the baby won't mind so much! It's also... I feel it, not as though I intend to ... not that I harden my heart. It's, I feel *myself* that there is a biological programme in me, drawing me back from them, just as there is clearly one in them sending them forth into the world. Jerome Bruner [*psychologist*] did, and is doing, I guess, research on the child's acquisition of language and one of the interesting things that comes out of his studies is that people really seem to have a genetically coded set of behaviours for dealing with young infants: turn-taking, playing peek-a-boo, and so on, aren't secret things that the parent learns and teaches the child to do. They are actually interactive rhythms that spring out of the child and the parent and there's something of that happening at the tail-end of childhood as well, that the child naturally, at 14 or 15, gets much more concerned about school friends than about parents.

But then this other thing, when they're 17 or 18, they seem actually to resort to anger against the parent. And, speaking from a sample of one, if parents react not with your typical anger which you might feel with a 14 year-old, — where you actually get into a quarrel — but here, you find that this is deeper and worse: you react with indifference, with understanding, with sort of "so be it"! And you're shocked to find this, but you would have to fake being angry back, because you're not angry. It seems right and natural that they should say it. What doesn't seem right and natural is that you should feel this way. You wonder where the twenty years of love went. You wonder why you're not upset, and since you're all alone, there's not much you can do about it, and you just find that you note it almost as a remote fact, that they're breaking free.

JANICE: Is it like the sense of the chrysalis where one thing is changing into another and you just look at the beauty of life, as you call it?

ALLAN: No! It's like death without the beauty. They're going on, and you're interested in them and involved with them. That's beautiful. To the extent that it sometimes makes you go back over those twenty years and feel again so vividly what it was like - when they were born, when they were three, when they were eight, whatever -- that part's beautiful. But this, what's happening right now, just seems like nothing, just a kind of emptiness.

MICHAEL: A vacuum.

ALLAN: Yes. I feel stupid, dull, dead inside. There is nothing positive in it at all [*feelings about kids leaving home*]. The future looks good, but as I head toward my own life or theirs, the past comes back sweet. And right now, it's as though they were strangers. It's not constant that way, but it's wrong, and it's taking up more and more of our time. I honestly think that they'll go a few days without thinking or worrying about me, or *feeling* anything toward me. They may think, but it will be in the thought-sense rather than in a felt-sense. And the same for me about them where, as long as we lived together, there was always the attunement. You're just aware of whether it is a good day or a bad day for them, what they're excited about, what they're looking forward to, what their disappointments are. I mean, you know, and you feel the tone of them as real as you know it's a cloudy day today and the weekend was sunny. In the same way, you're sort of always caught up in the other person's shoes, but not now!

JANICE: I think how I enjoy my children. I enjoy them. I enjoy their presence. I'm glad to hear them coming in the door at the of the day. I think, "What would it be like if that door doesn't open and these two little -- they're not little any more! -- people don't walk in again." I don't know what I would do then. I feel the same about you, Michael, coming home. I look forward to that.

MICHAEL: In listening to you, Allan, I was thinking that it takes a lot of maturity to live the moments of one's own story so that one doesn't get totally despairing or totally inflated. Right now, there seems no obvious answer to what you're going through, although you have an intellectual sense of it; but, there's not an obvious "you know, this all fits, and I feel good about it" answer. You have to really wait, and eventually, there emerges ...

ALLAN: But I don't think that it emerges as an answer to a tough question in logic, where you read it over and sort of think, "I might try this or I might try that." You think it over, and the next day something comes to you and you work on it and see that it does or doesn't work out. This comes just, it seems to me, completely out of one's conscious control. Things like losing her voice, or suddenly, just for no reason, being uninterested in one's child. Or suddenly, just being caught with the most hopeless belief that your child is gone. These sorts of shifts - you can make up little explanations to tack on to them after the fact: "Here's what I'm going through. Here's why I'm feeling this now," or whatever. But I hold all of these things in some contempt against the extraordinary complexity and mystery of life. It's the same with babies: they're just miracles! It's amazing that we make them in our bodies! If you compare the most complex things we can create, deliberately and thoughtfully, with our minds and how they work, and so forth, and then to even see a child play with its tongue, you realize it is all "straw," as Aquinas was supposed to have said of his work. They are wonderful things too, the things of the intellect. But they really don't encompass too much. They're really tiny forays into the foothills of reality.

MICHAEL: Dr. Carl Jung refers to the relationship of our conscious side to the unconscious as the relationship of the "flea to the elephant"! And we know who's the elephant here! [*laughter*]

ALLAN: Yes.

MICHAEL: What would you recommend for someone with this same experience? Anything come to mind?

ALLAN: At which point along the way?

MICHAEL: Well, widows we have talked to have all mentioned getting finances in order, for instance.

ALLAN: Oh yes! There are a lot of very sensible and practical things like that that need to be taken care of. I would think that, if it is within your power, the most important thing is to try to understand enough of your medical condition that you know what's going on in you, the way a doctor would know.

MICHAEL: You're talking about yourself as...

ALLAN: I'm talking about the two together. In sudden death, there really is nothing one can do except clean up after with things. But I say, if you know that you're facing a chronic illness -- and perhaps it's even the same for old age -- it's really very important to not put yourself in the hands of others, or in a kind of blind trust that the scientists may come up with something that in some way is a cure for it all, because there may be short-term cures for a lot of things, but there is no fountain of youth, no getting around death. Even if you get around *this* death right now, you're not hiding forever from it all. And you had best face up to it, if it looks like a reasonable doubt. I'm not saying that one shouldn't take proper treatment, or have surgery, or whatever. Of course, you should, but largely because it will improve the condition of life, not because in this way you won't have to face death, because you do have to face death. You do, right now! And I do. I think somehow we've split our society — those whose business is to face death, the death experts — and the whole rest of us who, because we put our old people in old-folks' homes and because anyone who is sick is taken out of the house and moved to this institution; because our chickens are butchered down in the slaughterhouse, not in our front yard. We don't really know anything about the end of life, the birth and the death of it all. And yet, to not know — we're really like little children having a nightmare — I think, it's worth getting involved, if not to be living the life we're living. As soon as you hide from what people are tempted to call the "ugly reality" — they call it ugly because it's not real to them — if they could make themselves real, they would actually see that it's kind of wonderful that we live at all! If your immune system is kind of "clicking on and off," what will amaze you is that it ever works at all! If you really came to have some understanding of how it does! The resources we do have, and strength, will impress you tremendously. Just see how much [killing] it takes to get rid of a human. I think that's the first thing: explain the facts. Our society encourages us to be frightened and put it in the hands of somebody else.

MICHAEL: Face reality.

ALLAN: That's the second part of this: facing reality; but it's also taking a kind of responsibility. It's not saying, "Well, I'll go to the doctor and he or she will fix it." This is *my* life; I *am* my body. It isn't like a car that's not working and I have somebody else take care of it. This is *me*! This struggle to exist, to hold out against illness, even to the failure of the system, is *my* struggle, *my* act! I might enlist others to help me with that, but it is fundamentally mine. If you don't have that you're like someone who has a treasure that could be stolen and taken away from you. You're not in the combat; there's no striving beyond that, only a fear of what's coming. But you won't even feel how good it is to be alive because you'll have to shut your mind off from what your body is like, because you can't do anything about it. But this is because you make a split between your conscious will and the animal will that's living in your body, making it live every moment it's living. We make a sort of rational decision to turn the body over to the physician as though it were a piece of property you could will to someone else, or for someone else to take care of it, instead of identifying ourselves with *this* striving and within the limits of this striving, to feel ourselves in unison. I think, however you can make that fit, the most important thing that anyone can do is to be active. And I think that -- what sort of advice? -- well,...

MICHAEL: For the survivor.

ALLAN: The advice I'd give is this: anyone who wants to come along giving advice is making a fundamental mistake; and the fundamental mistake is thinking that anybody else outside the situation has a sort of insight that they can come and lay in the lap of the person who's actually there. [*Instead*] I would ask, "What have you learned of the grieving process? What can you tell *me*? What don't I know that *you* now do? Where have you been that I may have to go one day, or that I have been, but don't know about?" It's a bit as though you imagine having raised a couple of kids: you know how to look after babies, and can sort of walk in and tell any young couple! I *could* tell the young couple, but the advice I'd give them would be that every baby and every parent are so different that you have to learn it yourself. I would want to know what they have learned; I would want to know what John and Shirley [*friends of Allan's*] have found out from Christopher [*their baby*] that I might have recognized that I found out, or discovered something anew! It isn't practical sense in this business of saying, "Turn around, look at yourself. You're just not a thing to be worked on. You're a *living* force in the world and you're *alive* now, for perhaps a shorter time than us. But, live it! And tell the people around us that they've got to understand that it's good and it's precious and that it's theirs. And then afterwards, it doesn't change because the dying person has stopped [*because the body has stopped*]; their time is up! If they have died well, then you have died. The necessity isn't a necessity that comes, out of an argument, but out of your loins and your pulse, and the living truth of your body.

What you've come to realize in all of this is that to be alive is to let yourself be. It isn't something you've decided: it's something you know already, that you can cut yourself off from this, not realize that it's happened. You can sit there and sort of realize, "God, what am I going to do with the rest of my life? I'd better make a plan!" We make a little plan and then we go out to live it, as though you can kind of create a thing. Well, I don't believe you can. I think what we must realize is: one, the living reality of us is that you must die; the other living reality is that as often as not, it is not a "true or false" [*as in an exam question; everyone laughs*], but somehow to accept those. It's not that one *shouldn't* plan; it's that one shouldn't just think that, unless I plan, nothing will happen! You have to turn around and say, "What is now happening?" It's like raising kids. You can't sort of say, "Let's get a good book on how to make babies and raise them, and then we'll just follow the instructions and we'll have a baby! You'll realize that when the baby comes along that it's a baby already on its own dynamic course. You can either look always at the book and just turn and *impose* what's the best. You can deceive yourself. Honestly, it won't work; it won't stick very much. Whatever happens to the kid will happen, a lot [being decided by the child], or you can see that a child is a process of growth, and of activity, alertness and consciousness and feelings, and so on, just going on, mingling with the processes of your own life.

JANICE: Follow the process; live the process. Wasn't it Jung who said that "the goal is the way and the way the goal"?

ALLAN: Yes! That's exactly right! The thing about what advice I could give out: there obviously is reasonable advice, but make sure the people are willing [to hear it]. All the sort of stuff Ann Landers would say about the fact that it's a good idea to decide who you're going to give little personal effects to, write the names on scotch tape, and put them in the bag. Yes! but, that's advice for everyday life anyway! For example, cut the grass, take out the garbage. It's not like that for this situation. I guess the advice for this situation is that it isn't that the living should take a preordained path, accept whatever path is preordained for itself! Whatever change it is, that is your whole living self. It brings up new ideas. Some of them will rise up to your consciousness; some will remain unconscious; you can feel them. Or, just knowing *that* they're there without knowing *what* they are, you will have a kind of openness to the mystery of it all. If you think that I'm going to have to do this, and this, and this, you'll be like the little tin soldier that never looked to the left and the right, and just marched steadfastly on! I have lived that way. I lived, that, I suppose, in the early years of my manhood, partly; being bright, you read books and you get a lot of ideas from them, and then you try to live those ideas instead of living your life.

JANICE: Is there anything you'd wished you had done that you didn't do before Meg died?

ALLAN: Oh!

JANICE: Like in the sense of...

ALLAN: Like, have two more babies? [*laughter*]

JANICE: I was thinking in a practical realm. There are no practical things you felt...?

ALLAN: I could have insured her for a million dollars before the diagnosis! [*laughter*]

JANICE: Before my father died, he helped me buy a car; it was in his name. It got paid off when he died. Michael asked me, when I first met him, "Why didn't you go ahead and buy a Mercedes?" [*laughter all around*]

ALLAN: Oh, there are many, many things that we did stupidly, or that we neglected to do, or were scared to do. There are lots of reasons people don't do as much as they might.

JANICE: But no one thing that sticks out, like, "I missed that," or, some have said, widows particularly, "I didn't have a will," or "no good pension", things that are important to them, now that they've got a lot of things to unravel as a result. Practical things.

ALLAN: No. But we were able to talk for nine years, and so we talked about a lot of contingencies. And if there was a simple, practical course of action to take to it. We made sure that we hadn't accumulated too much debt because for the first few years, we didn't know whether I might have a half dozen years of raising kids on my own. But then, some things we did that were a bit expensive. We bought a coffee maker that we could ill afford. But we did so. I thought about it, and Meg agreed with me: to become fairly well off in five years time, and to have done more when she was alive. Other things you'd wished you had done. If we hadn't been a bit daring here and there, I'd now be looking back and saying, "God, why didn't we go a bit in debt?" because we knew that my salary would continue to rise, you know, and all that! And here I'm sitting on all the prospects of her whole life spent being "too careful." So, it was a balance. Were we as bold and daring as we might have been? No! We didn't take a world cruise, or go back to Britain, or whatever. But, this *too* is part of the "privacy" thing; that you don't let the circumstances suddenly force you into becoming frantic, and becoming another sort of circumstance, as far as possible. Live within the normalcy of things, not sort of suddenly look for a miracle cure, or suddenly engage in a life style that you wouldn't have chosen otherwise. Try to be yourself! Part of being yourself — one of the things we enjoyed was managing our money well, having a lot to give to charity, being able to take good care of our girls and of ourselves, but not living in luxury, which we thought was [*not for us*]. I don't knock it either. It seems to me that North Americans spend too much of their attention and effort on purchases, and far too little on books and music, and nature. And we had a lot of time for that. We always read a great deal, and always talked an enormous amount, not just after Meg was sick, but throughout the whole twenty years of our marriage, we probably talked an average of three hours a day to each other.

JANICE: That's very unusual.

ALLAN: It was. We were an extremely unusual couple.

MICHAEL: I can't remember exactly, but from the communications research, I think they indicate that couples "talk" about twenty minutes to each other per week!

ALLAN: [*Laughs*] I think that three hours a day is a silly understatement. We would easily stay an hour or so in bed in the morning, with coffee.

MICHAEL: Is there anything that comes to mind that you would do over again?

ALLAN: I would say I would have done a lot of things differently, but I would not have done them in the time we lived together; I would have done them in time since. We *hardly started*! [*laughs*] So much to learn, about *everything*! Cooking, love-making, gardening, talking to each other, thinking things out. Things like the children leaving home. What I would have done differently is tack another 40 years on. What I don't remember [*is*] that there [*were*] enough good times to make it worthwhile. What I remember is that we grew up late and slow, because both of us losing our dads at 15, had, in a way, and being quite bright, become precocious adults, but also not really adults, with underlying deep insecurities and immaturities. And these took their time to work out. Still into our 30s we had personality defects, maybe even to the extent of disorders, immaturities, fractiousness, misunderstandings — all kinds of things that we were resolving. And I don't see that's changed in the 40's. Now, I'm working out some of the easy answers that I mistakenly gave in the 30s [*laughter*]!

Oh, this is going to get me on my hobby horses... which is North America's ideas of what it means to be a human being. To be a woman is to be like the centrefold of *Playboy*, and to be a man is to be, maybe, in your mid-30s. You're sort of [supposedly] physically at your peak; you're independent, and really owe nothing to anyone or anything. This is what it is to be a person! But I don't see this at all. To me to be a person is to be, not some state of the human being, before and after struggling to pretend to be that old and afterwards struggling to pretend to be that young, as if you're a kind of static thing that just sort of goes out to parties, drives sport cars, and does whatever those types do.

Instead, it's to be a baby. I was reading Dylan Thomas's "Fern Hill" yesterday, and it's so powerfully sound in the innocence and wonder of boyhood. The glory in the world when you're 8, and have a 22 [*rifle*], and a raft, and a tree house! That world is a world of greatness, but it would be an enormous sadness if one's child reached that mental age and stayed there. At the same time I could see loving such a child. But, how do we grieve? We are *not* one priceless moment, not even the sum of our priceless moments. We are what pushes through each moment into the next and casts back into the past, and takes up something else from it and starts up over again. Remember the kids' reading: they'd go through *Freddy The Pig*, and so on, and then they'd get into more interesting things, like Rosemary Sutcliffe, and so on. And then you'd to up to their room, and there they were — 9 or 10 years-old — reading *Freddy The Pig*! [*laughter*] and hugging the doll! That's all right too!

By saying that it's the passage through the years I don't want to suggest it's some nice straight line of growth. It isn't. Oh! ... I just has a visual image: I was sitting in the bathtub, bombing the duck with the soap [*all kinds of laughter*]... Well, the kids had bath toys! And I was going around — boom!! boom!! — and Meg was standing in the bathroom doorway, biting her lip to keep from laughing out loud. Finally, she made a noise and I knew. But, I'm sure that I *was* three years old there playing with the three year-old's toys! And that seems to me to be much more of what it means to be a person. To be this thing that casts about in time and follows some general rough direction, but generally, doesn't get it straight, doesn't get it right. There isn't a "right" to get it, except that there is getting it or not getting it. And, if you're worried too much about the "right," you're not getting it because then you're objectifying what it is to be a human being. You're identifying yourself with that externalization of yourself. I don't mean to be rude about your profession [*referring to me, and psychology*], but the idea of people discovering themselves in group encounter, seems to me a bit strange; like, thinking it all out, figuring it all out, or getting it right is all a way of intellectualizing ourselves. Maybe the better thing is to wonder when it's all messy and realize that this is the self. The self isn't hidden in this confusion of thoughts and feelings and inconsistencies, and some contradictions. You're got to sort through them and then, you'll find the self. The self is already there!

JANICE: It is all that!

ALLAN: It's all these edges and muddles; and it's the ability to untie knots and straighten things out. But it isn't what gets sorted out. It's the sorting out of things that is the self, as well as being unable to sort out. That, too, is the self.

MICHAEL: That is one of the reasons, Allan, in my "Human Journey" presentations that the metaphor of "story" is so valuable, because you tell me your story, you're telling me your "living." This is who you are, and your story can, from one perspective, look messy, but from another perspective, it looks pretty wonderful, very creative, no preordained path -- I'm just living my story. We make so many judgments that this "story" is better than that "story."

ALLAN: And that's wrong.

JANICE: Or, these parts or those parts are more or less valuable.

MICHAEL: Now, there are some parts of the story — you say, "maturities and immaturities" — I really like that; it's very 'Teilhardian' [*referring to Pierre Teilhard de Chardin and his writings*] I talked about that in my book, *Grippings*, where we outgrew a lot of our immaturities. Psychologists, I think, get sidetracked, concentrating too much on the "immaturities." When I'm 3, I play like a child of 3; when I'm 10, I playing like a child of 10; when I'm 37, I play like a child of 37. An earlier "immaturity" may be totally integrated by the time a person is 40.

ALLAN: There's a book by a man called Ronald Blythe, called *The View in Winter*. I highly recommend this: recollections and remembrances of people, I think, past the age of 75. And it is basically this with very little editorial work. He's taken 5, 6, 7 page interviews, put them together. But it's the most marvellous ... it lets you be a little bit inside the story that will be yours to tell, maybe, in 40 years; but not now! It lets you enter into this mind, and one of the amazing things about it is that it almost as precisely as it could be expected to, contradicts the American idea of our prime and our best years: "We're not yet fully human until we're on our own! by the time we're 55, we're pretty well past it! Oh, there are still some bits of humanity clinging to you [laughter], but not a lot!"

The interesting thing about *The View In Winter* is that, when you look back on the whole of life, you see that the times that were most real, are really from childhood through to really having to cope with the external world at 20, or so: taking up your course, studying at university, whatever! until you get to about 45 or 50, and know well enough your trade, and are well enough established, that you can start to calm down and *go inner again*! I mean, childhood was so long. A summer holiday lasted "years and years and years" [*we all laugh*]. Oh, there were so many days! Now gosh, you know, "I've got 2 things to do, and 4 months is hardly time enough to do them in!' And it's gone before you know it. Again, in old age the days slow down; and these people, looking back on the whole of life — and I think they're well placed to judge — find that their deepest, most human experiences, are the first and the last third of their lives! And that middle third is a bit of a loss — a price we have to pay! The busyness of raising our kids, getting our careers established, buying the house and paying the mortgage, trading cars every couple of years, and all the other busyness of life ...

MICHAEL: Unless you buy a Volvo! [*He owns one; all laugh*]

ALLAN: Does that make sense?

JANICE: The quality of life is lived as a child because you're not worried about acquisition; the quality you pick up in the middle, you're in the process of building and acquiring which doesn't, somehow, hold the quality of life that this wonder and appreciation do ... I don't even know if children appreciate the moment; they just live it! And older people learn to relive it, I would think, from that wisdom of looking back. I would think that that's the wisdom they have gained: is to re-appreciate, just live it!

ALLAN: Do you remember the distinction Heidegger makes between "meditative" and "calculative" thought? Calculative thought is to pose a problem which can have a definite answer to, like, whether it's better to finance the house *this* way, and a banker, or financial expert, could tell us. Meditative thought — there isn't an answer: trying to understand the relationship between Hamlet and Ophelia, or something. There isn't some "you've got it, or you haven't"! You really just summon up the known facts.

Well, I think, one of the changes with our life is that for the first and last thirds, there is a much higher proportion of "meditative" thought in them, of daydreaming, of wondering, of simply considering the facts. But these middle years get taken up almost exclusively with the programming thought of calculation: the jobs you've got to get through before the day is over, what you have to accomplish this year, how well you're getting on in the world, and where you've got some weakness that has to be corrected, and so on. We tend to see ourselves as problems to be solved in those middle years, instead of as things to be contemplated, e.g., works of art. And so, we're much more sort of "science-minded" in our middle life, "arts-minded" at the ends!

JANICE: I would think so!

ALLAN: Childhood is the time for dream and fantasy.

JANICE: Yes, the creative ... I just see as "living the process." Children don't choose to do A, or B, or C; they just go through the day. They're happy, or they're sad, or they're, whatever. We touch base with that again when we get older, and realize that all that calculating, or "calculative" thought, that you were talking about, is the quality of living. It enhances the physical aspects of living, perhaps, perhaps not, depending on your circumstances and choices. That fits in very beautifully ... I see living life, and going through the process as a cyclical, or circular, or spiral thing: playing with a "ducky" here, and you come around the next time and play with the "ducky" this way; and you come around and play with the "ducky" another way! The same thing: if you go in a linear pattern — ah! But, it's a big spiral. And you keep coming back to things again, new, and again ...

ALLAN: But even that, Janice, suggests a "neatness" that life doesn't have.

JANICE: Possibly. Perhaps we might be able to come up with a better image of what it might might look like. After all, even with the "messes," physicists are now showing us that there is a pattern to the randomness.

ALLAN: Or, just realize that any image is a simplified model. I don't disparage clinical counselling that tells us the pattern of things we experience, you know, like practical things from babycare books to the elderly, and everything in between. There is a reason to have some idea of how things generally go. It's the rigidity of mind that thinks things ought to go normally.

JANICE: That. That's normal!

ALLAN: Or the close-mindedness that won't see that when there is a departure from the norm, that too is normal. It's normal that all things shouldn't be typical and straightforward according to the book.

MICHAEL: I quoted it again in *Grippings*. I have some favourites over the years. Paul Valery, the French writer, says, "A great silence listens and I hear hope!" I love that because it tells me that what we consider ordinary can also be "unordinary": what is in our minds, and what we read about as the "pattern" (norm). In my moments of silence, how I'm living my life is much more coherent than the pattern.

JANICE: When you say "pattern", I think of my sewing that I've been doing. I always get a pattern, but never follow it [*laughter*]. Exactly! That's me! I may add more here, take it off here, sew it this way, sew it that way, or lay it on the chair in a different way from what they said. [*Pronounced*] *I don't always follow the pattern*! But I come out with something that looks "normal"!

ALLAN: But, you wouldn't want *not* to have the pattern at all?

JANICE: That's right!

ALLAN: It's sort of something that you play off.

JANICE: Yes, then it becomes mine. It's like "similar to" the original design. We find, though, that people who have no idea of what their "story" [life] means to them really get lost and have the key pulled from under them when they lose a spouse - if they don't have a sense of their own story, or the story that the two of them have together.

MICHAEL: No context.

JANICE: We need, a context to be who we are.

ALLAN: But I don't think that this is limited to death. I think that there are lots of other ways. People live a very precarious sort of life if they're not talking to each other, or if they are not listening to themselves. There may be a kind of "mutual convenience", a "pleasurableness of companionship"; but, also, I think they're prey to vacillation and to a lot of dissatisfaction. It's as though they're bored all the time, and so have the restlessness of boredom.

MICHAEL: We have many people in counselling with precisely that problem. They often "have everything," but are bored; and are asking, "What am I going to do with my life now?" They don't seem aware of any inner life for themselves.

ALLAN: You know, this thing about the "story": it's all just made up! You really do make it up as you go along. I'm not saying this in contradiction to ...

MICHAEL: That you create yourself.

ALLAN: Yes. I still believe you don't create yourself; but I believe the making it up is a kind of spontaneous effort at self. That is, there is a kind of creativity of the imagination that is from a mysterious source within us. And if there are two of you living together, what really is so self-sustaining is the interaction this takes place. We [*Meg and Allan*] lived a most uneventful life. We didn't do anything bold or wonderful, see strange sights, or exotic places. But, what happened, we'd be talking one day, and in that day's talk we might remember something that had been said a week before, or something read, or thought, or felt. And it would get brought in. And then, a month later, "Do you remember how we were talking about *that*?" And we'd go back and see that we'd missed a whole other aspect; and it would be doubly fascinating, first to fill in the bit we hadn't thought about when we were talking about it, and then to talk about how it is you fit in and don't fit in, and why, at a certain age, or approaching it one way, you'll see one side of it and miss another. All I'm meaning is, the thing just generates itself, this process of being alive. It's a dialogue that gives itself things to talk about. I think people who know a long life in silence gradually give themselves less and less to talk about, as if the words drain out of them, until finally, if you asked them, "Why are you married to this person?" or, "Who are you?" or, "What's been going on in your life?" - they wouldn't have anything to say. It's just all atrophied.

MICHAEL: We experience that in counselling; almost wrote a book on it!

JANICE: Yes.

MICHAEL: It's a sad indictment. That's why I like Jung's comment that the greatest tragedy is to come to the end of your life and find that you haven't lived it.

ALLAN: I know that [*quote*] and remember it well.

JANICE: [*To Michael*] I was thinking, if anything should happen to you, and someone asked me what would I have added to that time, or done differently, I would have been in the same boat you're in [Allan]. I would say, "I did everything I could do at that time."

ALLAN: [*Jokingly*] Maybe I should have had a lover on the side. [*Everyone laughs heartily*] Other than that...

JANICE: Keep you pretty busy!

ALLAN: I did all right!

MICHAEL: I'll get myself insured on the Mercedes, Janice!

JANICE: I'll go buy a castle!

ALLAN: But, it's obvious! I mean, you didn't need to say that. I don't mind that you did. But it's so obvious that there is just not the two of you there. There's really the one of you, and each is half of it. And you can feel that *fit*. My sister has a marriage that would leave Meg and me round-eyed after we visited with them. We kept the visits brief. They were pleasant, nice people; but they weren't obviously connecting with each other, hence, with themselves. You can't shut a bit of it off. You either open it all up or you shut it all down, but there doesn't seem to be, a middle ground, at least from my experience. Anyway, you can't sort of be selective and really know and understand yourself but not the other. Or, really tune into the other and lose yourself. You can play at that as a kind of game. Some people do; I don't. You know, "I've sort of buttoned my hatches, and locked myself into myself." But you pretty soon find that it's small in there [*laughs*]. What is easier for me is to lose myself in the kids, make them, you know, the whole focus of awareness, as a way of hiding from yourself. But neither one works. Anyway, they had a marriage [sister and brother-in-law] in which they really closed things off, and it really frightened us. Just to see how much strain there is on a human being to stop living!

MICHAEL: Harder to do that than it is to live!

ALLAN: You would think so, but the funny thing is [*laughs*], that all things wonderful are rare and difficult. But it is difficult just to be a little child. It's difficult to live unencumbered with a lot of crap!

JANICE: You've got to work at it!

ALLAN: It's difficult just to be natural and yourself. It's so easy to be anything else.

MICHAEL: Janice, is he saying we have to get rid of our 42" TV? [*everyone laughs*] By the way, Allan, your dining room, is like an "archetypal room!

ALLAN: It's funny you would say that. My sister and her husband would make good meals, but they wouldn't *taste* them. I mean, even if something doesn't turn out, it's hard to put other things in your mouth and not notice that you're doing that! And yet, they would chug-a-lug. And even if it turned out wonderfully, they still wouldn't, in an animal way, enjoy the taste of it. It would be a kind of intellectual satisfaction that they hadn't failed *this* time. But the positive side to it is that food is very, very close. It's probably as important as sex to us. But for a family to get together, for friends to get together — without eating — there is just one bond that takes place.

JANICE: There is a taking in: taking in of the relationships and taking in the food that sustains us to be there for the relationships.

ALLAN: At the Philosophical Days, when we have everyone bring dishes in, and the fact that the people in philosophy generally meet for lunch, it is much more than just sitting together: it is much more than words can say.

JANICE: Food for soul.

ALLAN: Yes.

JANICE: Food for body.

MICHAEL: A black-American woman in one of my classes once gave a presentation on "soul food." According to her, it had to do with the time of slavery. "Soul food," according to her, *connected* the slaves, one to the other; it was a sign of their relatedness.

JANICE: A mother can stay at the stove and dole out the food, or bring it to the table and pass it. These are two different experiences.

ALLAN: Feeding a baby, and obviously being fed as a baby when we were young, had to be a very, very fundamental experience.

JANICE: The first thing you do with a baby is put it to the breast. It comes out of the womb where it's been fed internally, now it goes immediately to the breast.

ALLAN: I can't think of one specific thing of merit, but if I had my whole life to do over again, I would want to do it as a woman and have babies! [*laughter all around*] If that had been my life, I might be saying, "I wish I could do it as a man!" But we really aren't complete in ourselves. There are our parents before us, but there is also the spouse we live with, and the children we bring into the world. And we don't make any sense as individuals. It would be like taking all the Hamlet lines out of the play, and just trying to make them apply. It isn't a play; it's the interactions that matter.

MICHAEL: Thank you very much, Allan, for your time with us, and your views on life, death and relationships.

"... the extraordinary complexity and mystery of life. It's the same with babies: they're just miracles. It's amazing that we make them in our bodies! If you compare the most complex things we can create, deliberately and thoughtfully, with out minds and how they work, and so forth, and then to even see a child play with its tongue, you realize it is all 'straw,' as Aquinas was supposed to have said of his work. They are wonderful things too, the things of the intellect. But they really don't encompass too much. They're really tiny forays into the foothills of reality."

— Allan, commenting on the mystery of life

COMMENTARY

What was most apparent in doing an interview with Allan was his deep concentration on the subject at hand, his sincerity, and his great sense of play. Allan loved to play and it was this quality, of enjoying the moment, enjoying good wine, enjoying good relationships that was very evident.

To listen to Allan's story is to listen to the story of two lovers. Allan and Meg were quite young when they got married. They had two children and always wanted two more. They were in love with each other and they loved their children. In one discussion Allan pointed out to my wife, Janice, and me that he was "a Michelangelo" with babies!

It was after ten years of marriage that Allan and Meg discovered that she had leukemia. Of course, there was total shock at first. This was unbelievable! Could it be happening to them? And yet they knew that it was happening. Interestingly, because of their love of life, they continued with the routineness of life. And so, for the next seven years, so as not to place undue stress on their daughters, they lived "richly and well," as Allan describe it. They allowed for their children to go into puberty as safely as possible. Of course, they did not know how long Meg would live. Statistics said possibly three or four years. Meg lived for nine years from the time she first discovered she had leukemia.

What one discovers in reading Allan's story is that his life and his relationship to Meg were his journey, and together, they were their journey. They lived their human journey intensely. For them, death became more and more a part of living. What is outstanding at one point in Allan's story is his sentence that they saw it as their task to face the worst, to take up the best. The lesson here, of course, is that they both learned that "attitude is the navigator"! and while they had death on their doorsteps more obviously, or consciously, than others, they still could make the best of it; and they proceeded to do so. They took each moment as it came; they savoured time; their cherished their relationship; and they loved their children.

Attitude as navigator suggests that, in spite of the troubles and difficulties we may have, we also have our attitude as a guide through these times. Our minds and our hearts have a lot to do with our focus on life. How we perceive the world has a lot to do with what we want to see and how we want it to be. Attitude again. I have mentioned in other writings that we become that which we love and we become that which we hate. It's our viewpoint in the situation; it's our perception; it's our philosophy of life and how it sustains us or not in our most difficult moments. Perhaps the *key* to how you and I cope with the death of a spouse is this philosophy of life that we have. This philosophy should have some viewpoint on death. From this vantage point we experience inner peace or we experience turmoil, depending on how developed this philosophy is. Victor Frankl, the Viennese psychiatrist who was in Auschwitz for three years, also pointed this out when he said that if we have a *why* to what we are experiencing, we can go through any *how*. Nietzsche affirmed this also many years before that. It is not the event itself, "but thinking makes it so," to quote an oft-repeated maxim.

Allan and Meg looked at their lives together, then, when they found out the news, and while going through the shock and human emotions that such news would engender in anyone, began to nurture the time that was actually theirs. What was before them was real; they could do something, be someone with that time. They found time to make love, and to be most tender. We could say that their love became more and more "exquisite" as Meg got closer to her death. In spite of her frail body, they even made love then! and "It was glorious," to quote Allan. They both loved so much.

Hearing Allan's story is an important reminder that you and I can do *something* about ourselves, our situations, whatever that may be. We can pick up the kernels of goodness that we see around us. We can be thankful for the little things, the things we take for granted so many times.

The prospect of death for Allan and Meg didn't make them happy, but their attitude to how they were going to live their lives with the knowledge that death was very much integral to their relationship made the difference. They searched for the best, and took the best, in spite of the worst. They did not give up; they went on loving; they cared and loved their children.

Another quality that emerges from reading and listening to Allan's story is that of honesty. He was very frank with us about his strengths and his difficulties. He talked about the difficulty of letting go, of Meg first, and then of his children going into adulthood; and yet, that too must happen. In response to a question about what kind of advice he would give, he said he would ask questions from the widowed spouse, like: what have *you* learned? what can you tell *me* about the experience? Allan was always the true learner: what may *I* learn so that I may grow? Allan also talked about his own human journey, and how he wrestled with his immaturities in his earlier years; but now, as time was moving on, these immaturities had been resolved, or, as Jung was wont to say, we often just outgrow them.

Intrinsic to his story is also the quality and reality of play. The world of play surrounds Allan. It is in play that the human spark gets a forum to expand. It's in play that we become ourselves. It's in play that we realize that babies are really miracles because they are filled with wonder and joy.

And finally, Allan loved the world. He loved the world as it was. He loved the sunrises, the sunsets, and babies again! He had tremendous respect for the body, and took care of Meg's body as his own. To make love was a most profound experience. It was to enter deeply into the "stuff" of the world and of mystery. He misses that now with Meg. "That's what death is all about," missing the beauty of the world, as he would say. But, in spite of all that, the world is still beautiful. Truthfully, in facing the worst, Meg's death, he did actually take up the best because he loves the world more deeply than ever; and he really loves babies!

"Hope is definitely not the same thing as optimism. It is not the conviction that something will turn out well, but the certainty that something makes sense, regardless of how it turns out."

— Vaclav Havel, poet, author, former president of the Czech Republic

---

CHAPTER NINE

ONE STEP AT A TIME:
THE STORY OF GLORIA

Michael first met Gloria, an Italian Roman Catholic, at a meeting for Parents Without Partners (P.W.P.) when he was a guest speaker that night at a meeting in her home. About thirty people were present. She agreed to have an interview. A week later, Janice joined Michael for this interview on a Sunday morning at her home.

MICHAEL: Gloria, could you provide us with some factual details to begin with?

GLORIA: My husband, Carlo, was 48 years old. He died in February. We had three children and had been married for 19 years at the time.

MICHAEL: How old were the kids?

GLORIA: They would have been 14, 16, and 17. My daughter was 17, the boys, 16 and 14 respectively.

MICHAEL: One girl and two boys?

GLORIA: Yes.

JANICE It must have been a shock to you when Carlo died.

GLORIA: Yes, it was a shock because he had never been sick a day in his life. Never, ever sick.

MICHAEL: Maria, what was the cause of his death?

GLORIA: Cancer, multiple melanoma.

JANICE: How long was he sick?

GLORIA: He was sick for a year. He was diagnosed in February and he died the following year in February. They told us right away at the time when they diagnosed him that it was one of the worst kind that anybody could have and he would be lucky to live for a year.

MICHAEL: So how did he get the information? Did he go for a checkup?

GLORIA: No, he wasn't feeling well. He had been home sick already for a month, almost flat on his back. The doctor thought he had a slipped disk and he sent him home for bed rest for a couple of weeks and said, "We'll see what happens." But, the doctor really actually dragged it on a little bit. If it wasn't that I'd pushed... I was at my wits' end. I phoned him [the doctor] this one day and told him, "You either get him into the hospital or I am going to call the ambulance and get him into one of the downtown hospitals, but you're going to take care of him."

JANICE: So it began as back problems?

GLORIA: Yes.

JANICE: Is that where it was, in his spine?

GLORIA: It was in the spine; it was in the lower back; it was in the back of neck. Sometimes the pain would travel under the rib cage also. He would get pains in the rib cage sitting around. But he didn't know what it was. At first he thought it was a strain because he did a lot of heavy work.

MICHAEL: What was his line of work?

GLORIA: He was a tile setter.

MICHAEL: There's a real art in that.

GLORIA: Oh, yes. He had his own business, and was doing very well.

MICHAEL: Was he as shocked as you were?

GLORIA: I remember him not feeling well even before February. It was around September, the year before, that he wasn't feeling too well. I remember that we went to bed New Year's Eve and he said, to me, "Well, what do you think? I don't think this is really 'nothing.' I think it is something. What do you think this year is going to bring us?" I said, "We don't know. Nobody knows what it's going to bring. We'll just have to wait and see." But I always had the feeling that when he really started to get sick, and he was in bed for four weeks, just seeing him in pain, jumping off the bed, the poor guy. And the pain ...

MICHAEL: It really hurt him?

GLORIA: Really, really hurt him. And he was always in constant pain, always! All through the year that he was sick. I thought right away ... I even said to one of my girl friends, — I'm terrible for that. I really have a sense, sometimes, not always, but for people who are close to me — I said to my girl friend, "Terry, I don't think this is an ordinary sickness. There is something more to it; I'm sure; I can feel it in my bones; there is something more to it than that. What the doctor says is a slipped disk. I've seen people with a sore back. They can still walk around. They're in pain, but ... that was different."

MICHAEL: There had to be a more pervasive pain than just a ...

GLORIA: Oh, yes! He was pale all the time. Actually when he did get bed rest for a week and started to get up, he tried to go to work. He was sitting at the bottom of the steps there; and he was shaking; his whole body was shaking. That's not a normal reaction to a back problem! I said to him, "Go back to the doctor." He was always the one who *never* wanted to go to the doctor unless he was really, really sick. He never wanted to take any pills, no pain killers, nothing.

MICHAEL: Gloria, just on the medical information, what did the doctors say was the cause of any of this?

GLORIA: They really didn't know! They really didn't know what the cause of it was!

MICHAEL: Could they have detected it earlier if he had gone for a checkup?

GLORIA: I asked one of the doctors at the hospital if they had been able to detect it before they did would he have had a better chance. He said that it wouldn't have really mattered in the long run even if they had detected it because my family doctor had let it go too far before they found out, and if they had caught it, and had given him "chemo," then maybe he would have lived longer. But this doctor at the hospital said "No," it wouldn't have made any difference at all in the long run.

MICHAEL: Initially, before you got all this information sorted out, did you have strong feelings that your own doctor let you down?

GLORIA: Yes, we did! I quit going to him! I'm not going to the same doctor any more!

MICHAEL: You were so upset ... you just quit going to him.

GLORIA: Yes, I just quit going to him. He's a good doctor; he really was a good doctor. But, you had to push him all the time to get him to do things for you. You were a number when you went in there, and you were treated as a number. He said to me one time, "You must be a psychic because you've *called it* now three times." I've called it all: my sister, my mother, my father all their deaths. I knew it two days before they died, on all of them. I said to the doctor [the one she quit going to see now that her husband died], "Please go see him and let me know what's happening. I don't see things right." He never went and he passed away in a matter of a day or two. Then the doctor would call me afterwards and give me his condolences, or whatever. I told him after the third one, "Now, will you listen to me when I tell you?" Things were not the way they were supposed to be. He let me down with my husband. So I said, "That's it! That's enough!"

MICHAEL: Did you nurse him here at home or was he in hospital for most of this final year?

GLORIA: He was in and out of the hospital. He was in the hospital from the end of February until the beginning of April. They sent him home after they started on the chemotherapy, and he was starting to go into remission, and he was home till the end of August, then back into the hospital for three more weeks. They then sent him to the downtown hospital and he was there until the first of November. He came home the first of November, and the way he was, the state he was, I was always praying that he would make it to Christmas; and then whatever happens then, happens. There's nothing anybody could do about that. He did. He lasted just barely till after Christmas. He went back into hospital January 7.

MICHAEL: He knew then that ...

GLORIA: Yes. He knew then that things were not going to work out. He was hoping that when he was in remission — he was always walking around with a cane — he could started walking on his own. But he couldn't look after himself when he was home. Just for a couple of months during the summertime, he was able to take a shower by himself, go to the bathroom. All the other times, even before and after that, he was in a wheelchair.

MICHAEL: That's quite a stress and strain having to do that for a whole year, isn't it?

GLORIA: Yes, and I was working at the time too. I worked part-time, up until 12 or 1 o'clock and then I would go down to the hospital. During the last couple of weeks, while he was still alive, I was practically living in the hospital.

MICHAEL: Were you with him when he died?

GLORIA: Yes [weeps here]. Sorry. I was.

JANICE: Was the hospital supportive of you?

GLORIA: The hospital was really good. They transferred him into a private room in the last week that he was alive. He didn't want to go into that. In his mind, he figured that once he was put in a private room, that was the end. He held on till almost the end, really. One of the girls downstairs, social workers, would say to me that she would like to put him in a private room so that they could put the cot in there for me. He always wanted one of the family to be there. I had my mother-in-law living at the house as well. She has been with us for twenty years, ever since we've been married. She used to go to the hospital in the morning while I was working, and then I would go to the hospital and stay from the afternoon on.

JANICE: How did the kids take care of themselves during that last year when your husband was dying?

GLORIA: Well, they were in school for part of the time. Then, of course, by 3:30 — 4:00 pm, they would come home from school, and my mother-in-law would be here. They didn't listen to her too much any more. You see, my husband was the disciplinarian. He always wanted things a certain way.. The children had to do this and this and this; that's all there was too it!

JANICE: So he was the structure ...

GLORIA: Yes.

JANICE: And it wasn't there any more.

GLORIA: That's right. It wasn't there any more. The grandma is the grandma. She used to tell the kids, "Don't do this, don't do that!" The kids would say, "Yah, yah, yah," and then did whatever they wanted to.

MICHAEL: Is she still with you?

GLORIA: She stayed until last November, but then she moved out to live with her daughter.

MICHAEL: Until that time though, she was living with you?

GLORIA: Oh, yes. 20 years! 20 years altogether!

MICHAEL: Gloria, what happened to you when you first were given the information about your husband's condition?

GLORIA: I remember going to the hospital the Saturday after he was admitted. He went in on a Tuesday. The doctor called me outside and he told me of the way he had deteriorated. They were looking for a malignancy somewhere, but they didn't know exactly where the malignancy was. When he was admitted into the hospital, he not only had the back problem, but he had also had nausea and other things. They admitted him; he had renal bleeding. His kidneys had given up almost already. The doctor asked me if he had any problems with his stomach or other organs. I said, "No. So far he has had no other problems, just that back problem. We decided then that we were going to do the bone marrow test [*weeps some here*].

MICHAEL: That's a tough one, isn't it, Gloria?

GLORIA: Yeah. And we did that on the Saturday in the afternoon after the doctor talked to me. I came home here; there was really no one here. My girlfriend had called, wanting to know how Carlo was. I couldn't talk to her. I phoned her back. I just couldn't talk to her. I was in shock, really. I knew, from before, I had the feeling, that when the doctor said he was looking for something — i.e., malignancy — that it was reality. I tried to think. My girlfriend said, "Don't go away; just hang in there; I'll be right down there." And she came straight down.

MICHAEL: Gloria, can you recall what went through you physically ... your feelings ... how your body reacted?

GLORIA: I was running on nervous energy really; I never stopped; I never stopped! I felt like someone had thrown a bucket of ice water on me. Everything just froze up. I couldn't eat. I went for months, not without eating, but I was forcing myself, really, to eat because I knew I needed the strength if I was going to keep on looking after him.

MICHAEL: What went through you, Gloria, in terms of how you looked at life and the anchors you could hold onto?

GLORIA: Um, the kids, first of all. I knew I had to look after them. I knew my life would probably revolve around them. I also hoped that maybe the doctors would come out with something that would cure him. I really would have kept him in a wheelchair. I really didn't care, even if he didn't get well, I knew it would have been bad for him. He was a strong man, and for him to be in a wheelchair would have been devastating. I'm sure. But I would have kept him, even that way, even for companionship, someone to talk to, come home from work, or the kids would do something, you know, still talk about things together.

MICHAEL: How did this all hit the kids?

GLORIA: I don't think it dawned on them when I told them. I sat down with them two or three evenings after that and I told them what the doctor had said, that he was very, very sick. We just didn't know how things were going to develop. Not until November or December [*he died in February*] — they knew then!

MICHAEL: They had to face reality then, of the death and dying ...

GLORIA: That's right! My middle son was the one who was shakened the most. He was the most rebellious afterwards; he was the one I had the most problems with. The other two were more accepting.

MICHAEL: They accepted it more ...

GLORIA: Yes. They did.

MICHAEL: What does rebellion look like?

GLORIA: In my son? Well, going out, drinking, drugs, breaking all the rules.

JANICE: Taking advantage of your situation.

GLORIA: Yes. Right up until a few nights ago.

JANICE: During this time, your mother-in-law was with you. How did she react to all of this? Was she supportive of you? Were you trying to hold her up? What did that look like?

GLORIA: I was trying to hold her up; yes; and she was very close to her son.

JANICE: Which son was he for her?

GLORIA: The youngest, of three.

MICHAEL: Gloria, when you say "close," what does that mean: "close" as "interference" or "close" as "intimate"? [*Everyone laughs*] Only one working with psychology would ask that kind of question! [*More laughter*] Your nonverbal expressions tell me the answer.

GLORIA: OK, I knew I had better not answer that because I think it would get me into something else altogether. [*Then picking up and pulling herself together after this musing, Gloria goes on*] She was actually devastated. She wasn't eating properly. I had to go to work during the day and I had no time to look after her and the kids at the same time. I had my hands full. When my husband died, he had a contract for an apartment building that they were doing work for; and that apartment building was a hundred suites, and he had managed to do half before he passed away. The other half were left. I didn't want to break the contract, so I had to look after that. I was looking after the kids; I was going to work. I just *couldn't.* I phoned my sister-in-law, her daughter, and I asked that she *do* something, maybe talk to her [*her mother, my mother-in-law*] whatever. But, she is a very stubborn woman [*mother-in-law*] and she had to go through that period, adjusting on her own.

JANICE: So, she was needing as much support as the kids.

GLORIA: Just about.

JANICE: How did she take care of herself? Did she go and see him, talk her feelings over with you?

GLORIA: She never talked about her feelings with me at all. She was really quite closed in. I guess I was in a way too. I had so many things on my mind.

MICHAEL: And you didn't need another kid!

GLORIA: And I didn't need another kid in the house! Another problem.

JANICE: She was physically healthy otherwise.

GLORIA: Oh yes! She's very healthy. She's 76. She's going to be 77 next month. She's quite healthy.

MICHAEL: Gloria, what would that have looked like — tell me if I'm probing too much — over the years if she had lived with you. You would have had a lot of those feelings about her being so "close."

GLORIA: I was, um, [pause] ... actually I resented her. You know, I kept thinking to myself, "Now, look at this: my husband was 48 years old; he's gone. I've still got her after all those years that I've had her already; I still have her anyways." You know, he's gone and she's still here, and I have to look after myself. If he had said to me, "You have to look after my mother," or, "Do this for me," then I could understand; I could probably still go ahead and do it. I couldn't see myself living together with her now that he was gone. I really resent that. I resented all those years — actually, I didn't have a life on my own with my husband because she was *always* here. She used to go to all the places that we went.

MICHAEL: Was it like having two women courting one guy, and then he died?

GLORIA: Yes.

JANICE: How was it that you ended up with her with you? Was that through an agreement between you, or, ... of necessity?

GLORIA: It wasn't ... My husband was still living with his mother when we got married because his father was quite inept' besides that, his mother and father didn't get along too well. His father died in 1971. At the time I got married, my husband said, "I have been living with my mother for a long time. We're pretty close. I don't want her going to live with anybody else. Do you mind if she comes and lives with us?" I remember telling him that I really didn't mind too much. I'm very basically an easy person to get along with, and I figured, *one* person! How many things could go wrong? [*making the assumption "not many" because of the 'one'*]. I said to him, "Well, what happens if we don't get along? What happens if things go wrong?" He said, "That's no problem! If we don't get along, we'll just move out on our own," but that wasn't quite the case!

MICHAEL: "I guess what I said at the Parents without Partners meeting the other night really hit home?"

GLORIA: It sure did!

MICHAEL: You know, Gloria, in my experience in this area of the psychology of relationships, what Janice and I call "soul psychology," as opposed to just "behavioural," I think *some* of the psychological base of cancer is related to people not moving out of those kinds of relationship dynamics. We need to leave father and mother psychologically and "cleave to our spouses." That is emotional health.

GLORIA: Do you think that has something to do with stress?

MICHAEL: That's what I mean! Yes!

JANICE: Taking on the burden — really the backbone — being the backbone of the entire family was just too much stress. You were holding onto the dynamic of mother, family, caregiver. You managed through it. But, there's a lot of stress there and you're holding it in.

GLORIA: That's true. I can see that.

MICHAEL: After the funeral, then, you made sure your mother-in-law moved on to some place else. Or, did she decide to go on her own?

GLORIA: She was here for almost two years after that [*funeral*]. She moved out last November, which would have been already a year and one-half after he'd died. I was coming to my wits end. I couldn't take any more. Looking back now, I think I was overreacting, but at the time, I really felt really, really bad. I asked her that maybe she could go and live with her daughter for a little bit and give me a break; just give me some breathing space to get on with my life, you know, be myself for a little while. Unfortunately, being the way she was, she took it the wrong way. She thought I was kicking her out of the house. I had to talk to my sister-in-law before I told her.

MICHAEL: Gloria, I know it feels rough, but you can see now that unless we take charge of our own lives, other things don't fit into place that well. Life itself will create conflict. And cancer is quite a conflict, isn't it? The one thing that Carlo needed to have done for himself was to basically have told his mum, "Look, find your own way in life. I'm not your 'mini—husband'! I'm married to Gloria!"

GLORIA: Well, he couldn't do that to his mother, I guess!

MICHAEL: And he died for her [*psychologically*].
GLORIA: Yes.

MICHAEL: I wouldn't blame you for being resentful. He was ambivalent. I'm not putting Carlo down when I say that.

GLORIA: No. He was a good man!

MICHAEL: That is a conflict with which every man has to wrestle. Every man has a mother and then he usually has a girl friend or a wife. A man has to make that choice: mother *or* wife! — but it doesn't always happen that way emotionally or psychologically; and that's where the trouble begins. A line in the scriptures says it well, "Unless a man leaves his father and mother, and cleaves to his wife

... " That's very profound, and it is also very healthy! A man can't be healthy unless he takes that stand.

GLORIA: I always say to my kids too, "When you get married, don't expect me to live with you. If I can't look after myself, put me in an old-age home. Put me anywhere, but with you." Once they get married, they have their own families, their own lives to live, and I want them to live them. I don't want them to feel responsible for me.

MICHAEL: What do you want to do for yourself now, Gloria?

GLORIA: I really don't know what I want to do with myself. Right now I'm going to have to stick around here and look after the kids until they get married, move out, or until they're old enough to look after themselves.

MICHAEL: How old are they now.

GLORIA: My daughter is now 19; my son is 18; and the other son is 16.

MICHAEL: So, there are still a few more years.

GLORIA: There's still two more years for them to grow up, need guidance, whatever. And I'm trying to do the best I can. That's really all I can do. I did join that Parents Without Partners (P.W.P.) just for something extra to divert my mind, really. Those are the basic goals in the my daily life, besides working, and looking after the kids and the house. I don't really think that's what I want. I like the activities [of P.W.P.]. I like the home activities and stuff like that. Other than that, I really don't think it's [P.W.P.] for me. No.

JANICE: Do the kids have responsibilities that they take care of now that they're older? Do they take care of certain things around here?

GLORIA: Yes.

MICHAEL: You can count on them.

GLORIA: I can count on — [*pause*] — actually my little one is the best for that. I tell him, "Give me a hand to do this or do that," and he does it. He basically looks after the outside of the house, shovelling the snow in the winter time, cutting the grass, doing the garden in the summer time. My older son is working full time. He left school. He didn't want to go to school any more. He's working full time, and basically, he really doesn't do too much around the house, except come home and sleep *and* eat. That's about it.

MICHAEL: Does he pay room and board?

GLORIA: No, not right now because he just started to work and I want him to get settled and get something going before he starts paying room and board.

MICHAEL: It's important now that you've gone through this experience — really, a tragedy — losing your husband is a tragedy, no matter how it happens. It's important that the son who is working does not have an experience of mother in the same way that Carlo did, because his mother protected him from all kinds of things, and then he died of it! The best medicine for anybody is to say, "Hey, this is reality. You work, you pay!" Much as they dislike it! If you don't like it, then try the world out there!" Very important, Gloria, not to let what you're doing with him to go on too long.

GLORIA: No, no. I wouldn't let that go too long. He does have sort of responsibilities: he has to pay for his own way too: he has to pay for the gas for his truck, any insurance; and he does have payments to make on his truck too, because it's not all paid for.

JANICE: He doesn't have to pay for accommodation?

GLORIA: No.

MICHAEL: That is really healthy [*paying accommodation*], even before any truck or motorcycle, or whatever! First of all are the house payments: room and board! They should be the very first ones. He can always take a bus or street car, or taxi.

GLORIA: Yes, I know. But, he was kind of fortunate because Carlo had the truck for the business before he died, and when my son got his driver's licence, he did work and helped me out through the whole summer. Of course, he got paid for the work that he did for the company, but that compensated for any effort that he put into it.

MICHAEL: Talking about practical things, Gloria, did you find that you had difficulty with financial matters to take care of after he died, or were you up on that area?

GLORIA: I was really up on it because I kept the books for him [*Carlo*] for his business. So I knew basically everything that was going on, what was there, what wasn't there. I was the one who was looking after the financial end of it before.

MICHAEL: The reason I mention this is that others — especially older women — would recommend careful knowledge around finances. I would ask them, "What would you recommend to other people?" They would say, "Make sure you get somebody to help you with finances. We never knew what they were. Make sure you have a lawyer, etc. But you didn't have those kinds of issues to deal with?

GLORIA: No, no, I didn't have those kind of issues to deal with. As I said, I was on top of everything already as it was.

JANICE: Financially, things were in place? Life insurance?

GLORIA: Ah, actually he really didn't have much of a life insurance at all, to speak of.

MICHAEL: If he had had the truck insured, it would have been paid for by now!

GLORIA: [*Laughs*] Yeah! Unfortunately, it wasn't so ... that still has to be carried on. I've always worked myself because; again having my mother-in-law here, I was always able to go to work; I was able to help him out financially. I don't know what I would have done if I hadn't been working, or, if I didn't have a trade, or the type of work that I did. I would have had to got to work in a factory, at $3 or $4/hour. Then I would have been really in trouble.

JANICE: So, having your own job was great security!

GLORIA: Yes, it was!

MICHAEL: What do you do, Gloria?

GLORIA: I'm a bookkeeper.

MICHAEL: That was a wonderful thing to fall back on to.

GLORIA: Yes, yes.

MICHAEL: What's the most difficult thing in having your husband die?

GLORIA: [*Ponders for awhile*] That's a tough one; that's a tough one. I guess, you want ... I hate coming home now. I know the kids are here. It's not the same as having a husband at home. You miss having him here to talk to. I actually still do not go to sleep on my bed. I still sleep on the couch. I very rarely go to the bedroom to sleep ... maybe once a month, or once a week. I *go* there, you know, ...

MICHAEL: You don't have the same relationship to what you both did together?

GLORIA: No! No! I still have all his clothes in the closet. I haven't gotten rid of all his stuff yet. I just can't bring myself to it. No, I think the toughest thing is trying to get on with your life; but the memories are always there. It doesn't matter: you come home; you go into the family room. It's not the same; everything is completely changed! There is nothing the same.

MICHAEL: How have *you* changed, Gloria?

GLORIA: I don't think I've really changed very much, really. I'm still basically the same as I was before. My feelings towards things are different. I feel that if there is something that you want to do, or you have to do, it's better to do it today than wait till tomorrow.

MICHAEL: And get on with it.

GLORIA: Just get on with things!

MICHAEL: Gloria, you mentioned that Carlo was the disciplinarian, etc. That would mean that you were, therefore, more in the background.

GLORIA: Yes.

MICHAEL: Now that you are alone, you've trained yourself to be in the foreground?

GLORIA: I think so; I think so.

MICHAEL: So, there's been a real change in that.

GLORIA: There's been a real change in that! Yes!

MICHAEL: It feels good, right?

GLORIA: Yes, it does. It feels a lot better than it did before. As you say, I always felt in the background. My husband and his mother were the ones who were out "in front."

MICHAEL: Your husband and his mother were over to one side and you had to sort of "tag along."

GLORIA: Tag along, and whatever went, went! If we had to go somewhere, and my mother-in-law didn't want to go, she'd kick up a fuss — that wasn't for her, that type of thing — then nobody went! Stay at home!

MICHAEL: Wow! Talk about power!

GLORIA: Yeah.

MICHAEL: A *real* Dragon Lady! [*all three of us laugh and laugh; and it feels good too*] You know, my impression is, Gloria ...

GLORIA: She is basically a very nice lady. I felt so bad ...

MICHAEL: Oh, I'm sure!

GLORIA: ... when I asked her to leave, she took it *so* much to heart. For her, I was more of a daughter than her own daughter was.

MICHAEL: I am sure of that!

GLORIA: But, I was always saying, "Yeah, yeah, ok, that's fine."

MICHAEL: You were a daughter, Gloria, but what a daughter has to do is *obey*!

GLORIA: *Yes! That's exactly what was happening*!

MICHAEL: And if you had that relationship with a woman like that, then you have on the surface this nice, sweet, person, etc., but, the energy involved in the relationship was Dragon Lady.

GLORIA: Yes, yes!

MICHAEL: And that surfaced when the crunch came, i.e., "OK, you need to find your own place." Gloria, what would you do differently, or do over again?

GLORIA: What would I do differently? If I could go back to when I got married, first of all [*laughs here, but it's serious*] I wouldn't live with my mother-in-law! Second of all, I would make sure that the man that I married would have the same type of ideas that I had, and that is, to do things *today*, not leave them till tomorrow. It may be too late. I find that with a lot of people: they're in the same situation. They're saving and scrimping and doing things for the future tomorrow. Yes, that's good to do; you have to look after that.

MICHAEL: Some wisdom, somewhere!

GLORIA: Yes, *but* — also, we really never took a holiday together. We never really went away, anywhere! That was bad. I think he regretted it in the last part of his life too that he didn't. He did try to make it up to me, but it was a little bit too late then. He always felt that he didn't want to leave the kids. His mother would be left with the kids and she wouldn't be able to cope on her own, etc., etc. It was all right to look after the kids during the day because we both came home at noon and everything was fine. We took over and that was the end of her role then, — but it was never the end of her role. We never really left them for a week or two; we couldn't do that.

JANICE: That would be taking advantage of her goodwill.

GLORIA: Yes, yes. [*agreeing with Janice's thinking on the matter*] But, that's what I would do. That's what I would tell people to do, to really stress: to really make time for yourself, and take time out. If you like to read, sit for an hour and read; go for a walk; or if you want to go away on holidays, take the time. If you have the money and you can do it, take the time and do it, and don't wait until tomorrow. Do things together with your husband.

MICHAEL: That's one of the things that Janice and I have done for ourselves. We each have our alone time, our retreat time, but we set up our lives in such a way that we do things together as well. We do conferences together around the U.S.A. and Canada. We combine different things so that we have "together time." It's really important that choices be made around these areas because if something happened today and Janice died, or if I were to die today, we could not regret that we hadn't done certain things we should have. There are things we would like to do, but, looking back, I would never say, "I wish we had done that together!" because I know we have done marvellous things together!

JANICE: Trying to make sure we live life along the way!

GLORIA: Yes, that's *right*!

MICHAEL: The interesting thing with these kinds of choices, Gloria, is that these are healthy choices; these are *life* choices; and life is very supportive with us when we make those choices, and finds us the money to do them without having to "break the bank" and without having to be stretched out. That's the irony of that. And people sometimes don't realize or don't believe that that's possible. One time we were in San Juan and as we walked along the beach, we talked about how nice it would be to have the kids experience something like this as well. We promised ourselves that the next time we were in a wonderful place, we would have them join us for a week or two as well. We went to Hawaii the following year to do a conference, and they actually joined us for the last two weeks! It was all possible because the idea was good to begin with; it was healthy; and it was life! We had our goals and we *made* the time.

Gloria, what do you believe in about life, what it looks like, and where you go from here now?

GLORIA: [*Laughs*] I believe that life is a gamble. It really is. You never know about tomorrow. Where do I go from here? I don't know. I have a tendency of taking it now from day to day and not think about what I'm going to do a month from now. I'm just taking it on a daily basis, really. I might be here today and might be gone tomorrow. I would like to do a certain thing, and I would like to do it today. Just take it on a daily basis, whatever happens, whatever comes...

MICHAEL: Live the rhythm as it goes.

GLORIA: As it goes, yes.

MICHAEL: That's really healthy!

GLORIA: [*sigh*] Yes. I wish a lot of people could do that. Sometimes you can't do that either, you know. I like to do that. That's basically "my thing," but there are things that happen during the day that sort of backtrack, and you can't do what you had planned on doing; but that's ok too. Just take it the way it comes.

MICHAEL: Perhaps another way to say that too, Gloria, is that all the worries that each of us has about today and tomorrow, a month from now, if we just do a good job today, these worries never turn out to be the way we imagine them to be anyway!

GLORIA: Most of the time I find that most of the worries that you do have, or whatever thing happens along the road, it does, um, not get better, but it sort of works out for the best. I think a lot of people make the mistake that whatever happens today that is really, really bad, and you really get burdened down, that it's the end of the world. And they make it worst than it really is. Just take it one step at a time, and it wouldn't be so bad.

MICHAEL: Death is a reality that forces that issue onto us. Death tells us that "we're here today and gone tomorrow." Death tells us how tenuous is our human journey.

GLORIA: I have come to accept that as a part of life, really. And it is part of life. I have gone through it not only with my husband, but, I've lost my family on my side; it is practically all gone. All that is left is my brother-in-law and sister. In a matter of three years I lost three people: my sister, my dad, my mom, and my husband got sick two years after my mother died. So, in the space of five years, I have lost four people!

MICHAEL: So, you have met Death!

GLORIA: I think so. Yes, we have become friends all of a sudden!

MICHAEL: Gloria, we lost a baby "in utero" at five months. Now, there wasn't the long-term relationship that you have experienced with your situation but when you say "living today and the moments," that lesson came through very clearly for us then. Death makes us think about the priorities in life and where it is all going, and what do I value the most.

GLORIA: I think really health is the most important thing, and being able to do things the best you can. You can't look at the material things in life because if you do that — if your look at money, for instance, — the more money you have the more money you want. You're going on an ego trip like that.

MICHAEL: It keeps escalating — the hunger for money.

GLORIA: That's right. Money is nice to be able to live comfortably. I really can't complain about that myself. You can keep going the way we are now, for a little bit. Mind you, it's expensive to live these days: four people in a house.

MICHAEL: You know what we found, Gloria? Teenage boys *inhale* food! [*laughter all around*] Gloria, what have you learned from all of this for your own journey in life?

GLORIA: I am basically ready to accept death when it comes. Really.

MICHAEL: Do you have a religious philosophy of life?

GLORIA: Yes, I do believe that there's life after death. I'm Roman Catholic. We have that belief and I think that a religious belief is really very, very important in life because if you don't have..."

MICHAEL: A context?

GLORIA: A context to believe in, you really don't have anything.

MICHAEL: It must be awfully empty and hollow.

GLORIA: Yes, it is.

MICHAEL: To me it would feel very scary.

GLORIA: Yes, it is very scary. And you hang onto that belief. I really hang onto the belief that when I die I will see my husband again. Actually, I'm a dreamer [*laughs, almost apologetically, as if to bring up dreams is "weird"*].

MICHAEL: Talking about dreams, anything come up?

GLORIA: [*Very animatedly now*] Oh, gosh, yeah!! I remember one particular dream that I had not very long ago. My husband was here sitting at the kitchen table. We had some friends over. [*Gloria then explains: "This is a dream mind you!" as if not realizing that we are very accepting of this reality*] It's not real, but it's so real that it's unbelievable! My kids must have done something because my mother—in—law started to say something to them, sort of yell at them. To me that wasn't really too important, to yell at them. I remember saying to my husband, "Tell your mother to mind her own business and don't interfere with the kids. I will look after the kids!" He never talks to me in the dreams. I remember him sitting there, smiling at me. All of a sudden he got up and he came over to say goodbye. I sort of held on to him. I said, "No, wait a minute! I must not have remembered that he was dead. Then I remembered saying, "Well, if you have to really go now, ok, don't forget, that when it's my time to go, you know where I am. Come and get me!"

MICHAEL: What a dream! Wow! Did your husband every tell you any dreams, Gloria, during his time?

GLORIA: He never used to dream; he never used to dream. Myself, before he got sick, I had the weirdest dream, that I was in the bedroom. Somebody was, I know somebody was in the bedroom. I thought I had wakened up. Actually, I did wake up, *screaming*. My mother had passed away already. In the dream I was at the foot of the bed, near the dresser. There was this kid, with red eyes. My mother came in and I had this kid and I wanted to push this thing away. And my mother kept saying to me, "Don't look at his eyes! Don't look at him"!

JANICE: It was a baby?

GLORIA: It was like a baby. I could see by the reflection in the mirror that the eyes were bright red. I got goose bumps!

MICHAEL: And this is a little baby that you're holding?

GLORIA: Yes! I'm trying to get rid of it. My mother was there and she's trying to take it away; and I'm trying to push this thing away. It didn't want to go; it didn't want to go!

MICHAEL: You could see the eyes by looking in the mirror?

GLORIA: Yes, I could see the reflection. Yes, I could see the redness of the eyes. They were really red eyes. I was so scared, I guess, I woke up; I was screaming. Carlo said to me, "What's wrong with you?" I've never had dreams like that!

MICHAEL: What did you make of that dream, Gloria?

GLORIA: I think maybe perhaps it was some sort of warning, that something was about to happen.

MICHAEL: That death was around you.

GLORIA: [*Very quickly*] Yes!

MICHAEL: How would you associate that with the eyes and the baby?

GLORIA: I, um, for some reason or another, my mother thought that it was the devil.

MICHAEL: In the dream?

GLORIA: In the dream. That's why she kept saying to me, "Don't look at it."

MICHAEL: Death disguised as a baby and as evil, at the same time, a double figure?

GLORIA: Evil. Yes. I would think so.

JANICE: Conjures up images of Death as being a new life, as well as an awful dreadful experience.

GLORIA: Yes. I guess because of the pain and everything else that is associated with death, because I'm sure that you go through some kind of pain, whether it's heart attack or whatever, which doesn't take that long. Death is painful. It is.

MICHAEL: Was Carlo aware in the last stages that he was leaving this life and going into death?

GLORIA: It's funny that you asked me that because in the last week that he was alive he kept drifting in and out of sleep and waking up. I remember at one point or another I did ask him, "Did you dream of something? Did somebody say anything to you? He said, "No. I dreamt that I was downstairs in a very dark room, dark room, and it was very cold down there." I said, "Do you remember anything else? anybody there?" He said, No, there was nobody there, but it was cold, very, very cold, and it was very, very dark." He kept drifting off into these things. Sometimes he would think there was a priest outside his door. He would say to his mother, "Close the door, mother. There is Fr. Jim. Fr. Jim is there.

MICHAEL: He would tell his mother actually there in the room?

GLORIA: Yes, I think so.

JANICE: Was he on medication at the end, a lot of medication?

GLORIA: He was, yes. On morphine. And he took his last medication at 6:00 am, but he couldn't swallow it. I gave him the Tylenol. Then he put it in his mouth and I tried to give him some water to send it down. He just took it out of his mouth and put it back in my hand. He said to me, "That's enough. I don't want any more! I've had it!" Those were the last things that he said. And then he would sort of collapse, not into a coma, ... I think he still needed those people around him, that I was there.

MICHAEL: He knew that it was time "to move on."

GLORIA: Yes. I think he knew it then that it was time. He was just sort of moaning all the time. There was one word that he kept saying over and over again, but we couldn't understand it. At one point I thought he was calling "Jeff," who is my son. But, the more I think about it, I think he was saying, "When? when? when?!"

MICHAEL: Did you experience all of this as a passage, or did he as a passage from this way of being to another way after death? Do you know what I mean by a "passage," as a journey?

GLORIA: No, at the time, I really didn't. I was there. I knew it was happening, and I knew it wasn't going to be much longer.

MICHAEL: It was more of a clinical experience.

GLORIA: Yes, it was; it was a clinical experience. They came in to take X-rays and then asked me to leave the room then. I had problems letting go of his hand because he was holding on to my hand so tightly; he just didn't want to let go. I had to pry his hand open so I could leave the room. I would have stayed but they didn't want me to, and I left the room. And when I went back in he had already started ...

MICHAEL: Slipping into death.

GLORIA: Yes. But he was still moving his mouth, still moving as though he was trying to say something.

MICHAEL: Isn't it amazing, the whole experience!

GLORIA: I went back into the room and as soon a I saw him, I realized, "This is it! the end!" There is really nothing ...

JANICE: So, Gloria, you went the whole journey with him.

GLORIA: Yes, I did.

MICHAEL: One last question, Gloria. I don't know if it is redundant: what would you recommend for others in your situation?

GLORIA: I know there are a lot of people who would not be able to take that kind of thing.

MICHAEL: Not deal with reality.

GLORIA: *Yes*. But, if you can, I would strongly suggest that you stay with him the whole time. That's an experience that you'll never forget, really! And, as I said, this last one made me friends with Death. I really don't think I'm afraid to die now. If it came tomorrow, it came tomorrow. I wouldn't like to go tomorrow, because I'd like to see my kids growing and settled; but, if it comes, it comes.

JANICE: Do you think that happened because you went right through the process with him and didn't leave out any of the parts? If you had left out any of the parts, perhaps you would not have the same feelings?

GLORIA: Maybe not. No. But I think it's because I went through that, the whole process.

MICHAEL: You don't regret anything at this point.

GLORIA: No, no, I don't. I don't regret being with him at all.

MICHAEL: Any regrets?

GLORIA: No, no, I think I did what I had to do. And I did the best that I could, really. As I said, he was like a baby. I washed him; I cleaned him; I fed him; I pulled him up when he wanted to get up. He was a big man. There was nobody there. He would wait for me to go there. If he wanted to get up he would wait for me to go to the hospital, and then when I was there, he would say, "Well, maybe we should get up now for a little bit." He would hang on to my shoulders and I would sort of just pull him up to the edge of the bed and then he would get his legs down.

MICHAEL: So you lived the human journey in its living and you lived it in its dying.

GLORIA: Yes.

COMMENTARY

To meet Gloria is to meet a woman who, in the very best sense of the phrase, has spent her years "attending to." She has attended to her husband; she has attended to her children; and she has attended to her husband's mother, her mother-in-law. She weaves together in her personality the qualities of simplicity and genuineness. Today she is friends with Death. That may sound strange to some people, but, for Gloria, after four deaths of relatives in the last five years, she has lived the human journey in its living, and she has lived the human journey in its dying and death. She has met Death. As she says, "I don't think I'm afraid to die now." It wasn't always that way. But she has learned to deal with reality, to face life and to face death, and to stand tall as a woman.

As became evident during the interview, the main troubling spot for her in her relationship with Carlo was the realization now that his mother was *always* really first. In a way it seemed as though he was "married" to his mother first and foremost, and Gloria was "tagging along," as she put it. Her feelings of what this dynamic really meant to her came out in the dying and death process of Carlo. Gloria realized that that dynamic wasn't right and if she had to do it all over again, she would have made Carlo make a choice, or, have taken him away from his mother. She [*the mother*] could very well, twenty years ago, take care of herself. It was a convenient situation that she move in. "Convenient" here means, of course, "convenient psychologically," especially for Carlo. He never did make that most important break. Gloria would have it differently today if she had to do it all over again. There would be room for vacations, for fun, for play, for travel, for things for the two of them to do together. She would make choices for life and not for convenience. That, she found out, was too costly. Carlo was gone now, and her realization of independence would have to be lived by herself. Carlo was now dead.

The lesson that Gloria learned about having her mother-in-law in her home since she was married was that a couple needs to live for themselves, establish their relationship, get clear in their priorities, their lives, their choices. A couple needs to choose for each other. Nothing else is more important than that. Nothing. This is the most important task for any couple, and now, after Carlo has died, Gloria realizes that for herself. Naturally she has resentments. Perhaps she is more angry with herself that she allowed this to happen. Of course, she was young at the time, and it takes a tremendous amount of energy to make that step alone [*to have one's husband "cleave" to his wife and not his mother any more*], without having an actual mother-in-law physically present. To make matters worse, Gloria goes on to say that she really was a "nice" lady. That's true, but Gloria also came to see that behind a lot of that "niceness" was a "power base" which kept her son, Gloria's husband, "in tow." The excuse that was used was that they could not leave the kids with "grandma" for too long. After all, she was "putting herself out" to look after them, and they didn't want to burden her more than was necessary. But, in so doing, Carlo and Gloria also cut themselves off from each other, their alone time, their couple time; and now, naturally, she misses him. How she would like to come home and see Carlo there, be able to talk with him, discuss things of the day, plan new and different things, and expand their lives. For Gloria, home is not home, is not the same without Carlo there. There is a hollowness, an emptiness; and she lives with that. Thus, Gloria is very clear about doing for oneself, in the most positive, creatively selfish way. Gloria would also say that a couple must choose their relationship, not just let it happen. This takes courage, but it must be done. What Gloria means by "choose" is that each of us must let nothing interfere with the primacy of our spousal relationship — nothing! There needs to be time for self, but also couple time, children time, and time just to be. That's why "one step at a time" is so integral now to Gloria's philosophy. Horace, the Latin poet, had a saying which was "carpe diem," meaning "to seize the moment, opportunity, day."

That's Gloria's philosophy now: don't waste time. If you have something to do, do it today. Don't procrastinate; tomorrow may never come. And Gloria speaks with conviction and with experience because in four most important relationships (mother, father, sister, and husband) there are no tomorrows, just memories.

Gloria has realized that consciousness of one's goals and purpose means that one gets into life today. One does not delay. It was Jesus who said that once you put your hand to the ploughshare you shouldn't turn back ("And Jesus said unto him, No man, having put his hand to the plough, and looking back, is fit for the kingdom of God," Luke 9:62) Don't turn around and doubt when you know the way, when you know what you must do, when you know what is healthy for your relationship.

If what one envisions is filled with life — and anything that enhances relationship is — then life has a unique way of providing us with the means to accomplish most of our dreams. Life wants us to create, to live, to play, to dream, to feel the wind on our face. Gloria knows now that life demands that.

Death has a role in teaching us many lessons. Gloria has learned hers: Today is the first day of the rest of her life, and she will live that fully. She takes each day as it comes, and it is here that the years of attentiveness and solitude have their greatest value because she listens each day, to its pulse, to its moment, to its message. Today is the most important day. All the tomorrows will only be todays when we "get there"!

Gloria looks ahead now, to see that her children get out on their own, independent, "settled," as she calls it. She did not talk of another relationship with another man, and I didn't ask that. There is a sense of the contemplative with Gloria and her experiences now of death have brought her closer to the real fabric of life, to that edge of reality where the inner and the outer work in harmony, where the human journey is a sacramental journey because she can say that when Carlo visited her in her dream, she did ask him to be with her when she was about to die, and "to come back" for that.

Thus, Gloria reminds us of the woman who was attentive. She attended to Carlo till he "slipped into death." She bathed him, fed him, changed him; she was "there" for him. She's attentive in small things and that is why today is important.

In listening to her story it became apparent to us that because Gloria is attentive in small matters, life will also grace her in "big" matters. She is herself today more than ever. What greater gift: the gift of oneself. And to that self she is most attentive. She is living her truth and, for that, Carlo should be very proud.

CHAPTER TEN

GO FOR IT! A LOVE STORY:
THE STORY OF JAMES AND VIVIAN

James and Vivian are each respectively a widower and a widow. When we first met them, they were deeply in love. He was 68 and she was 63. They were not married yet, but were discussing it. A most beautiful couple! After their respective spouses had died, they had picked up their lives and were continuing on the human journey. Their story is somewhat different than the others since it involves both of them; but we wanted to include it here to highlight that "love blooms eternal!" Within a short time after this interview, we received a phone call from Vivian telling us that she and James were now married! We wished them the very best in everything.

MICHAEL: I personally want to thank both of you, James and Vivian, for taking this time to talk with us. I would like you to provide some background information first, if you will.

JAMES: I'm James. I'm 68 years old. I was married for 38 years.

MICHAEL: How about you, Vivian?

VIVIAN: I was married for 35 years.

JAMES: My spouse's name was Adele and Vivian's spouse was Roy. Now, I was 30 years in the banking business and moved from branch to branch, as bankers are wont to do. When I came back from overseas, I met Adele in the bank, and after that we got married.

MICHAEL: When did Adele die, James?

JAMES: Adele died in June, 1986.

MICHAEL: And Roy, Vivian?

VIVIAN: Roy passed away in May, 1983. It is nearly four years now.

MICHAEL: And both of you met?

VIVIAN: Basically, we both grew up in the same home town. I partially grew up there. James's sister was married to my first cousin! So it's almost a family connection here. I missed [*did not see much of him*] him in my growing up years. James was six years older than I and in the war; I missed him because he was away. And then I drifted away. So, we really did see each other.

JAMES: I knew of Vivian.

VIVIAN: We knew of each other, but really did not see the other.

MICHAEL: Were you living in the same town?

JAMES: No, no.

VIVIAN: No, no.

JAMES: Vivian lived in one place and, since I was with the bank, I moved to various towns. And I never really met Vivian at that point then.

VIVIAN: Actually, we met last November.

MICHAEL: [*Chuckling*] Was that by accident?

VIVIAN: No, not really! James, we should tell him about this little story. This is a good one!

JAMES: Adele passed away in June. I was having some problems with concentration, depression, and just generally keeping my mind on things. I had very little interest in my work.

MICHAEL: Everything just "bombed out" on you.

JAMES: Yes. I just wanted to get away from it all. So I called my sister and I asked her if it would be all right if I came down — I think this was on a Tuesday — and spent Wednesday, Thursday, Friday, Saturday, and possibly Sunday, with them, and just have a quiet ... get away from for a few days. She said she would be very happy for me to come down; so I went down there on Tuesday evening. Wednesday morning — they had an appointment to meet Bob's sister, who was up at Huntsville.

MICHAEL: And Bob is?

VIVIAN: That's James's brother — in — law, and my first cousin!

JAMES: ... to go up to Huntsville; and I think that Bob thought that Vivian would be up at the lake, because Vivian left at noon.

VIVIAN: I had been there, but left before James got there.

JAMES: My sister and her husband wanted me to meet Vivian; they thought I wanted to meet her.

VIVIAN: Matchmaking now! [*laughter*]

JAMES: Matchmaking! [*laughter*]

MICHAEL: It was a set-up! [*laughter*]

VIVIAN: A set-up! [*laughter*]

JAMES: Anyway, we drove up there and Bob's sister, Lois, was there. So, we had a nice afternoon with her. It was a lovely spot there.

MICHAEL: [*James goes on to talk about a past convention where we met his Adele and his daughter*] James, how did Adele die?

JAMES: She died of cancer. In September of 1985 she was undressing one evening, she noticed a very small lump or bump on one of her breasts. I said, "My goodness!" She called me in to have a look at it. I couldn't see too much. But anyway, I said, "You must go to the doctor." The doctor, when he saw it, called me. So I knew it was serious. He wanted to do a mastectomy and they wanted to take the breast off, if they had to, if it was malignant. They didn't know if it was malignant or not; they suspected it was though for all the reasons that they had. That was it, before Christmas. They didn't do the operation till January. By the 7th or 8th of January they took the breast off. The next time I saw her, she had her breast off. Then she came along quite nicely after, but Adele was a great believer in natural health. She had very little confidence in some of their cancer clinics. I think, if anything, she leaned too heavily on this one vitamin product that she was taking. Adele knew of a doctor from Loyola University in Chicago who had a clinic in Tijuana, Mexico.

MICHAEL: Laetrile?

JAMES: Laetrile. I didn't want to leave any stone unturned. In the meantime, in our home town, the oncologist there gave Adele *perhaps* a year and one-half to live. Adele took the attitude, "I will *beat* this thing!" So, she decided that we would go to Mexico. We called them there, made an appointment, and we went into retreat there for 21 days, followed their diet, habits, and so on. The big thing was, of course, that she was on Laetrile. Whether it did any good or not, I don't know. I went with her and went through all that with her. After the 21 days, we came back, and in May, early in May [*1985*] she had another appointment with the oncologist. This time they had detected that the cancer had spread to her bones. That was the next phase.

MICHAEL: And she died in June.

JAMES: That was a year from then. It was a trend the disease was taking. So they called it "breast cancer of the bone." I believe that's what they called it. Adele had another lady friend in Toronto who had cancer as well who was going to Mexico again. Adele determined that she would go. I drove her down to Detroit, put her on the plane, and sent her to San Diego where she met this other lady and went again to Mexico. I didn't go with her this time. But, by this time, Adele was getting so she had to travel by wheelchair. She just couldn't get around otherwise. I met her when she had been down three weeks, I believe, in Mexico with the other lady; and when she came back, I remember the first feeling I had: "I'm not going to have this lady very long!" She looked so tiny, withered up. That took a lot out of her, that trip too. She was sitting up on the top of the ramp of the airplane — they were getting her down from there — she looked like such a tiny human being. But, anyway, we went home, and I kept her at home as long as I could. Eventually, we were afraid she might get up at night, fall down; so we put a bed in the living room at home. She found sometimes that when she went to the bathroom, ... she almost fell down a couple of times. I was afraid that I couldn't stay up all night and go to work too. We didn't have an all — night nurse at this time. I did sometimes, but not continually. Eventually we got an opening; so we put her into the hospital. She then kept going down, just as the doctor said. A year and one-half, in June, she passed away. She never gave up hope of coming home again!

MICHAEL: Vivian, how about your situation? How did your husband die?

VIVIAN: He died of cancer too. He found out in May of '81.

MICHAEL: How old would he have been?

VIVIAN: He would have been 65. It was prostate cancer and it had already spread to the bone when we found out. So, he had to go into the hospital for about ten days, have some minor surgery done. Then he went on hormone therapy. For a year and one—half — it took a little while to get going — he did exceptionally well. He gained weight and was back up to 200 lbs. Then in January of '83, his hip started paining him again. It was constant pain; then he was on Tylenol 3. Eventually, he went to the hospital for radiation treatments. That was in March. He was in there for ten days of radiation, and then he came home. I thought within the first two weeks that he was picking up and then he seemed to backslide. He went into the hospital; he was only in for six days, and he died in May, 1983. He had pneumonia.

MICHAEL: And they ...

VIVIAN: No, they didn't treat him, which was really a good thing. My daughter's a nurse. I didn't know that he wasn't to be treated intravenously. She's a nurse and she knew it. She said, "You were lucky you got the doctor that you did. Another doctor may have prolonged it and prolonged it. You have no idea what bone cancer will do and the pain it causes. He would have suffered and then still go down slowly, day by day." So it's similar.

MICHAEL: We have bone cancer in these two cases. Now, James, Adele had bone cancer too. Did she suffer a lot with it as well?

JAMES: Yes. She was on the morphine. She was almost delirious a lot of the time. Her mind wasn't clear, and yet, she knew me.

VIVIAN: James and Adele had a longer drawn out last period than Roy and I had.

MICHAEL: Then, he was spared a lot of suffering. A merciful act.

VIVIAN: Yes.

MICHAEL: Now, to get back to the match—up ... [chuckles]

VIVIAN: Then, through the visit up to Huntsville through the cousin there who had the unit — she also took a unit, what do you call them, a time share unit — in Tennessee in November. So James got invited to go down to Tennessee and so did I [laughs].

JAMES: Vivian got invited, and Lois was very reluctant to drive so far. She too was working, and she called me to say that she and Vivian were going down there and didn't want to drive and that this would be an excellent opportunity for me to meet Vivian. So, she [cousin] was working for me too!

VIVIAN: So the three of us — three singles now! — this is another widow lady now — the three of us went to Tennessee on a holiday together, all singles! Another widow lady, James and I.

JAMES: We had a lovely condominium down there.

VIVIAN: It was a beautiful place. I had a good time ... a beautiful place [*laughter all around*].

JAMES: ... a place for mainly golfers to go. Three golf courses there. What made it all worthwhile for me is that I had a client in Chattanooga, a doctor down there. So, I called my doctor friend, and told him that I was near Nashville for a week or ten days. He said, "By all means, don't go without coming down to see me! As a matter of fact, I'll make a date. You come down Friday afternoon. I'll be out of my office then and we can have dinner together, and you can meet my family."

VIVIAN: And bring the two ladies with him! [*laughter*]

JAMES: This is the odd part!

VIVIAN: Lois didn't go because she thought she might get car sick! I *think* sometimes she stayed home on purpose so that James and I could go alone! I *think* this is what happened! [*laughter all around again*].

MICHAEL: Scheming behind the scenes!

JAMES: [As an aside] I had a big jacuzzi bathroom in my room, [*at Huntsville a big bed and a large jacuzzi*! Three of us could get in there together! [*laughter all around again*] Every night we'd run the hot water [*laughter, laughter*].

VIVIAN: Bathing suits, of course!

JAMES: And every night the three of us would get into the jacuzzi bathtub! This gave us a kind of "commune" effect!

VIVIAN: A fun time!

MICHAEL: And this is back in last November [*1986*]?

VIVIAN: Yes.

JAMES: Well, anyways, the long and short of it is, Vivian and I went off to Chattanooga, and we had dinner with our good friend, the doctor, in Chattanooga. When we were coming out of the house, there was almost a hail storm, ice, and the doctor told us, "Be very careful of ice down here because they have no salt on the highways. And these hills are bad! They might not be icy at the bottom, but you get up to the top, they could be icy. So, if you have any problems, turn around and come back." Well, we didn't.

VIVIAN: We got back!

JAMES: We got back all right, but I said to Vivian, "It could have been ... maybe we could have got stranded and we could have got to know one another earlier!" [*much laughter*] But we weren't so lucky! But anyway, we got back. Lois greeted us when we arrived. That was on Friday. So the next day we headed back to Canada. I went off to my home, and Vivian went off to her home. What happened then, Vivian?

VIVIAN: Well, when I left your place, you said, "I haven't your phone number!" I said, "I'll call you!" Now, that's Saturday night. I phoned him. No. I phoned him and I said, "Well, if you'd like to go out to dinner Saturday night, I guess we could go out to dinner within a week." And we've been going out ever since.

MICHAEL: Isn't that wonderful!

VIVIAN: In January, we went down to Florida for two weeks.

JAMES: I had an invitation that I could have a lovely condominium down, right on the Gulf, outside of Tampa there, a quarter of a million dollar condominium. I got it for two weeks. We have other friends in Tampa; we thought it would be a good place to go. So I went to Vivian's elder daughter, Ann, — she's the nurse in Sarnia [*Ontario*], the one we alluded to in connection with Roy's death. I put it to Ann, "Would you — how would you feel if I, or would you object, if I were to take your mother for two weeks, take her to Florida, with the object of wanting to get to know one another better, and possibly ... who knows where this thing might lead to, I guess matrimony for me." Ann looked at us kind of startled, and said, "Go for it! Go for it, mother!" [*laughter*] "You've been sitting for four years now. You haven't been out with anybody. You haven't had any dates. We like you, James, and we'll trust mother!"

MICHAEL: Isn't that neat! You had some invitations ...

VIVIAN: I had had a couple of invitations, out for dinner. It was too soon. But, other than that, I hadn't had any invitations out. But, I got to the point where I was ready to go!

MICHAEL: Looking at your philosophy in life, you seem buoyant. You're oriented to life, to producing life rather than mulling over ...

VIVIAN: You can't back up! There are only two ways to go in this: you either (1) go down, or (2) climb out of it. There are only two ways.

MICHAEL: That's an interesting expression.

VIVIAN: And some people do slide back, further and further. But there's no point in that!

JAMES: I was taking some instructions from a minister and my daughter had requested that I go and talk with him and get a little instruction. So the first lady that I took out — well, first of all, like my wife, she worked in the bank. This lady had three boys. She had been left a widow when she was perhaps 35 years old, and she was now, I think, 52 or 53. So, the boys were off her hands and raised. She was very, very similar, actually, to Adele. It made it seem very comfortable. She had a lovely apartment over near the park, and she invited me to come over whenever I cared to. She too had a swimming pool in the apartment building. So we could go swimming every night, even in the winter. She would go every night. She was a real health one. But the thing that I thought about was, I don't think, — she was within three years of getting a pension, having spent most of her life — 25 years — in the bank, and I think it was her interest — I don't think she was particularly interested in marriage. She seemed to like my company; she seemed to like to swim with me, but really, there was no discussion, no interest to get married, or anything like that! There was no talk about that at all!

But anyway, I told Tom, my friend the minister, about this girl that I was taking out. He said, "You're fine, James. But it wouldn't be that you're going with this girl because she reminds you of Adele, would it?" I said, "By gosh; you know it might be! She is Adele all over again!"

VIVIAN: You see, you can't replace!

MICHAEL: You can't replace.

VIVIAN: It's important to see that.

JAMES: The minister said, "I wouldn't get too deep in there. You can never replace Adele. If you're looking for this lady to replace her, you're going to be disappointed. On the other hand, if you get involved with her, and you start comparing her with Adele, then you're going to be into trouble too!" He said, "I would recommend that you tread lightly on this!"

MICHAEL: So, then, with you and Vivian, it's like a fresh start!

VIVIAN: Yes, it sure was for me!

JAMES: I have something else also. I have one more episode to bring in. [*laughter all around*] While I was up at Huntsville — to go back to that — Lois said to me, "James, I have this nice place here. You're looking for a few days holiday. You stay in Huntsville till the weekend. We have a big party here Friday night. The play group from the district comes in. They put on a play and serve a nice meal. It's one of those theatre things," she said. "You will enjoy this. You can stay down at the motel down the highway," which I did and I stayed with Lois till the weekend. In the meantime, the next day, Lois took me over to Warren's, a mutual friend. Warren had been left a widower; his wife passed away very much the same way as Adele did, only a year before Adele did. I went over to visit Warren. Of course, Warren was very interested in having me. Warren, in the meantime, had found himself a new wife back home where I live. A lovely girl! And I was so happy to see that they had a happy marriage. So I said to his new wife, "It wouldn't be that you had any sisters, would it?" [*laughter galore*] This is just about what I'm looking for. "Well," she said, "James, to be frank with you, I haven't. But I have two nice girlfriends of mine. I'm going to ... I want them to come up to see our new home here anyway" — they [Warren and his new wife] have a beautiful home up there, a $200,000 home [which is a lot in a rural area] — "I'll be inviting them up, and when I do, I'll get you to drive them up. This will give you an opening to get an invitation, to get an introduction." So, one evening, I came home from my daughters. I had been over to my daughters for Sunday meal, and I came home Sunday night; and there was a note to call Warren [his friend], in Huntsville. So, I called Warren. Warren said that they had invited these ladies up the following Saturday. He would give me the telephone numbers. I would call them and they would be very happy to ride up with me. One of these ladies was the senior secretary of a large corporation. She had been secretary to the president. She was a very, very — how would you call it? — all dressed up!

MICHAEL: Sophisticated?

JAMES: Yes! A sophisticated lady! She was a very sophisticated lady. She had always been pampered in the business. I could see that. She was spoiled! Then husband had died. She had been a widow, and she was looking for a man. She lived in the top apartment, high class apartment, in her city. Anyway, when I drove up to the door to pick her up, I could see that she was very impressed with my Mercedes [*laughter*]. [*Aside, Just what she wanted, you see!*] Now, the other lady — we had to drive to another address to pick up the other lady. But, this first lady I picked up, she jumped right in the car, got in the front seat. I could see that she was settling right into the front seat. The other lady, if she came, would have to take the back seat [*laughter again*]. So, we drove over to the other lady's address, picked her up, and sure enough, she had to get into the back seat! Well, sir, I got along very well with her. She was playing right up to me, this one here was, and we drove up to Huntsville . The next day, Warren announced that their son was and two or three children were coming over to the house; and this [*first*] lady, she came up to me. I was outside of the house. She said, "James, Warren's children are coming over here. This kind of turns me off. I'd like to get out here for an hour or two, a few hours ..."

MICHAEL: Now, this is the "sophisticated" lady?

VIVIAN: Yes.

JAMES: She continued, "I wonder if you could make yourself scarce." [*laughter in room*] I said, "If you can arrange it with the host, I'll be glad to." So, she went, and came back, and said, "Well, I've fixed it all up with Warren's wife. The hosts said they would be glad to because there would be too much commotion around here with the children." So, we jumped in the car and we drove to North Bay [Ontario]. We found a lovely old home out on the highway and by this time; she was "eating out of my hands" [*gales of laughter all around*].

But, I still had this one commitment [*that he recounted earlier*]. Well, shortly thereafter, I was back to work and Lois called me one day; and said she had this condominium in Tennessee. She had Vivian going with her. She would like very much if I would drive them. I said I would drive them. I told this other girl, "I have one commitment — don't get your heart too set on this thing! — I have to take two widows to Tennessee!!" [*laughter for a long time now*] She said at that time it was all right. But when I got back from Tennessee...

MICHAEL: Things had changed!

JAMES: Things had changed! She said that I had been away for a week with these two other ladies, and in all probability I had made love to them, or something like that, and this had bothered her to no end. She thought I was ...

MICHAEL: A no good scoundrel!

JAMES: A no good scoundrel! [*laughter all around again*] She made it easy! Her name was Wilma. I said, "Wilma, let's just call it off. In two or three weeks, I haven't damaged your life *too* much! [*laughter all around again, especially from Vivian*] I'll just step aside!" About this time Vivian called me and I took up with Vivian. It has been Vivian ever since.

MICHAEL: Isn't that great!

JAMES: Then we had a week or two weeks in Florida. And I mentioned the trip down here [*Barbados, where interview was held*], and we have been very happy.

MICHAEL: Isn't it wonderful here!

JAMES: Isn't that nice!

MICHAEL: Vivian, do you want to add anything to this. This is all very interesting!

VIVIAN: No, not really, I don't think so. Oh, I do have a cute little thing I could tell you. James told you about my daughter, Elizabeth, telling us to *"Go for it!"* I went west for Christmas to visit my children. My oldest boy is thirty-five. I told him, "I am going to Florida on the 17th of January with this chap whom you have never met. What do you think of that?" He said, "I think it is just fine as long as you're home for midnight!" [*laughter again*]

JANICE: Isn't that cute!

VIVIAN: I said, "Midnight will be the 31st of January! He said, Well, it's all right, mother. Just give me 20 minutes to think about it, and then, whatever you want to do is fine!"

JANICE: How many kids did you have, Vivian?

VIVIAN: Five children and nine grandchildren. The rest of the kids have met James. Two boys at home have met James. It's fine with the family at home. They're all for it!

JAMES: I have one boy; he's just 21. He is his mother's baby. We just thought that maybe he might be the one who would have a little difficulty with this [relationship]. But, oh, a few little things that Mark has said ... I don't think there's a problem with Mark either, because when I was getting ready to come down here [to Barbados], I asked Vivian if she minded coming in a day or two ahead, and do a little laundry for me, and help me pack my shirts in my suitcase, and she graciously did come in. Mark asked me, "Is Vivian coming in?" I said, "Yes, she's coming in a couple of days early to pack my shirts, and so on." He said, "That's good, Dad!"

MICHAEL: Isn't that terrific!

JAMES: So you can see, he's not too bad! They don't say much — kids, but, you just have to be there with them.

MICHAEL: Let me ask you: obviously things have changed in your personal circumstances with your husband dying, Vivian, and your wife dying, James, but what has changed? I don't mean practical kinds of things, — but even that maybe. Your outlook on life — anything changed at all from the past?

JAMES: Well, I'll tell you, I think I took a — you know, you say, "Why me, Lord?"; that's the first thing. Adele was the most meticulous person in her eating habits, in her living habits. She always strived for pure foods and natural foods. If we went into a restaurant, she'd be the first one to return things. And yet, she's the one who's gone. Roy was a man — I don't suppose he ever drank to excess? [looking at Vivian], never smoked to excess. He was close to the soil; he was a cattleman, dealing with cattle all his life. And you wonder. I guess everybody wonders ...

MICHAEL: In spite of good intentions!

VIVIAN: I really think there's a plan for all of our lives. That was the way it was meant to be. That's how I feel it is.

JAMES: On the other hand, Vivian had 35 years, — right?

VIVIAN: Yes.

JAMES: And I had 38 years. That's better than the average!

VIVIAN: It is. My parents didn't have 10! I always thought I was quite lucky to have 35 years. We have to look positive.

JAMES: Here's another thing I'm going to say: We both had good marriages, and that speaks highly about her husband and my wife, that we're anxious to get into another good solid relationship!

JANICE: Because you've got good feelings that you're bringing with you.

JAMES: That's right! You don't want to be away from [a good relationship].

VIVIAN: I don't have any negative feelings about going into another relationship with James because it will be all right.

MICHAEL: Did you find your own personal philosophy of life — whether it's religious or not — helpful to you when he, or she, died?

VIVIAN: I think I had a positive attitude about living. I think that was one thing that helped me through.

MICHAEL: Vivian, you're very young looking!

JANICE: Yes, it shows!

JAMES: I was born in 1918! So, I'm 69 years old!

VIVIAN: I'll be 63 in May!

JANICE: You, don't look your age at all!

JAMES: But, this romance of ours — may I say this? — this romance of ours is almost like a new ...

MICHAEL: Like a new lease on life?

JAMES: As good as the first, the second time around!

JANICE: All the excitement, the good feelings ...

JAMES: I think the reason they're so passive [*meaning, not saying too much about Vivian and James's relationship*] is possibly because they think, "Oh well, they're probably "over the hill' anyway!" [*laughs*] This is a fallacy. If your health is good, you can enjoy one another just as much at 69 as you do at 39!

MICHAEL: What would you recommend for others in losing a spouse, or, needing a new person like this?

VIVIAN: I think it happens. I don't think you should be out looking for someone, and certainly, not too soon. That's the way it was with me. I had a feeling that probably I would meet someone and remarry, because I think I really wanted to have someone to look after. If you've had a husband for 35 years and five children, and nine grandchildren — that's been your life! Taking care of someone. That's the one thing you miss.

MICHAEL: A relationship.

VIVIAN: Yes. I think I felt that one day there'd be someone. But I didn't go out looking. And it happened.

JAMES: [*Going back to his friend, Warren, above ...*] Now, when I was talking with Warren, he and I took a walk (he, by the way, is brother-in-law to so-and-so, a well-known Canadian; his wife is this well-known person's sister. So you know they're good people, and smart people) Warren's advice to me was, "James, don't ever go looking for a woman. That's the worst thing you could do, especially not at this time." I really hadn't had a wife for, ah ... Adele was not a wife for me for over a year before she died; and I suppose it was the same with Vivian and Roy [*looking over at her*]. Most cancer victims are not themselves; they're only shadows of themselves. I would say that Adele was not in normal health for four years before she died. In retrospect, you could see it coming on.

VIVIAN: When you look back, you've really lost long before he/she has died, especially with cancer. Your life together is ... well, you just keep on going. You really haven't lived together. You're not able to go anywhere, or do anything together, and you're always caring. It's a case of caring. But you're not really *living*. When you're going through it, you don't realize it.

JAMES: It isn't the day they die that they die!

JANICE: You go through a whole mourning process through the period with a person dying of cancer.

VIVIAN: Yes, you do.

MICHAEL: Janice's dad died of prostate cancer.

VIVIAN: Oh, you [meaning, the spouse as well, in a symbolic manner, had the disease because the dying spouse needed so much care and attention] had it too! The day we learned that he [Roy] had it, that was the most devastating day ever, not the day he died. That's a relief.

JAMES: That's a relief!

MICHAEL: That's why, even now, James — it's not quite a year — a new relationship is so comfortable.

JAMES: Yes.

MICHAEL: It makes so much sense because it has really been five years! Some people would say you have to wait three years.

JAMES: To me, to put a time frame on it of three years of waiting is absolutely ridiculous! There's no sense in it at all!

MICHAEL: Go with life!

JAMES: Go with life! In the first place, how many three year periods does a man of 69 have, that is, productive years? I haven't got the time to afford that. I can't afford the time. Vivian is 62. She's waited four years. I think she's put her time in, as far as that goes!

MICHAEL: Life is buoyant; it is up; and it's got a real zip to it!

VIVIAN: Yes, it has!

JAMES: I wouldn't have missed the last three months for anything.

JANICE: Isn't that great!

JAMES: The best times really.

MICHAEL: What would you recommend to others?

JAMES: *Go for it!*

VIVIAN: GO FOR IT! It's unorthodox, you know, to do what we're doing [to be going off on trips, unmarried, with a person of the opposite sex]. It's not the way I was brought up. I had to about bare my soul to take off to Florida, you know.

JAMES: You have to be sure [*in your heart about the relationship*].

VIVIAN: Some of my neighbours yet ... I live in a small town in southern Ontario. They don't know yet what I'm up to, I don't think [*i.e., going away to places with James*]. I feel like shoving my bag in the car after midnight, you know, this sort of thing. I feel like sneaking "down corridors" [*laughter all around*]. My in-laws — I haven't confronted at all! [*laughter*] I guess they've heard; I don't know.

MICHAEL: Let them!

JANICE: It's wonderful you have the courage to live your own life.

VIVIAN: I'm just going to do it anyway!

JAMES: [*Still pondering earlier parts of the interview*] I had two other ladies, I guess, that I took out. And now, I think, not really one of them would have worked! So, I've been kind of lucky. I think when it's right, you'll know it. That's what my friend, Warren, told me. He said, "When it's right, you'll know it. You won't have to worry about it." By the same token, I think you're well to expose yourself to the other one because there might be certain idiosyncrasies — I might chew gum or something like that that she might not like.

VIVIAN: I smoked; I quit!

JAMES: She smoked and she quit. That demonstrated to me that as soon as Vivian found out that I was a non-smoker, she quit smoking. That was pretty terrific; that took some will power.

MICHAEL: Isn't that neat!

VIVIAN: I had some incentive; that's all I needed.

JAMES: It told me something.

JANICE: That's a wonderful story. There's a lot of sadness in the background, but, I know what you mean by having gone through the process of mourning, because we did that with my dad, and his death was such a relief.

JAMES: Life really ... happiness is more and more short—lived. That's life, isn't it? One day has to end, so that another day can start.

JANICE: So, facing death again doesn't affect you in the same way it might have before then. Do you have a different perspective on death now?

JAMES: I'll tell you ... when my dad died, the minister told a story. My dad was a pillar of the church. I don't think he was missing from the choir very often. And the minister said, "Today, Billy ... [*James's father*] will be singing in heaven!" If you look on it like that, he's gone on to another life.

MICHAEL: That's right!

JAMES: That's the way I look at it. I think that Adele was too good. She has a better life now! And I expect Roy has too!

MICHAEL: For Janice and me, we say that after death, a person is in the resurrection. Roy is in the resurrection; so is Adele. That's our way of expressing what you're trying to say.

JAMES: That's right.

MICHAEL: James and Vivian, Janice and I would like to thank you for sharing with us your sorrow, and also your love story. As you said, GO FOR IT!

"I think it happens. I don't think you should be out looking for someone, and certainly, not too soon. That's the way it was with me. I had a feeling that probably I would meet someone and remarry, because I think I really wanted to have someone to look after. If you've had a husband for 35 years and five children, and nine grandchildren — that's been your life! Taking care of someone. That's the one thing you miss."

— Vivian, commenting on her role as wife

COMMENTARY

We first met James about three years before this interview. His wife, Adele, was with him then. According to his story, she was already one year into the illness that would claim her life — cancer. The next time I saw James, he was with his new "friend," Vivian. I had a wonderful feeling about them instantly — *real people* — and that feeling was more than brought out in their generous time with us.

James and Vivian — a true love story, she 62, he 68! Both had been widowed, and both had met again, having really not since each other since childhood! They show each of us that one can be proud to stand tall and love openly; they show not only that hope springs eternal, but so does love. They have that fresh look about them — seasoned because of the years, realistic because of experiences, but open to the future, and to life. They love life; they share life; they live life; and they give life!

For us, as interviewers, we loved their playfulness, and especially their sense of humour. James loves to tease, but he does it ever so softly and gently. He is tender and innocent at the same time; Vivian is caring and so supportive. They each look at life positively, and take this fresh outlook with them each day. We both admired them for the courage to *live* their relationship. They are "going for it" with as much energy and hope as possible. Vivian would say that going off to these distant places together [*while being unmarried*] seems "unorthodox"; but, that does not stop her. To stop life here would be to place artificial barriers in front of life; they will not do that.

Both James and Vivian also look back on 38 and 35 years of marriage, respectively. They have lived marriage. And so, when they contemplate their own relationship today they know what to expect; they want quality; they want genuineness; they want stability; they want love. And they are living it all! Life is good to people who are true to themselves, in spite of their hardships or sorrows. There is a peace beyond understanding. James and Vivian know about this peace; they live that too. They radiate life. They are doing what many of us so often are reluctant to do: going for it. When everything or everyone around us might be telling us that 'it is wrong', or 'are you sure you're doing the right thing?', or 'aren't you too old to be thinking of *this* stuff?', James and Vivian have searched their hearts, plunged into life and are "going for it!"

The experience of being with James and Vivian told us loudly and clearly that *Life* is what is important, that life is not determined by age, but that life is the substance of everything. In this regard, we are reminded of the greatest moral principle that we have followed and taught and written about over the years: that what gives life is moral, what denies life is immoral. Giving life, therefore, is the basic benchmark against which we unify our lives, give ourselves a direction, and make decisions that enhance who we are and what we do. In problematic situations, therefore, we ask not so much "should I do this or that?" but rather, "what will give life?" And whatever that is, that is where I need to go and that is who I must become.

What a wonderful reality: the buoyancy of expectation, the joy of children's excitement, the naiveté that life holds out to us all the time greater and greater dimensions of living. It's all there before us; we have only to reach; we have only to believe it's there; we have only to take that first step.

James and Vivian's story tells us that they have the courage to do precisely that. They have the courage to say that life is more generous than we ever thought possible. They are courageous enough to believe in their dream, in their vision, and in their love. They are doing what we all must do in life: they're going for it! Truly, theirs is a love story!

"The greatest misfortune of all
is not to be able to bear misfortune."

— Bias, a Greek sage (circa 570 B.C.)

CHAPTER ELEVEN

LIFE HAS TO GO ON:
THE STORY OF JIM

> Jim was a very successful businessman with seven children. He was 51 years old at the time of the interview and had raised the children by himself after his wife died. We interviewed him when we were on a lecturing tour in Barbados.

MICHAEL: What are some of the factual data about your wife: when she died, how did it happen, how long were you married, etc?

JIM: All right. We we're married for almost 25 years. We had seven children, and we had just had the youngest one who was just a few months old. Susan [his wife] was complaining — actually what happened was that I was complaining that she did not get back into shape after the birth of this seventh child. She got into shape for the rest of the other children. She said she didn't know what it was; she had been doing exercises and the swelling just wouldn't go down. I thought that my vasectomy after the last baby hadn't worked! [and she was pregnant again] I went to the doctor and he said, "No, it wasn't that." He said that there was probably a cyst on my wife's ovary; and so we made an appointment for her to see the doctor, and about a month later we found that it was cancer! They told me she had two years, but she died within six months!

JANICE: Oh, my gosh!

JIM: But, in this way she didn't struggle on like some cancer patients.

MICHAEL: What year would that have been, Jim?

JIM: That would have been 1973. It really blows the hell out of you. I couldn't believe it when they told me she had cancer and was at home with seven kids.

Things were just starting to go well in our lives. We had bought our first home. We had never had a home before. We could now do things together. All of a sudden this came along. First myself, I fell to pieces for a couple of years.

MICHAEL: It blew out all the circuits!

JIM: I went on a couple of years' drunk and blew everything I had ever owned. I had a roof over the heads of the kids, but I wasn't giving them any love and understanding.

MICHAEL: How old would she have been then, Jim?

JIM: She was 34.

MICHAEL: And you were married ...?

JIM: We would have been married ... I made a mistake ... almost 20 years, not 25 years. My oldest by the time was 15. I got married very young. She — it's so hard to remember back that far now — I know what happened to my life after. I had a couple of things happen after that. I sold my house because I wanted to get out of the bad memories, and we bought a new home. A few months after we bought the home, the home burned down to the ground. I didn't have any insurance on it! How I got a mortgage without insurance, I don't know. But here I am now $100,000 in debt. Just after that happened — it was a rental house — and I was on the phone one day and my son came running in and interrupted me on the phone. I told him, "Be quiet." Then he yelled out, "Andrew got hit by a car!" I ran out the door and there was my five year old lying out on the ground completely out, bleeding at the nose and ears. I thought I was going to lose him. And I fell on my knees and prayed; and he was all right. They told me he would never walk again, he would never do this. Now he is a big 6 feet 2 inches; he's the only 6 feet 2 inches one in the family. ... What is he going to be? He's going to be 19 this birthday! He's a big, strong husky kid. Everything worked out just perfect for him.

Things went pretty rough there for a while until I started realizing that life has to go on, that she's gone and not here any more. I think that from all my experience from being a single parent, and really people who go through divorces, I think a widower is much better off, or any type of person who is widowed; they're much better that way than going through a divorce. It's traumatic, but only for a short period of time. You have to finally get them out of your mind, and life goes on. At least you're not worrying about the fact that the person you love is living with somebody else, or you get the kids involved, and they go to live with the mother, and then live with the father, and they're playing one against the other, as I hear all this stuff from the divorce people. My wife is gone, and nothing is going to bring her back. And life has to go on.

The hardest problem I have is with my children, as far as life going on, because they don't want me to get deeply and emotionally involved with anybody. They don't mind my having several different girlfriends, but when one starts to get serious, they start pulling back. They don't want me to get involved. Jealousy, or whatever it is: but they don't want me to get involved.

MICHAEL: How old is the youngest one now, Jim?

JIM: Fifteen. He's going to be fifteen in August. And that little guy! He went through, I mean, I could tell you stories! He went through such stuff as — I remember, perhaps because he was young he never got potty trained. He was only six months old when his mother got sick and just a week short of a year when his mother died! She died on the 23rd of August and he turned a year old on the 30th of August. And from constantly being pushed from one place to another, he was never really potty trained. I always say that, "Before a year old it's [shit] like custard: it's doesn't smell, it doesn't [soil]; it's easy. But after they get into that heavy stuff around a year and one-half." I couldn't handle it [laughter all around]. I'd be trying to change him and I'd get sick. So I had to come up with a solution. I'd take all his clothes off but the diaper, turn on the shower and shake! [laugh, laugh, and more laughter!] The diaper fell off [laughs], and I cleaned him all off, fluffed him up. You'd think he'd be scared to hell of showers; but he loves them! But he runs around and jumps up and down [gales of laughter from us all]. Then after I'd finished that I'd clean him all up and I would run cold water in the tub so that it [shit] would kind of gel, and then I would clean it all out. Oh God, if I found out it was really loose, I'd just pull the plug, and "Vroom, vroom," down it would go! [laughter again] But, it worked!

JANICE: I love that [*story*]!

JIM: I guess the biggest problem with having a big family as a widower is the kids. I'd come home on Friday night, and I'd start doing the laundry Friday night and I'd still be doing it Sunday night, at midnight! The old washer is going "Ka-blum, ka-blum, ka-blum"! doing this and trying to cook meals in between. I did this for about six months and I just couldn't take it any more. I'd just come home and do that, and then on a Saturday night, I'd just go out and get loaded and calm down for Sunday!

JANICE: Did you have babysitters, or someone else to come in?

JIM: Oh, the older ones. We had some help but it didn't work out. Every time you would get someone they'd be dishonest, and it just didn't work out. The kids said, "Let's just do it ourselves." But these laundromats, especially for a widower with a big family — I could go down there, and with fifty machines, I could be out of there within three hours! It was the folding that took all the time!

JANICE: Oh, I know all about that!

JIM: So, laundromats were a great saver. But the hardest part, when I smartened up, oh, the first two years, I still did the laundry and did what had to be done, but I didn't do a lot of loving, getting involved. I was drinking an awful lot. Then I got back involved with the kids sports as I used to before with my boys, things like that, and things started changing. Somebody sent me *The Power of Positive Thinking* by Norman Vincent Peale. I read that book, threw it into the corner, and read it again, and I started reading parts of the bible which said the same thing. And my life started to change. I started getting more positive. I said, "Hey, there are lots of people. You feel sorry for the guy with no shoes until you see the guy with no feet!" That sort of thing. It was the same thing with me. That's what I went through. So, I guess, in 1975 I really started getting back on my feet again, and worked myself up to where I am today. I worked myself completely out of debt; I just paid my last cent off, except for the income tax. I think I'll always owe them no matter how much. But I own 20% of my company which is the second largest company in the country [*in the industry*].

So, I'm doing pretty well financially now. I'm probably worth — oh, I don't know what I'm worth — probably a couple of million dollars, I'd guess. I did that since 1975 till now, in the last 11-12 years. It was a lot of work, but I had a lot of support from my kids, a lot of love; and we have a lot of fun at home, you know. Now, we get out and play ball together and I get involved with the kids and the rugby, the girls and the baseball.

God, they had me at the school. The little guys were upset because their mothers would come to the school on Mondays and Wednesdays; they didn't go to school on their sport days with their groups, and all this sort of thing. Both of my kids went to kindergarten and grade one together. Geoff was in that accident; that's how he missed a year of school. He was in a coma for 38 days! They told me that they didn't know whether he was going to live or die, what he was going to be. Then they told me he was going to live, but they didn't know how much brain damage, you know, and so on. Anyway, they went to school together; and they came to me one day, crying: "Everybody has their mommies going; we don't have a mommy, daddy! Won't you come to the school and be the mommy?" And so here I was in school with all these women — thirty-five mothers there and I'm up there doing the hula hoop! [*tremendous laughter*]

JANICE: That's terrific!

JIM: I met a few single women there; it wasn't too bad! I've got to laugh about all this. I got to know everybody on the school board and got involved in everything. If you're widowed and you have children — people say, "How did you ever do it with seven kids? How did you bring them up?" I don't think it's any harder to bring up seven kids than it is to bring up one or two. In fact, it is probably easier because they help look after one another, and there's so much love. I mean, you can go out and blow up the whole bloody world; kids don't care. They love you. [*you can do anything.*] Love can make a lot things happen.

MICHAEL: They must have been just darling with you!

JIM: Ah, we had ... I mean ... I figure a lot of times how I neglected them. Now I am getting so heavily involved with Lisette [*fiancé*]. We're probably going to get married next year. One of the big problems is that Lisette thinks I spoil the kids, and I say to her, "Look," but she's right. Harry is 30 years of age now. He's just working in our business as a handyman. He does just about everything around the company. I don't even know what we pay him. I think he gets about $1,500 a month which is not enough to bring up a family if he gets invloved with a girl; and I haven't done anything. I got him this job. He was 15 when his mother died; it's fifteen years now. And he had to come home from school, pick the kids up from the daycare centre, bring them home and look after them. He never had any teenage life; and neither did the two oldest girls. They took their turns; so [they don't owe me anything]. So I let him stay at home till he was 27-28. I said, "Hey, it's time. You've had your rest now. It's time to get to hell out and get to work!" And you learn, from what you do, and the older you feel, you have a guilt complex because, even though it's not my fault that my wife died, you have a guilt complex because you're still only one parent and they don't have a mother. You try to be both to them. But you can't, you know! And it's tough. I think that's the toughest part, and the fact that you don't have anybody really to sit down with and talk to and tell your problems so that you know that, no matter how bad a thing it is that you're going to tell them, that it's going to be between the two of you. It's just like talking to yourself if you can. I can't get that with any other women. Lisette is the closest I've come to. I can talk to Lisette, and it doesn't go other places. The first time I told her something, and it came back to me, I told her, "What I told you was very private." It is very important to be able to sit down after coming home and say, "How are you today? I had a fight with the boss. What an asshole he was! Was I ever an asshole! I shouldn't have done this! What do you think of this?" And they sit there and they tell you that they care!

My wife was my best friend! When we got married, she was only 17; I was only 18. We started out right away. And all of a sudden, wham! she's gone! She was never sick a day in her life! She was always healthy, and then we find out she's got cancer!

MICHAEL: What kind of cancer was it, Jim?

JIM: It was a rare, rare type of cancer. That's why she never had any pain with it or anything before it was doing anything. It was a little thing, the size of a dime, up in the bowels. It started in the bowels. And by the time they found it, it had just gone right through all the body. It was into the liver and everything. There was nothing they could do. They did a complete hysterectomy, but the cancer was in the liver. It was probably the hardest time of my life. I couldn't sleep at nights. I would go to sleep at night; I would cry; I would go to church, and I hated the Lord! I used to call him, "You son-of-a-bitch!" and everything else! "What are you doing to me? First, you take my wife. Now you throw fire bolts at my house! Now one of my kids gets hit by a car! What the hell do you want from me?" I used to scream at him.

I'd go down to the ocean beach and say something to him. I used to smoke a little bit of pot when I was [*in Korea*] and stuff like that. After that I would go down to the beach and take a joint and smoke it by myself on the beach and scream and yell at God all night. And I found out that that's not the way to get along with people! [*laughs*]. You've got to be a little bit humble! [*all kinds of laughter from each of us*]. And you've got to get along. You know, you have a tendency when something like that happens to blame the whole world for everything that's happened, to go into a "self-pity" trip.

If I were talking to anyone who has been widowed, or who has lost anyone they cared about, or lost anything they really care about that's really deep, the worst thing you can do is go on a "self-pity" trip. But, it's the hardest thing to tell anybody. I can cope with other people who go through these problems; I'll go talk with them and bring them out of it, because I've been there. *You have to be there*!

I have a brother-in-law and a sister-in-law — the closest relatives — always very, very selfish. My brother-in-law lost his daughter to cancer when she was only 15. He changed, and he understood what I went through. We became the best of friends. He just died last year of cancer! He was my age, and just like that! Now his wife who was always very cold toward me and my family is very close to my kids. When we go over there, she wants to visit with them. She is very friendly to me, and so on and so forth, because they *understand*. *Nobody understands until they go through how dramatic a shock it is to you*. A person just doesn't understand, I always said, "If I had to sit in a wheelchair, I'd blow my brains out." But I don't really know because I'm not there. And you talk to these people who've felt the same way; they go on living. And you get this guy

Hansen [*rode his wheelchair*], running all across the country and people like that who make you feel that life does go on. It's the same if something like this happened to you. You can help somebody else who's been in the same position because you understand.

I have given a lot of thought, and I realize I went through two years of self-pity and self-destruction. I would come home at night. The kids always had their meals, a roof over the house, but then I was gone. I would say, "I am gone." I'd be out of the house at 8:00 PM. I'd leave for the bar and stagger in around 2 or 3 o'clock in the morning.

I think the thing that really smartened me up was the following: on Bill's sixteenth birthday, about a year and one-half after his mother died, I walked in the house about 3 o'clock in the morning. I had left him a card with 50 bucks [dollars] in it. I said, "Hi, son! Did you get your birthday present?" He said [rudely], "I got it!" He's never spoken back to me in my life. You have to understand: my kids do not talk back to me! I'm very easy, but I'm very strict! When they get big and get on their own ... my kid, the 30 year old, jumps at me once in a while. I just laugh and say, "OK." He's on his own; he's a man now.

JANICE: But, they have respect.

JIM: Yes. They have respect. The young ones, they get it when they say something [*back to me*]. Here he was, fifteen years of age, just turned sixteen, and he turns around and says, "Yeah, I got it! and you can shove it up your ass!" Here's a kid who has never said anything bad to me in his life! "And furthermore, I'm quitting school tomorrow and looking after my brothers and sisters because you're not doing the job!" I was *so* mad that I took a swing at him. Thank God I missed him. You know, I'm a pretty strong person. That was fifteen years ago; I was also in better shape, you know! And then I went and lay down on the couch and I couldn't sleep. That was 3 o'clock in the morning.

Finally, at 6 o'clock in the morning I said, "This is crazy!" And I turned on all the lights in the house and woke everybody up. The baby, everybody. I got them upstairs and said, "We're having a family meeting!" We sat around the table. You should have seen them, a little kid with his nose dripping, and their little cold, bare feet, and I said, "We're going to have a family meeting." Then, I told them. That's all I could say. I said, "I'm sorry. Bill has brought it to my attention that I have neglected you kids." What he said to me was, "You know, you might have lost your wife, but we lost our mother! It hurts us too, and nobody is helping us! You're not helping anybody!"

JANICE: What an incredible thing!

JIM: At the time I was furious, but then when I got to thinking … So then, we had a meeting, and life started to change for me. We were all sitting there. I was crying; the kids were crying; the baby was crying, not because he knew what was happening. He didn't like being wakened up at 6 in the morning! [*laughter all over*] Here we were: all sitting there, this four or five year old, having this conversation, and I have tears running down my face, and I have my arm around them, and I'm saying, "I'm sorry! Let's see what we can do to start over!" And then, things started to change; and I started thinking about positive things: how many good things happened to me after my wife died, how the community rallied because I did have seven kids, and how they came over and looked after them while I was away with my wife being sick for six months, and how they helped me out after she died; and every day I'd come home, there'd be some kind of casserole sitting on my front step. I had so many casseroles in the freezer, for crying out loud, … what they didn't realize, the neighbours, was that one of the things that helped me was that I always liked cooking, and I always helped my wife around the house with the heavy stuff. I never thought that she should wash and polish floors while I was there. I could help with that, or do the windows, or even wash the dishes with her, you know, especially the hard times when she was going out to work to help bring in the money. I always thought we should share those things. And my dad was the same way. The going was tough. A lot of people — I don't what it is about males; they do the chauvinistic thing that they can't do any of the housework, that they can't do anything like this; it's degrading. I said, "I think that's a bunch of bullshit!" I would have been in a hell of a mess if I didn't know how — I know guys who don't even know how to boil water!" [*Janice laughs and laughs*] I usually got up every Sunday morning and made my wife breakfast. Every Sunday morning she got breakfast in bed. I like doing that.

JANICE: What a neat treat!

JIM: I do that for Lisette now. I believe it was on the weekend, but I said, "You sit. I'll go down and make the breakfast." And you enjoy doing it if you're doing it for somebody else whom you love. And the same thing: I cook for the kids, and my kids all say, "Oh, dad! When are you going to cook a meal, huh?" Linda [our housekeeper] has been cooking meals. "When are you going to cook a meal?" I make a big turkey dinner; I make a roast, or I bake a couple of pies, or something. When they find out, [*they say*], "Dad's making dinner (in a whisper)!" All the ones who are out on their own are at the house eating [all the stuff]! [*laughter all around again*] But that helped me because I knew that stuff.

If there's any advice you can give to someone who doesn't know how to do these things is that they should go and learn how to do them, take a course in cooking, or something. You know, you'd be lost. But, I can bake casseroles, make my own bread; I can do all that sort of stuff. Whereas the neighbours weren't sure what I could do, and so they sent over these casseroles all the time! Then when they stopped sending them over, that's what I used to do every weekend: I'd make up enough casseroles to last the whole week. I'd make maybe a salmon, a tuna casserole, or macaroni and cheese, chicken cacciatore; and I would just throw them in the freezer. Add a microwave; they'd throw it in the microwave, and zap! and it's ready for their supper. I'd just phone up and I would say that I was not able to come home for supper, but there were casseroles downstairs in the freezer. I'd say, "There's this, and this, and this. Which one do you want for supper?" The kid would pull one out, throw it in the microwave, and ...

MICHAEL: Away they'd go!

JIM: That was it!

JANICE: So, they learned a lot of skills to take care of themselves too.

JIM: Yes. But they learned a lot of bad things. Being a single parent is very tough on the kids. I mean, all my kids are tough; they're generous, to a fault, just as I am. They also learned that from their mother. She was also a very generous person, but she was also frugal: she knew what to be generous with and not. I do stupid things like jumping into the pool, and saying, "Let everybody this afternoon drink beer on Jim!" For three hours I wouldn't let anybody buy a drink, just me. I don't have to do that. But I enjoy doing that. I've got some money and I ought to do something like that.

MICHAEL: How old are you now, Jim?

JIM: 51. I don't look that age, do I? Well, you see one good thing about being widowed is that you can get a younger one, as I have. [*laughter*]. I think women keep you young. My kids keep me young. I get involved with my kids: I go to a basketball game here; I go a rugby game, sometimes even play with them. I coach football; I coach baseball; I coach hockey, and I get out there with my stuff and do it with them. I get with the kids — honest to God! — I get with them and my kids are into something, and I forget how old I am, and think I am one of them! That Walt Disney movie, "The Basset and the Hound," and they have the great big dog like this [*pointing*] and the little dachshund — he's running under the table and knocking it over and he can't understand why he's always getting into hell! I think I'm their age, and then I run across a mirror and I say, "Who the hell is that old bastard? That's *me*!" [*laughs and laughs*]

I just decided that I think the only way to live is one day at a time, and forget about what's happened in the past. You have to go on living in the future. There are lots of things I did in the past that I am not happy with, that I'm disgusted with myself for, and things like that; and I can't rectify them. They're done; they're gone. And if I let them eat me away and say, "Well, I never should have done that, I shouldn't have done this stupid thing, I shouldn't have done that stupid thing," in your lifetime, you destroy yourself. And so I say, "Those things are in the past; I'm a different person now and I do this, you know, and then I just do [it]." I did not value my life there for a while. 1981, I guess, was the last of my bad years. I went through a really bad time; I grew a beard; I really didn't like myself, didn't like shaving myself. I looked at myself and hated myself. Things weren't working out for me in my life and I was doing things I knew I shouldn't have been. I wasn't caring about people; I was caring about me.

MICHAEL: Did you have a religion that you shared with your wife?
JIM: Well, we never had, you see, my wife and I went through rough times. I don't know if you know anything about Québec. In Québec they have such a thing as "Lacombe" law: old laws where you can consolidate all your debt, and you pay so much every month if you get yourself over, instead of going bankrupt. Well, I was into [*that*], right at the start of "Lacombe" law. I used to have bailiffs at my house. They'd come in, clean out all my furniture, if I owed some guy $200, or something like this.

The industry I'm in now was easy to get started in. When I used to go out on a sales call [when first in this industry], I made sure that when I sat in a guy's house my feet were flat on the floor. I had a habit of crossing my legs. I would always talk to the guy like this: my elbow here [on table], but I tried to keep my feet on the ground because I had holes in the bottom of my shoes. I had two day-old newspaper in them to walk on, in -30° [F] weather and in snowstorms. Also, I used to have a car that I parked three blocks away in case somebody would see me coming with it. I'd say, "I couldn't find a parking spot!" or, whatever.

So, we went through the rough times; we had a pretty hard time, but we stuck it out. I didn't make a good income, and there were no more jobs, and I was into this, and I just stayed with it and stayed with it and stayed with it. My wife said, "That's what you want to do; that's what you're built for; you're going to make it pay." And just when we started to make it, she died. So, it was really tight, especially on $5,000-6,000 a year, I guess, in '66, '67, '68. I paid off everybody I owed over these years and everything, and we were just getting into the place. I had a philosophy, one philosophy, that we had to go to supper at least twice a week together. Just the two of us. We usually went on a Wednesday and on a weekend. We got a babysitter, and we went out together. We didn't look on the prices on anything that we wanted to do. If we wanted to stay overnight, we'd make arrangements to stay overnight. It didn't have to be far, just so we could be alone together and do some of the things that we wanted to do. We never had the money to do that before. My wife never got out of Canada except to the United States. These trips here [*in the Caribbean*], every time I come on one of these, I think, "Wouldn't she have loved this place here! Wouldn't she have liked that place! Wouldn't she have liked to have done this!" Christ, you know,

I bought Lisette [*fiancé*] a diamond ring there that cost me $25,000. It didn't cost me that, but that's what it's valued at. Hell, that would have been four — *five, six* — years income! in those days! So when things got good and we started paying the bills and everything, that's when it happened [his wife died]. So, it was kind of a shock; but it's gone.

And now I have a philosophy in life. My philosophy now is that you can't look back; you have to look ahead and do whatever you can do. Lots of times I'm quick to jump on something and say something to someone. And my philosophy on that is that if I say something to you that's wrong, and I realize that I made a mistake, then I have no hard feelings and come up and say, "Gee, Michael, I'm sorry; I made a mistake on that. I was way out on second base on that. Would you please forgive me?" And apologize. I think if you make a mistake, you should apologize and it should be finished. I hold no grudges with anybody! except one person! [laughs] And, life has been pretty good. There are a lot of things I have done in the past that I learned lessons from, that I'll never do again; and that's the important thing. That's the important thing, to learn the lesson from what you did before, and not to do it all over again.

MICHAEL: One last thing, Jim, what would be the most important thing that you would recommend when someone goes through this experience?

JIM: I think ... it's hard for people who don't understand. I believe very strongly in a Superior Being, and whether you call him God, or not.

MICHAEL: Life Force.

JIM: Life Force ... I believe in it as God, but I always tell people when I tell them that that "G-o-d" spelled backwards is "dog," man's best friend. So, it doesn't matter what you really call it, as long as you have something to reach for. I believe that if you go to church, and you pray, and you believe in what you're doing, then it really helps a lot. And then you have to forget what's happened in the past ...

MICHAEL: And get on with it!

JIM: And go on, and start just like Alcoholics Anonymous say, "Live one day at a time, and don't say I'm never going to drink again in my lifetime." Just say, "I'm not going to have a drink today. Tomorrow is another day." And so on, and so forth. Well, I think you're got to live your life like that. We all do things that we're not proud of. The thing is, we can't dwell on those. We have to dwell on, not the negative things in life, but — I think that's the biggest thing — not to dwell on the negatives and try to pick out the positives. I mean, when I really get down on myself, down on what I feel, I go for a drive in the rough part of my city, look at the slum area, the people lying there, and the kids playing on their streets, and say to myself, "I'm pretty lucky, you know, to come to a country like this. The Caribbean may be a beautiful climate and everything, but I say how lucky I am to live in the greatest country in the world [*Canada*]; and how lucky I am to have seven children; and how lucky I am to have Lisette, and all the other things." When you put them all together — if you take a piece of paper and write down the pros and cons — the pros far outweigh the cons. I think that's what you really have to go at. You have to think about what you're going to do in the future, not what's happened in the past.

MICHAEL: A real posture of thankfulness.

JIM: I really think that that's the biggest thing that's made me succeed: that I don't ever dwell — if something is negative, i.e., she [*Lisette*] gets mad at me because she wonders how I could forget that — well, it was a negative thing. I forget it, but I don't forget it. I plant it back here [pointing to back of head] so that I don't make the same mistake again, or try not to make the same mistake again. I'm not going to remember that we had an argument a year ago and what it was over. That's gone because those are negative things. You have to get rid of them and throw them out of your mind and go on for whatever there is for today, and the next day, and the next day. I think that's the only good advice I could give to anybody. These are mostly the things I've gone through; these are the things.

JANICE: What a story! Thank you for sharing your story with us.

MICHAEL: Thank you very much, Jim, for sharing with us the painful moments but also your tremendous positive philosophy of living.

COMMENTARY

So there you have it: Jim's story. His story is one of deep emotion and deep conviction and deep laughter. But it wasn't always that way. Somehow his wife's death had shaken "the foundations" for him; but in the shaking of these foundations, he came to see what was of real value to him and what would not, in the best sense of the word, make him a success in life.

Without a doubt, the core of his success today as a person is his ability to ferret out the positive in life and in the situations which he encounters each day. It also helps to have Jim's attitude, of course, too, which is to begin life and to go out into life each day *expecting* the best, looking for life, and enhancing it wherever possible. Jim has learned that to spend one's time on the "negatives" gets on nowhere; it does not build; it destroys. Jim has learned the lesson that I write about — which we all must learn and live by — that we think in images; and in so doing, we become the image in our daily living. If we think negative thoughts and hold negative images of ourselves and the world around us, then we will live a negative life, and attract negative results into our lives. On the other hand, though, if we learn to see ourselves, to *envision* ourselves as living and breathing in a positive environment, we reap the results there as well. *We become that which we love and we also become that which we hate!* Where we put our energy is where our life will take us. Our lives are filled with the practical things that were first of all just inner images for us. If these images have been positive, our outer practical affairs will have this positive tone as well; and positive events and people will come into our lives. Success, therefore, comes from positive imagining, from seeing the world from the point of view of its beauty. In both Michael's books, *Reflections* and *Grippings*, he writes: "It's better to nurture the light than try to dispel the darkness." That's what Jim has learned to do. He went through the darkness, but now cherishes the light.

Jim was left with seven children when his wife died. She was only 34. The oldest child was 15. As he says, for the first while, he went through hell and back, and interestingly, it was his eldest, a son, age 16 now, who reminded him of what he had, even though his wife, "and our mother," is now gone. He called them all together one morning at 6:00 AM, and through tears and apologies said he was sorry for not looking after them well. Everyone cried; they hugged; and a new day, and a new future began for them. They could manage together; they could go on somehow without their mother and his wife. When he emerged from that time of self-pity, he realized that *life has to go on*; and a little later, he tells us that *life does go on*. Because of that reality, one picks oneself up, dusts oneself off, and begins afresh, except that there is more wisdom now, and more experience. That is why Jim is able to say that while he is not proud of some of the things he has done in the past, they're over with now; one cannot dwell on them; one has to build today, to create today, to love and laugh and play today. "Today is the first day of the rest of our lives" could be the core of his philosophy. He likens his philosophy to the Alcoholics Anonymous philosophy: "One day at a time." And he is very wise in doing this. He also sees and believes in a Supreme Being, call it God, the Life Force, but a presence and a power in the universe that does guide us and give us wisdom and new days, and children, and joy.

Jim is also incredible in his spontaneous laughter and in his generosity as he would put it, to a fault. Yes, he is generous, and he laughs a lot; and he is honest and straight as an arrow. If he finds that he has said or done something to offend someone, then it is not beneath him to go to the person and make amends. In this way he continues to reinforce his philosophy that one must forget the past and go on living for the future, because life, does, indeed, go on.

The reader, I am sure, has many funny images of this man, a widower, a single father now, trying to take care of these seven children. But he found that this was probably not any more difficult than having two because the older ones just pitched in, and relationships were created through the interactions of their home. One can see him shaking the baby who was being changed in the shower! And the child, now a teenager, still liking showers! The image is wonderful and very real. We can laugh at it now, but for Jim, right after his wife died, we're sure it wasn't all that funny then.

Perhaps the most obvious characteristic of Jim today is his great openness and generosity with people. He loves people. He loves to talk; he loves people around him; he protects relationships, and expects that in return. Jim has found that to look at life through the eyes of positive expectation fills his life with wonderful things, with his love today, Lisette, and with a deep, deep love and appreciation of his children — the oldest being 30, even though Jim is only 51! He has found that life is good to him these days. He has grown; he has matured. He has allowed life to test him in the crucible of his wife's death, and he has found hope, love, prosperity, and on-going life and vision. Is there anything else more important?

"But the hardest part, when I smartened up, oh, the first two years, I still did the laundry and did what had to be done, but I didn't do a lot of loving, getting involved. I was drinking an awful lot. Then I got back involved with the kids sports as I used to before with my boys, things like that, and things started changing. Somebody sent me *The Power of Positive Thinking* by Norman Vincent Peale. I read that book, threw it into the corner, and read it again, and I started reading parts of the bible which said the same thing. And my life started to change. I started getting more positive. I said, "Hey, there are lots of people. You feel sorry for the guy with no shoes until you see the guy with no feet!" That sort of thing."

-- Jim, commenting on how he changed his life

"Don't walk in front of me,
I may not follow.
Don't walk behind me,
I may not lead.
Just walk beside me
and be my friend."

— Albert Camus (1913-1960)

CHAPTER TWELVE

I'M NOT FINISHED WITH YOU YET:
THE STORY OF CONNIE (A)

We had known Connie and Michael for about two years. At one point they had come to see the both of us for counselling. The couple were of Italian background, both young, in their early 30s, and they had a young daughter, Lisa. During that same summer, Michael fell ill with what was diagnosed at the time as menningitis, and died within about three weeks. Connie went into deep shock. This is not a very happy or pleasant story – at least, at the beginning. Michael interviewed Connie ten days after her husband, Michael, had died. Connie was disoriented, angry, confused.

Part B (Chapter 13) of Connie's story is told in an interview nine months later. The reader will see and feel the difference in Connie in just this short period of time. We feel that both accounts are worth telling.

MICHAEL: The questions I am going to ask, Connie, are just questions for you to talk through your story; and we'll just follow our hearts and serendipity with that. My first question is this: "What day did Michael die?"

CONNIE: The 11th. That was a Saturday night, at a quarter to six.

MICHAEL: Today is the 21st. So it is only 10 days later. How old was he Connie?

CONNIE: 37. He just turned 37 on April 12th.

MICHAEL: Can you provide some background on how he died.

CONNIE: He first told me that he had a sore leg. He was always complaining about his leg.

MICHAEL: Was this quite a while ago?

CONNIE: No. That was about a week before he took sick at home. One week he was at home, then at the hospital. He didn't want to go to the hospital. I used to scream at him to go to the hospital. So finally, that Sunday morning, I took him. That was after he had been in bed for a week with a high fever. He was already sick. His face was swollen. He had come home from the cottage Wednesday night and told me he was shivering and cold. The weather, however, was very hot but he was still shivering. He went to bed; he was so cold. All of a sudden he said he felt very sick. In the morning he got up but he was still sick. He managed to get himself to work but came back home. He just couldn't make it.

MICHAEL: He felt so lousy?

CONNIE: Yes, he felt lousy. His fever was so high. So then I said, "Why don't you stay home and I will go to work?" [*Both Michael and Connie were self-employed in exhibiting and selling paintings*]. He just got sicker, sicker and sicker. Finally I called the doctor and explained to him the symptoms he had. He said, "That is not normal; take him to the hospital." So I went upstairs and figured that if he wouldn't go to the doctor...

MICHAEL: He was the type who wouldn't go, right?

CONNIE: Are you kidding? He has never been to a doctor. He would always complain that his bones hurt. I used to scream at him and say, "Go to a doctor, for God's sake!" On Sunday night when he got up he was hitting the corners of the wall. He was walking into the wall trying to get to the bathroom. I would say, "Look at you! Your face is swollen! Are you going to wait until you are all swollen to go to the hospital?" So I tried getting him to the phone next to me, and he said, "No! I don't want to go." So I put the phone down. He said it was the flu and that he would get over it, but this man could not get over it. The next day he said he couldn't take it any longer and said I had better take him to the doctor. I rushed him down to the hospital. I waited seven hours for a doctor.

Every three hours I would scream for a doctor. "When is my husband going to be checked?" "Well, we are waiting for a specialist," was the answer. Finally the specialist checked him, called me in and said he had meningitis. He explained to me what meningitis was. I thought maybe Lisa [*daughter*] and I could get it.

MICHAEL: How old is Lisa now, Connie?

CONNIE: Nine. So the Doctor said it was not fatal meningitis; it was viral meningitis. The doctor said, "He is going to have to pull through himself but we are going to have to keep him here for observation to look after him." I kept telling the doctor, "What about his leg?" They checked his leg. He had all the tests done, a scan on his brain.

MICHAEL: A brain scan?

CONNIE: A brain scan. He had blood tests done. At week later I was still screaming at the doctors, "Aren't you going to give this man any medication? Only Tylenol 3?" He said there is no medication for meningitis. But when he saw that Michael was hallucinating, that he was telling me all kinds of things: for instance, that there is a fly in front of his eyes! He is making fun of me; I am asking him if he would like to get up. "No! I don't want to get up!" I said, "That is not Michael!" So the doctor ordered the nurses right away to take a spinal. It had to be checked. He told me it would take two days before they would get the results and then he said, "There is nothing wrong with his spine." But infection in the head was coming down because he could bring his head forward.

MICHAEL: He was stiff before that?

CONNIE: He could not even get out of bed. He couldn't even feed himself. I fed him for five days.

MICHAEL: That must have been wild because he is so independent.

CONNIE: He is so independent. He thinks he is indestructible. Nothing can get through to this man. As a character I could never get through to him.

MICHAEL: A real "macho.".

CONNIE: Macho, right. "I can take on this room and nothing can break down because I can hold this room in my hands."

MICHAEL: Except meningitis. So here he is lying in the bed; you're screaming at the nurses and the doctors to do something, and he is babbling on. Is that correct or is that too severe?

CONNIE: By this time his mind is not Michael any more. He has lost his mind.

MICHAEL: Did he ever recover it?

CONNIE: No.

MICHAEL: He never did? How long did he go on like that? What would that be? three days, five days?

CONNIE: Two weeks in the hospital. I think he was in the hospital about ten days. Then I went there Thursday. He ordered me to continue work so that he would not get behind in his work. He was saying, "You will have to do the work." He still was all right the first five days. He said to get hold of his brother, tell him to set me up, go to the mall and exhibit. I said all right. His fever was coming down now. I had cancelled his display and he screamed and yelled at me because I had cancelled his display. I said, "But you're not coming out of the hospital yet. We have to let the mall manager know that you're not going back to work." He thought that every day he was going to wake up and the hospital was going to tell him that everything was going to be great and he could go home. That's what he kept thinking every day and every day he was getting worse instead of better. That whole week I fed him. I had to wear a mask the first two days. I had to transfer all his food onto paper plates because he was in isolation. They really didn't know what he had.

MICHAEL: They would destroy all that.

CONNIE: Yes. They just wanted to do it for health reasons I guess, because they didn't want it to go back downstairs or in the hallway, whatever.

MICHAEL: Did they ever determine that it was contagious?

CONNIE: No. Three days after that we didn't have to wear masks. The doctor said it wasn't contagious. I asked him. I felt that he wasn't giving me much satisfaction. Towards the end of the week I was getting very angry. The tests came out all right. The last week that I was doing Michael's exhibits, the Saturday that he died, I had spoken to him at 7:30 in the morning. That was because his mind would always be going; I knew his mind wasn't there. The Thursday night that I saw him he was saying to me, "If you were not a snob, you and Lisa should move into the little house [*that was purchased last year when they separated*], sell everything and you will have enough money to take care of yourself." I said, "Do you always have to think about money? Would you just let it be and first get well? Then we will worry about that."

MICHAEL: He was very concerned and hung up about money, wasn't he?

CONNIE: Always. So then, I would say, "As soon as you get well we will go up to the cottage and finish off what we started there." Friday I called him all day; he was actually feeling better. That Thursday night he got up from the bed himself. I said. "Michael, look at you; you are getting better." I brought him endive; he always liked that. I figured if I boiled the vegetable, where he could suck it through a straw, it would be easier for him, but he ate himself. The first five or six days he couldn't even get the spoon into his mouth. He could barely reach for the phone.

MICHAEL: So this was the Thursday before the Saturday when he died?

CONNIE: That's right.

MICHAEL: That is uncanny.

CONNIE: The next day I said to his Dad, "Go up there and make sure he eats because those nurses don't go in there. They want him to feed himself." No intravenous or catheter. He would drop his food and not reach for it. Every time I was there, from morning to night time, he would talk to me whenever he would wake up; he would talk to me for half an hour and would go back to sleep again.

MICHAEL: Was he coherent when he talked to you? Was he able to think straight?

CONNIE: He made sense when he spoke. It was just that he would jump from one thing to another.

MICHAEL: Nothing was connected?

CONNIE: Right! I thought he was driving me crazy. I wasn't thinking that he was losing his head. I kept thinking, "What is the matter with this man." He was getting me angry. I was thinking he was doing this more on purpose, just being bitchy because he was in the hospital. I knew he was angry because he didn't like being sick and that's what I thought it was. "This man was driving me crazy!" I felt like he was a little boy and I wanted to spank him and tell him to settle down. That's how he was acting. That's what I wanted to do to him just to settle him down.

MICHAEL: Connie, at this point, you never thought he was dying?

CONNIE: Never, never in my life. So then that Friday his Dad said, "Oh Wow! Michael is fine. The doctor says he is going to be out in a week; he is on his way to recovery." "That's great," I thought because I was working 9 am - 10 pm and had missed going to the hospital. It was only that Friday that I missed going. I would call him constantly from the mall, but he wasn't making sense. That Friday morning I called him at 7:30, my usual time, and he says, "Oh, who is at the mall?" I said, "Nobody now; it is only 7:30." "No one is at the mall? You left those paintings all by themselves!" I said, "Michael, the mall is not open yet!" And that's when I began to realize that Michael was really losing his mind. I had realized that earlier on the Wednesday previously, but it didn't strike me until maybe three or four days later that Michael's mind was going slowly. I still kept thinking that he was just being silly, you know, immature just because he didn't want to be in the hospital, just getting angry with me and his situation. So I would not think that he was losing his mind. I felt he was making me lose my mind because of the way he was being silly. So then that Friday morning I said, "I am going to try and get hold of that girl. She can come and take over the display." The girl calls me up and tells me that her brother had an accident and wouldn't be able to come. That kind of put me in a bind because I couldn't leave [the mall]; so I called him up and said the girl can't come. He said, "That's okay, goodbye." That's all he could say half the time. He was too tired or he would give me hell for calling. You wouldn't believe the hell he would give me for calling.

MICHAEL: Do you think, Connie that the illness brought out a lot of his disposition that you expressed a couple of years ago in our counselling sessions?

CONNIE: Yes. You mean it would all come out when he got sick, about how he treated me when we were married?

MICHAEL: There were no barriers to hold the stuff back. He was a very frustrated man.

CONNIE: Very.

MICHAEL: And when he was sick, it all poured out.

CONNIE: He never showed me any frustration. He was very controlled and "all-together," and nothing would get through to him. No matter what I called him — I called him every name in the book — nothing penetrated this man. How can a person, any human being just sit there and nothing ever hits you? I think if I threw him sticks and stones they wouldn't even hit him.

MICHAEL: He would just laugh it off.

CONNIE: Toss it off half an hour later; that would drive me nuts!

MICHAEL: Even if you could get *some* reaction...

CONNIE: Yes. Even if he would hit me. I used to tell him then, "Why don't you even hit me?"

MICHAEL: Then emotionally and psychologically all of that stuff just kept getting bottled up.

CONNIE: When he was in the hospital, he tried to control it as much as he could in the beginning. That's why his mind was going. He was mouthy. Mike was never mouthy in a serious way. He could be when he was fooling around with me though.

MICHAEL: So he was mocking you?

CONNIE: He was mocking me. Why would he do this to me?

MICHAEL: I would assume that since he had this "macho" image of himself, when you were helping him he was in a vulnerable position and he "took care" of his vulnerability by laughing at you about it.

CONNIE: I don't know how many times I wished that he would die.

MICHAEL: A defence mechanism.

CONNIE: Is it?

MICHAEL: Well, it comes across that way. It comes across as if you were the biggest pain that God created.

CONNIE: That's right. That's how he showed it to me. Exactly.

MICHAEL: It was his inadequate way of dealing with his frustrations. What I'm hearing at this point, Connie, is that since Michael bottled up his emotions and did not communicate over the years, that all of a sudden, now with his sickness, this reality hit you right in the face.

CONNIE: Because I couldn't understand him I was getting angry. Do you know that when I took him to the Emergency I told him I was going to leave him because, you see, we had an argument; that was my anger.

MICHAEL: So you were taking him in and the argument...

CONNIE: Yes. When we went back together [*after they had separated the year before*] he had this other woman that he had met.

MICHAEL: Now this was over the past year?

CONNIE: Yes, he met this girl and we would fight over that. I didn't separate because of that. I separated because I could not get through to him. Everything else would get me more and more frustrated and cause me to run. I would just run. Usually it was that or we would probably kill each other or something very drastic because of the frustrations that were building inside me.

MICHAEL: Your relationship was very stormy.

CONNIE: All this time, all I ever wanted for him was to sit down, get through to him about how I felt as a woman. He could not handle it. He just kept walking away from me. Again, I had to understand his 'women things' that he would do; when I would want something it would never get done; and then yet, when he wanted something done from me he expected it just like that, instantly; and, when I wouldn't do it instantly, he had to put me down all the time and I stayed down: through the women, his drinking, making me feel inferior. My complex was getting bigger and bigger; maybe it's just me. I would go to the psychiatrist; I would go to the psychologist.

MICHAEL: Because you thought it was your problem.

CONNIE: I thought it was my problem because he said there was nothing wrong with him. I was always taking the blame and carrying this load all the time.

MICHAEL: Connie, would it be about a year ago then that you moved out and got yourself another place?

CONNIE: That's right. Then he went to California and one of his latest girlfriends called at the house. I *thought* it had been going on. This was the Christmas before I moved out. So I yelled and I screamed and I scratched and all that. I carried on for awhile; then I slowly calmed down. I had this other man; he was a psychologist. He was a friend of mine too and he came to the house and he tried getting us together again and said, "Don't be crazy. He is a good man. You all have to try to understand him. Go on a holiday, but just be together as a family." So we took off for California. But all we did was look for homes. He wanted to move to California. I said, "I don't want to move to California. Get it through your head. I don't want to trade Toronto for any city in the world." That's the way I felt. "If you want to go, then pack your bags and leave. If that's how you feel, then go." He wouldn't go. He wouldn't leave Lisa and me.

MICHAEL: How did Lisa do with all of this coming and going?

CONNIE: Not good. She did not begin to understand until the day that lady called, which was a year before I moved out.

MICHAEL: Did you have emotional problems with her after that?

CONNIE: Yes I did.

MICHAEL: What would some of the emotional problems look like?

CONNIE: She became very sad. Very quiet for awhile. She said, "Can't you two ever get along? Can't you be like Phyllis and Doris [*neighbours*]?

MICHAEL: So, she was trying to put you together in her way?

CONNIE: All the time. She cried for eight months at the other house [*the one she and Connie moved to after Connie and Michael separated*].

MICHAEL: Did you buy the other house?

CONNIE: He bought it. He put up the money to buy it. He wanted to make sure Lisa would go to the same school. He wanted to buy a German Shepard to protect her. He didn't want a separation. He wanted to go to this other counselling where you go away for the weekend [*marriage encounter?*]. I said, "I don't want to hear about it any more. I've taken it to the lawyer and that's final. I don't want you to change my mind any more," because every time we got to the point where I was going to run out, that's when Michael would try to pull me back in again.

MICHAEL: He would be bending then?

CONNIE: He would be bending just a touch, not a lot, just a bit and then he would try to convince me.

MICHAEL: Connie, as you are telling your story a lot of anger and frustration in trying to deal with this personality for years is very much on the surface; and in addition, there is also the death. Is there a collision between your anger and any possible guilt?

CONNIE: I don't know.

MICHAEL: Do you feel relief today?

CONNIE: No, I'm still angry. He wasn't supposed to die. I still wasn't finished with him.

MICHAEL: Connie, what was unfinished? That's important for you to look at.

CONNIE: We decided that we were going to go back together again. I called. We got together and it was like we were always together.

MICHAEL: Yes, even though you were living apart. How long were you in the other house?

CONNIE: In the other house? I moved in July, the same time, the 31st of July. He came and he cut my grass and made sure everything was all right. He saw that I had everything that I needed, made sure I would get enough paintings to get me going, made sure to bring drinks for Lisa for her lunch. He made sure everything was all right. He would sleep over because Lisa would ask him to. He didn't have the heart to say no to her. He read books and assured her that nothing was really wrong. Then suddenly after Christmas he would ask me to go away. At Christmas time we went to our neighbour's party. We went to a Halloween party; I said yes. And then at New Year's he didn't come to the house any more. He said my sister and nephew moved in. He felt that it was not right for him to be there any more. They moved in with me because I needed help to pay off some of the bills. So my sister came in from California and said she'd live with me for a while until I could pick up; and I said, "Oh, all right. That would help me." So then he would just come up to the door and pick up Lisa. Before that he used to walk into my house. It would hurt like hell inside. He wouldn't even say hello to me. He'd pick up Lisa and that would be it.

MICHAEL: It must have felt really cold.

CONNIE: Cold, like he would just turn cold. I think what it was is that I had a full house and he had an empty one at that time. Before that both our houses were empty of other people.

MICHAEL: When did you move out of that house?

CONNIE: July 31. Then we started seeing each other after Christmas, after the California trip. That's when I took him to the lawyer because he wanted to go back again. He went back to California.

MICHAEL: That was because the woman was there?

CONNIE: No, she was not in California; she was in Mexico. So then...

MICHAEL: You were moving out?

CONNIE: Oh yes. He had taken so many trips and I was having such a hard time with money. Every time I would speak to him I would scream and yell because I was frustrated and didn't have any money, and yet, he could afford to take trips to Acapulco. He took three or four trips in three months. He didn't call Lisa one week when he was away. He wouldn't call her. He wasn't doing anything any more. I think he was giving up. At New Year's I marched down there and I said, "Well! You have taken so many trips and you have left all the load on me and Lisa and everything, and I want you to take care of her for New Year's because I'm going out." He said, "No, I am not going to take care of her for New Year's." We had this huge fight; we hit each other. It's the first time we have ever whacked each other physically. Lisa was there and saw this. I just grabbed my girl and said I would never see him again as long as I lived.

Lisa went through this whole pain. I went home and cried and cried, just like I'm crying today. It is the same type of pain, only this is a stronger pain. I cried and I was getting weaker and weaker because I didn't have the support any more. I didn't have him to run to as I used to. I had a spare key that he didn't know about. While he was away I picked up his mail and in the mail he had this letter from that same girl that he knew five years ago whom he had met in Mexico while we were together and I began to wonder: he doesn't want to come back because he has someone else; and that hurt even more. Then I tried getting through to him. I really wanted to. I didn't want to be alone any more. I would take him anyway he was. I'd go back to him and live that stupid life that I had lived before since it was better than this kind of life I was living now.

MICHAEL: Just like living "pillar to post."

CONNIE: It was awful. So then he said he would like to take Lisa and me some place in the March break — to Acapulco. "I want to tell you now that I want to take her there. Do you mind if I take her to Expo?" I said No. She had never been on a plane. I'll never be able to afford to put her on a plane so you might as well take her. So that went by. He didn't take her to Acapulco. At March break he said, "Would you like to go to Florida?" I thought maybe that woman wasn't all that important; so I never talked about it. He knew I knew about it; so we went on a nice trip. We went to Florida, and took Lisa to Disney World. After that for three weeks I was going back and forth from my house to his. I would only stay with him on the weekends. I wanted to stay there all the time; I wanted to move in right away. But he'd always kept saying, "I just want to try it out." So then finally, after I came back from Florida, I just kind of stayed there. He never told me to go back. I just kept staying there day after day. I never went back home after that. Before it was like weekends only and then I was straight. Straight. It was great. I was very happy. We were both very happy.

MICHAEL: Would this be late March?

CONNIE: Late March, April. April was great. Then at the end of May one time when I was in bed with him I turned around and was going to hug him. He pushed me away. I got hurt, started crying, and then said, "You always had those letters in that drawer [from the woman in Acapulco]. Are you ever going to move them? How can this marriage go on if you don't remove those letters? *I* can't move them; it has to be you." He said, "I don't think of those letters." But, to me, for him not to move them still meant that he did [*think of them*]. So, every day I would check to see if they were there; they were still there.

MICHAEL: Did he ever explain to you, Connie, why he pushed you away?

CONNIE: Nothing. He told me he was confused. He didn't know what he wanted. He never knew what he wanted.

MICHAEL: Was he seeing someone else at this time?

CONNIE: No. The only contact he had was this girl in Mexico. He had no one here.

MICHAEL: At this time, would you have sold the other place?

CONNIE: No. We tried putting it up for sale. The bills were coming in for this house and the other house. It was getting harder and harder. Pressure was getting bigger and bigger for him and he was pushing me further and further away. I said, "There is no use for me to stay here if you don't want me." "Well," he said, "you are going to be lonely over there and lonely here. You might as well stay here." I said, "You're sick; you really are! How can you say that? You're right. I would be lonely there and lonely here. So, I'm going to live life like this?" He didn't make love to me for one month. He cut me right off; he did not want me to touch him and that's when the fights started. Then he got sicker and sicker until I took him to the hospital.

MICHAEL: When he started to get sick had he already been working at the cottage?

CONNIE: Yes.

MICHAEL: So he picked up the meningitis there?

CONNIE: They don't know yet. I have to get to that part of the story.

MICHAEL: Do you consider, Connie, that when he turned you away, that was a turning point as well in the relationship?

CONNIE: Turning me away? What do you mean?

MICHAEL: You wanted to give him a hug and he pushed you away in bed.

CONNIE: I thought he just didn't want me any more. He was more interested in Mexico.

MICHAEL: You never really did come back together after that because he started getting sick. You hadn't had a chance to reconcile?

CONNIE: That's right. I wanted to find out; that's what I was angry about.

MICHAEL: Connie, in the same way in life that you were left hanging many times with him...

CONNIE: All the time.

MICHAEL: So with his death you are still left hanging.

CONNIE: I would scream and yell at him. On the Saturday morning [that he died] I phoned him from home, "You know, I am at the Mall and will be working right up to six o'clock; then I am going to see you." He called me that morning as well. I said, "How are you feeling?" He said, "My armpits hurt." I said, "Did you call the nurse? Did you tell her to give you Tylenol 3? Call the nurse and tell her to give you Tylenol 3." And that was that. He said, "Okay, goodbye." Eleven o'clock came and I started to get ready for work. I got to work, opened up the display and got everything together. I then called him. I had paid some bills on Friday and had seen Acapulco on the telephone bill with the same name and number of that girl. I felt such anger. I was going to choke him. I said to myself, "Here I am, taking care of you; I shouldn't even be feeding you!" I hated him, and I was going to give him hell. But I had to wait because he was too sick for me to give him hell. Apparently when he had that argument and had cut me off, he had called her. "I took care of this man and he is still playing games. He is playing tricks on me!"

MICHAEL: This first phone call was Saturday morning then?

CONNIE: At 7:30. That's when his armpits were hurting him. I still didn't say anything to him. I was going to hold it. When I called him at eleven o'clock he said he wanted to be by the sea. When he said that, I answered, "Sure, which one? Acapulco with your girl friend?" He answered, "What are you talking about?" "Oh," I said, "just forget it." I didn't think it could be Italy; it could have been. It could have been the Mediterranean Sea. I'm thinking the sea, like the ocean, So, I'm thinking Acapulco right after I see the bill because he has already talked to her. He's planning another trip again. Here I am: working for him, doing everything for him, taking food and taking it up. I didn't tell anybody about that. When I called back at one o'clock the nurses told me he was not feeling well; he was not up; he couldn't answer the phone. They couldn't get hold of me until six o'clock. I kept calling.

MICHAEL: This is the day he is dying. What time did he die, Connie?

CONNIE: At 2:30 pm apparently they took him down to intensive care. That's when I kept calling the room and no one would answer. No one would answer. But do you think I had any kind of brains to call the nurse? I had his direct line and would let it ring no more then three times and hang up. I didn't want to disturb him because I knew he was ill. The nurses had just finished telling me he was sleeping. Because he was sleeping for ten days, I knew that was what he was doing — sleeping! His father even came to me and said, "My son is fine; everything is great."

MICHAEL: That was the same day?

CONNIE: Yes, that's when he came that Saturday to help me take the display down.

MICHAEL: What time would this be?

CONNIE: Five o'clock. His father and brother always had to help me bring down the display and drive the truck.

MICHAEL: So they didn't know that he had already died at this time?

CONNIE: No, they hadn't contacted anyone. They couldn't get hold of me. Anyway, my brother-in-law went to visit him. They grabbed him and said, "Where is his wife? We have been trying to get hold of her!" He said, "She is at the mall." The doctor called me there and said, "We have brought your husband down to intensive care and we want you to come to the hospital right away." I started screaming at the doctor. "I knew something was wrong because you doctors were not doing anything." I hung up on him.

MICHAEL: Did you know at this point that he was dead?

CONNIE: You know what, Michael, I had a feeling. I was crying; I thought they were going to tell me that he was really close to dying. Not dead, close to it, like it is really bad. Maybe an operation will pull him through. God knows what will pull him through, but it is serious. I know that for them to call me at the mall meant that it was bad. I turned around and went to Roberto, his brother. "I think we are losing him," He said, "Don't say anything. Just go to the hospital and I will take care of everything." So I went to my father-in-law and said, "I'm going to the hospital now; you'll have to take care of everything." So I ran to the car. I was crying. I was saying, "Michael, we're going to fix everything up; you'll see." All the way up there I was crying. I drove all the way up there, no problem. I don't know how I drove.

MICHAEL: You didn't remember the trip except that you were crying.

CONNIE: I was crying. When I got there the nurse said to me, "Just go in there." Meanwhile tears are just pouring. I ask, "Now what's happening? What has happened?" She said, "The doctor is going to talk to you." I walked into the middle room, where intensive care is. My brother-in-law asked, "Would you like a cup of coffee?" He was just was sitting there. Finally this doctor came in. He tells me that they brought my husband down at two-thirty and that he went into a seizure. Then he turned around to Tony and said, "Didn't you tell her?"

MICHAEL: The doctor said that to your brother-in-law?

CONNIE: Didn't you tell her? Don't tell me he is dead! He can't be dead! I was jumping everywhere, groaning to the doctor, "He can't be dead! How can he be dead? No one was there!" When I calmed down I crawled to the doctor's knees and I said, "Tell me: how did he die?" He put his head down as if he just didn't know.

MICHAEL: The doctor didn't know?

CONNIE: I asked, "How can you not know?" By this time I was going to kill him. I still didn't believe it. I didn't want to touch him [*Michael, her dead husband*]. But I went in. At first I thought he was sleeping. Then I went to touch him. He was dead; he was so cold. I knew he was dead and I didn't want to touch him any more. I felt angry.

MICHAEL: You were angry with Michael?

CONNIE: I screamed at him and called him every name in the book and I said, "Now! Are you happy? Are you happy being in there? Why couldn't you pull through?"

MICHAEL: Do you think possibly, Connie, even his act of dying was his way of mocking you? Did that ever cross your mind?

CONNIE: I was mad at him; he was dead. I was still angry. He wasn't about to die because I wasn't through with him. I wasn't through giving him shit because of what had happened before.

MICHAEL: What an incredible amount of anger in death.

CONNIE: I picked out his coffin and couldn't understand why I did that. It didn't matter which coffin he was in. How do I tell my little girl that he died?

MICHAEL: How did you tell Lisa?

CONNIE: She was at my mother's place. I didn't tell her that night because I just couldn't. I had to first calm down. I had to dry out my tears. I said [*to the family*], "Don't tell Lisa; please don't tell Lisa anything right now." That whole night I was screaming at him, yelling at him; I got no sleep.

MICHAEL: So when you went home you were still just wound up.

CONNIE: I was still screaming at him and was still angry. I was angry at him. How could he have done this to me? And I still screamed at him. I think I only had an hour's sleep. I was too tired then to scream at him.

MICHAEL: You were exhausted.

CONNIE: I exhausted myself till I couldn't scream any more. Early the next morning I went down and I said to Lisa, "Remember at the hospital when dad was very very sick and I had to stay at the hospital all night. Well, he is very very sick; he got really bad. The doctors really tried to help him but his heart stopped and he just died." Lisa then said, "You mean, he's dead?" She cried, but not a big cry, kind of a sad cry. She wiped her tears, carried on. The next minute she was back to doing whatever she was doing. I thought it was going to hit her like 'a ton of rocks'! I was more relieved that it didn't hit her that hard. That afternoon I asked my niece if she wanted to come to the funeral home. I asked her to get someone to get me down there. "I will come down," she said. Before that had happened, the first time that I saw him in the casket I screamed at him. They couldn't take me away from him until I was through with him.

MICHAEL: While he was there in the casket?

CONNIE: While he was in the casket I was still screaming at him [*not out loud, but in her mind*]. I was still angry at him. When I would look at him I was angry. I could not control my anger. If there were no people I would have screamed at him. I would have told him I out loud. I quietly screamed at him [*pursing her lips imitating what she had done*].

MICHAEL: With Lisa now, ten days later, how is she managing her feelings?

CONNIE: She wants to be beside me. I find she is getting a little more hyper. Is that anger inside her?

MICHAEL: Yes.

CONNIE: I can see that. Just the other day she said, "Will I ever have a daddy?" That's up to her, I tell her. "If you go upstairs you will see pictures. If you look in his wallet, there is a picture of you. If you look in his truck, there are pictures of you. Your daddy loved you very much. We both loved you very much. He loved you so, so much. You want to cry; I want to cry. You have all the right to cry. Look at me: I'm crying." She would hug me and hold on. Everything would be all right. Daddy was in heaven. We would be strong. She would wipe her tears and be off to play.

MICHAEL: So then, Lisa wrote the note [*something that Connie told me earlier*]?

CONNIE: She then wrote the note and it says, "Love Daddy, when you get to Heaven, let me know how it is." What does that mean?

MICHAEL: Well, she certainly has made a connection with him and the hereafter is very much a part of her mind and her psyche, at least now.

CONNIE: Does she believe in the hereafter?

MICHAEL: I think it is hard to say. Possibly in her own way at nine years of age. Connie, what you are saying is that she never did see him dead in the casket.

CONNIE: No. Halfway through I went upstairs and she decided, "Yes, I want to go and see him." So Tony [her girlfriend] brought her up. Someone brought me a message because, by this time, I was at the casket. But now Lisa didn't want to come. While I was there I was waiting for her because I had got the message saying that she was going to come in. I was going to meet her halfway to bring her in slowly. I just wanted her to see him from far away because she was afraid I would let her go out. I wouldn't push her to see him; I didn't believe in that. Everybody was telling me she had to see him, she had to see him. I said, "She doesn't have to see him." So halfway through she got as far as the flowers. There were so many people it frightened her. She ran back out. She didn't come back till the day of the funeral. Then she said, "Do I have to look?" as they were bringing him out from the Church.

MICHAEL: This was after the Mass?

CONNIE: This is after the Mass. She wouldn't come in for the Mass. She said she was too scared. She still wouldn't come into the Church; she waited outside, you know, in the hallway.

MICHAEL: Yes, the reception area.

CONNIE: As I was coming out behind the casket I saw her. She had her head in between my two friends. She hid her head.

MICHAEL: Sort of in the armpit area fashion [*i.e., slightly cocked*]?

CONNIE: Yes. I don't think she saw the casket. So anyway we went into the limousine, or whatever you call that car. My sister-in-law went into the car with me. I explained to Lisa that now we were going to take him to the cemetery. We were going to bury him under the ground, but, for now, it was going to be a box in the wall. He is going to be away from the ground for now.

MICHAEL: He's in a mausoleum?

CONNIE: Finally she convinced herself, and I said they are going to put him in there for now and in later this year we would take him out and bury him in the ground. I told her that there was nothing to be afraid of; the coffin was closed, and it was just a box now. We got out of the limousine and right up to where the casket was. I said to Mark, my father-in-law, and everybody else too, "Please! Don't cry! Don't yell out and scare her! Don't yell!"

MICHAEL: As in, don't do wailing.

CONNIE: Yes. Don't go crazy on me because I have my little girl. I have convinced her this far. Let her stay. My mother-in-law and father-in-law were fantastic. They did anything I said. If I said to keep quiet and — if it was my son I would have burst out — but they listened to me. "Do it for Lisa." I just wanted to make it feel as if it was a natural thing. Maybe it was wrong but that's how I felt like doing it. So then I said to Lisa, "Do you want to kiss the casket goodbye?" I said I would hold her.

MICHAEL: She didn't want to do that?

CONNIE: Then this man screamed out, "Michael!" My father-in-law was so mad he pushed him away. Lisa got scared. She left.

MICHAEL: Connie, what holds you, gets you through all of this now? You and Lisa are back living alone. You don't have family or people staying over with you. At this point, what holds you through this now? Is there any belief system, religious philosophy or anything of this kind?

CONNIE: No, I don't have one.

MICHAEL: So that in spite of your growing up in an Italian Catholic family, you consider yourself an atheist.

CONNIE: I am an atheist. As far as Jesus Christ is concerned, there might have been a genius at that time and everybody thought he was God. I believe that average people should use normal intelligence. I always believed at that time that there was this great man. He must have been a genius and everybody else just kind of made a god of him. He made everybody else believe that he was the Almighty God but not God in the sense of the Bible.

MICHAEL: Along with that philosophy, then, you wouldn't see a concept of afterlife then.

CONNIE: I don't know what you mean.

MICHAEL: When Michael died or when people die, that's all there is, as far as you are concerned? When Lisa says, "I hope I will see you in Heaven"...

CONNIE: I taught her to believe in God.

MICHAEL: She goes to a Catholic school?

CONNIE: That's right. I wanted her to believe in God because as I was growing up, with all these financial problems, I began to realize halfway through my life that when people are weak or at their weakest point, they need something or someone to believe in so that they can carry on with themselves.

MICHAEL: So what is helping you right now?

CONNIE: Nothing.

MICHAEL: That must feel like despair or a total vacuum.

CONNIE: The outside world now is just dead. No one is really living now as far as I am concerned. Nothing is really moving. The cars aren't moving; the world isn't moving; it's just dead.

MICHAEL: Death hangs over everything.

CONNIE: Yes. Death has dropped me here right now and I keep telling myself that I know that about myself. I keep saying, "I will be in my mind; my mind is strong, in spite of the fact I'm breaking down and my emotions are too." The doctor told me that it was the aftershock, that your body starts shaking, and you tend to get weak. I did not eat for seven days. I had to force food down. I did not sleep. The only way I could sleep was with 20mg. of Valium. That is the only way I slept. If I didn't make it with 10mg. I took another 10mg. because I would wake up screaming.

MICHAEL: Connie, are you having any dreams?

CONNIE: Yes. I have dreams. This afternoon when I was napping I remembered all kinds of things. It was different in the dreams. I walked into so many rooms and there were people there. They knew that Michael had died and I knew that Michael had died. When I walked into this one room, there were two people hanging upside down. I screamed and ran out and went into another room. All these rooms were connected. You know how there would be one room here and one room there but they all lead to everywhere, not like separate rooms but kind of like here [referring to my study], but no closed doors, all open. Then I went into another room where it looked as though there was a party and I reached out for a cake. I was so hungry; I wanted to eat it, but I couldn't get it to my mouth.

MICHAEL: The cake.

CONNIE: The cake. It was chocolate cake and I wanted to get it to my mouth because I was hungry in my dream. Then I told this lady that my husband had died. She just fell! She was holding onto me and she fell and I held her down. I put her down; I put her down on the floor.

MICHAEL: She went into a swoon?

CONNIE: Yes! She melted on me and I helped put her down. I thought she had fainted so they put this thing on her mouth to come to.

MICHAEL: Like smelling salts or something?

CONNIE: That was when I got a call. I was coming down two stairs and I got a call. I got on the phone and it was a guy who wanted to know about Michael. I was trying to explain to him that he was dead: "Can't you get it through your head that he is dead!" The guy didn't want to take it. He didn't want to accept it. He said, "Ah, you're joking!" So I had to convince him two or three times that he was gone.

MICHAEL: When the people were hung upside down, were they hanging from the ceiling, Connie? Just hanging there upside down?

CONNIE: Just hanging there. Men, in suits.

MICHAEL: It must have frightened you.

CONNIE: I was screaming in the dream.

MICHAEL: Have there been any other kinds of dreams over this time before he died?

CONNIE: No.

MICHAEL: So this one broke through very vividly?

CONNIE: It was in the afternoon. It wasn't at night time [*when she takes 20mg. of Valium*]. I was only on my 10mg. of Valium.

MICHAEL: 10mg. of your drugs?

CONNIE: 20mg. of the drugs at night. Yes, or else I would not have gone to sleep. For one thing I could not sleep. I would be awake. I needed 20mg. of pills. My girlfriend would be lying in the bed with me screaming at her. She would be lying there, but I don't remember when the pills did take effect. I would fall back asleep out of exhaustion.

MICHAEL: In the morning you would feel tired?

CONNIE: No, I would just go! I wouldn't scream any more. I would wake up thinking, "Oh my God, I am just so refreshed now!" and it was only a little while since I slept. I would get a coffee. I thought it was morning time. I felt wide awake and Tony [*girlfriend*] would tell me that it was night; and she would tell me that he was dead. I just couldn't accept what had happened to me. It was a nightmare. I would sleep for a little while and think it was morning. Everything was off! I was "just not there" at all during those first days! Now, a little more of the reality is settling in. But, I have so much anger at Michael. *I still haven't finished with him!* For now I am going to have to do my best, get through this as best I can. I even forgot about Lisa for a while during these days. I've got to get on my feet more and be there for her. I'm her mother; she needs me. Little by little we'll make it though. Why did he have to die? There's so much I have to tell him? I'm so angry with him! He died before we had a chance to talk, to settle things.

MICHAEL: Connie, you have been very brave to spend time in an interview like this. Michael has been dead only ten days. I know that when the reader of this interview reflects on your struggle, he/she will recognize a woman who is suffering greatly at the moment, who is "a bundle of feelings" for the most part, but who also is strong inside. Connie, you are suffering deeply right now; you are in deep anguish and turmoil. You are angry; you are hurt; you are alone. It's important to trust at a time like this, and even if you can't, then let me carry that trust for you: a trust for a more hopeful future, a trust in the transformative power of life *and* death. That trust will not be broken either.

> The usual commentary for this interview is to be found at the end of Chapter 13: Part B.

CHAPTER THIRTEEN

I'M NOT FINISHED WITH YOU YET:
THE STORY OF CONNIE (B)

This is the second interview with Connie. Nine months have passed since her husband, Michael, has died. When we left her at the end of the first interview (Chapter 12 - Part A), she was taking 10mg. and 20mg. doses of Valium all day and night. She was waking up screaming; she was angry with Michael. She had not finished giving Michael "the piece of her mind" that she wanted to, but couldn't, because he "died on her," as she says. During these nine months she had visited the tomb and had really let her feelings out. In addition, Janice spent a number of private hours with Connie, helping her adjust to her new life without Michael. We think the reader will agree that we have a new Connie emerging here. During a five minute period near the end of the interview when Connie was talking, we thought she looked just radiant! She had learned — albeit painfully — about herself, and she was living life for the first time.

MICHAEL: Connie, Michael died nine months ago.

CONNIE: I know [*said very deliberately*].

MICHAEL: Our first interview was ten days after after Michael died. What I want to do in this interview is to have you talk about (1) what happened and (2) what has changed for you. Connie, if you can, roll your memory back to that week when he died, and, in your own way begin discussing, for instance, as a starter, how he died.

CONNIE: Ten days before he took sick, he had a headache. He thought he had a cold. Then he decided that it wasn't just a cold any more, that he had to go to the hospital. [*Connie is describing all this in a very factual way, certainly not in the very emotional way she described events last summer*] He was diagnosed with meningitis, but he was going to overcome the disease, he was going to get better. I helped him out during the whole ten days that he was in the hospital. Then he died of a blood clot. His actual death was from a blood clot.

MICHAEL: A blood clot. A blood clot? So, it wasn't really meningitis?

CONNIE: It was encephalitis in the brain when they did the autopsy. They thought it was ...

MICHAEL: Meningitis.

CONNIE: Yes, but it was encephalitis, once they did the autopsy. They didn't know that till the autopsy was performed — *after his death*!

MICHAEL: When you were found out later that you were told one thing and something else happened, how did you feel?

CONNIE: I was angry. I thought it was malpractice. I felt that the hospital didn't do what it was supposed to do. Even as I was taking care of him at the hospital, there were no nurses for me to call, and I wanted a nurse. That's true. Because his food had to be transferred into another dish, he wouldn't be fed until 6:00 pm; food comes at 5:00 pm! And then when I would get there, I would say, "But your food is still sitting here!" So that meant that nurses were either too busy, or there weren't enough; and I would feed him, take care of him. And when I wasn't there for five days, I felt he was disowned. Because he had to fight this on his own, the nurses only went there when it was necessary to feed him, when nobody was there. As soon as I would be there, the nurses would disappear.

MICHAEL: Was he a good patient?

CONNIE: Was he a *good patient*? He couldn't even move! So, what do you mean by "a good patient"? He couldn't even move off the bed!

MICHAEL: He didn't complain?

CONNIE: No. The only thing he complained about was that he was in so much pain. He had such a high fever; he was running a very high fever. He couldn't move. "That's what caused his blood clot - bed rest," the doctor said. "That's how you get blood clots." I said, "Well, if you knew that, then why wasn't anything done?" The doctor responded, "Well, if that's the case, then we would need a doctor and a nurse for every patient. And that's impossible!"

MICHAEL: So he died from a blood clot from too much bed rest.

CONNIE: That's right.

MICHAEL: That's what the doctor said.

CONNIE: That's what the doctor said. I investigated the matter. My lawyer talked with another doctor — who had nothing to do with the hospital, or the doctors, or anything — because he just wanted a rundown of how meningitis or encephalitis or when a patient ends up in a hospital. What are their procedures? And apparently, the procedures are *exactly* what they did with Michael.

MICHAEL: So, it was normal what they did.

CONNIE: It was normal what they did.

MICHAEL: But it's also acceptable to feel angry about how "normal" it was.

CONNIE: *Yes*! Because you're seeing that they're not taking care of him properly the way I felt they should. Maybe in their way they were taking care of him properly. But, in my way they weren't. So, I just felt, "Yes, I was angry with the doctors." The doctors even knew that I was angry with them.

MICHAEL: Connie, how many months has it been?

CONNIE: Nine months. It will be nine months on April 11.

MICHAEL: Nine months on April 11. So tomorrow it will be nine months.

CONNIE: Yes.

MICHAEL: And at the end of nine months most women who are pregnant give birth.

CONNIE: Uh huh! [*meaning, what I was saying was right on target, symbolically speaking*]

MICHAEL: Connie, do you have feelings around that theme, that perhaps you are "giving birth" as a result of the death?

CONNIE: To my own body. I feel as though I am a new person again. I feel as though I have slept for thirty-four years and I can't remember a lot of things that happened through my own life besides just being with Michael. When Michael died, it seemed that my life died too. For nine months everything was on hold. I couldn't remember any more what my life was with Michael. I lost all track of that. I lost all track of memory. I couldn't even think straight. I couldn't even remember I had a daughter. And that's very scary. Not to remember that I had a daughter — I only remembered when someone would say, "Where's Lisa?" And I would say, "O my God, where is she?" That's when I would remember I had a daughter. I even forgot I had Lisa.

MICHAEL: Today, just before we got into the interview you didn't even recall much of the fact that I interviewed you nine months ago, ten days after Michael's death.

CONNIE: No. Only the time that I came here and started crying. But I cannot remember what I said to you. Not at all. Not one word. Nothing. Nothing.

MICHAEL: Nothing. So, Connie, when you say that you were asleep for thirty-four years, and then Michael died, you're saying that you got the biggest "kick in the pants" ever?

CONNIE: That's right.

MICHAEL: And it was almost like the waking up of the first time.

CONNIE: I was waking up because the first thing I said when he died [*raising her voice noticeably now, as if in emphasis*] was, "Where was I for thirty-four years? Where have I been?" I was in total shock for seven days I remember. My mother-in-law said, "My son has been dead for seven days." I said, "Seven days went by?" Which meant that I didn't know that seven days went by. At all!

MICHAEL: Connie, when you saw and realized, "Where have I been for thirty-four years?" how did you feel and what did you think?

CONNIE: Scared. Fearful. Very scared! Scared. That's all I can remember, just shaking inside. Not knowing who I was for thirty-four years - I was scared. I said, "Who am I?" That's what I was saying for a long time.

MICHAEL: Who am I.

CONNIE: Yes. "Who am I?" And also, "What happened?" and, "Why did he die?" Those are the only words I remember saying for seven days, for seven days straight.

MICHAEL: "Who am I?"

CONNIE: "Who am I?," "What happened?," and, "Why did he die?"

MICHAEL: The image that comes to my mind is that all of a sudden you found yourself standing in mid-air.

CONNIE: Yes! [*meaning, "You're darn right!"*] I thought that the world wasn't ... I thought that the world had stopped. I thought the cars weren't moving. I thought people weren't doing what they normally do, go to work, doing their thing, etc. [*emphasis*] I thought everything had stopped!

MICHAEL: In the movies that's known as suspended animation, when everything is just suspended.

CONNIE: Yes.

MICHAEL: Somehow things are going on but nothing is clicking.

CONNIE: Nothing is clicking. That's right! When they stop a movie, everything is still going on. Is that what you mean?

MICHAEL: Yes.

CONNIE: That's exactly how I was. Exactly. At the beginning I had thoughts of suicide.

MICHAEL: Connie, when you realized that, that you were basically "on hold," sort of "suspended," how did you get out of that?

CONNIE: I really don't know how I got out of that.

MICHAEL: Was it recent?

CONNIE: Yes. It was actually not too long ago. Actually, I would have to say six months later. I stopped and I said, "If this is what life is all about, then I am going to have to go out there and fight the battle the way my husband did because I suppose this is what he did." I didn't understand that. I had no idea of what Michael was doing while we were together.

MICHAEL: It was almost like "playing house."

CONNIE: Yes! I didn't know what he was doing. It was as though I was playing house with the dollies, ...

MICHAEL: And the only problem is that Lisa, your daughter, is a "real dolly"!

CONNIE: She was the "real doll." Michael, he was taking care of all the other things which I didn't know. I didn't *know* that life was like this.

MICHAEL: Because he didn't communicate that to you and kept that away from you.

CONNIE: Yes.

MICHAEL: Is that typical of ...

CONNIE: Italian background. Keep the women in the dark.

MICHAEL: And many traditional Italian women literally are "in the black": with their clothes, knowledge about the "real world."

CONNIE: That's right. And, oh! There's another thing too: I was the one who was always against wearing black. [*Lowering her voice*] And I was the one who wore it.

MICHAEL: So you went right into the role.

CONNIE: I went right into the role. I always considered myself a non-Italian, as non-accepting of the traditional, typical way of thinking of the Sicilian family.

MICHAEL: Everything's laid out a certain way.

CONNIE: Yes, laid out a certain way, and you follow these traditions. I always had in the back of my head, "No, that's not me." And when he died, the *first thing* I wore was black; and you couldn't take it off me! And I'm saying, "But this is not like me." But I couldn't take the black off either. And up till now I still feel kind of guilty when I wear coloured clothes. I still feel that it's not ...

MICHAEL: Not quite being fair.

CONNIE: Yes, not being fair.

MICHAEL: Honouring a memory.

CONNIE: Yes, honouring a memory.

MICHAEL: Sort of being disloyal.

CONNIE: Yes. Being disloyal. That's right.

MICHAEL: Can you see in all that, Connie, how being asleep for thirty-four years you now are forced into growing up, and it's tough work.

CONNIE: It is.

MICHAEL: You're going against a bunch of traditions.

CONNIE: At first I used to think how hard Michael had it. I don't think Michael had it hard now. Michael was raised with the fact that he was the breadwinner, that he had to go out into life and fight all this battle that I'm fighting. Now, of course, I have had to do it in three days [right after his death]. He grew up fighting this battle. I didn't get that chance. So that's why in the beginning I said, "Oh my God, is this what life is all about?" because I didn't get that chance gradually; I got it *all at once*!

MICHAEL: Think how wonderful it is, Connie, that at your age now - that while it was, and is, very painful to grow up and be awake - what it must be like for people who are widowed when they are fifty or sixty in the same situation [*being asleep*].

CONNIE: Yes. I knew of a woman — not too long ago — she lost her husband. And I really felt pain for her because now she has only herself. She's fifty-five. But, she's so lonely. Even lonelier for her. She's gone through the hard times, the growing up times. I don't know if she was awake all her life. I don't know. But now, the fact that I have a second chance - -this lady doesn't have a second chance.

MICHAEL: She doesn't think she does.

CONNIE: Or she doesn't think she does. Her chances are a lot slimmer than mine, in other words, because of her age.

MICHAEL: Because at the age of fifty-five I think she would see herself as having limited options.

CONNIE: *Options*! [seizing upon the word] That's right. Whereas I have more options.

MICHAEL: You have opportunities.

CONNIE: Opportunities. Yes.

MICHAEL: Problems can be seen as opportunities. When you're thirty-four, and in this dilemma, problems CAN be opportunities, if you can work your way through them. At the age of fifty-five, problems are problems in many respects.

CONNIE: Yes. Problems are still problems! and you have to sort your way through them. I said after Michael died, "If I thought I had problems then, what are *these* [*great emphasis*]?"

MICHAEL: [*Big laugh*]

CONNIE: [*Laughs out loud*] *These* are *problems*!

MICHAEL: So, what are "these" now, Connie?

CONNIE: "These," in general, are the mess that I was left with...

MICHAEL: Finances?

CONNIE: Financially. Problems I had waking up to this 'wonderful' world which I didn't think was too wonderful when I woke up!

MICHAEL: [*Playfully*] Imagine Sleeping Beauty.

CONNIE: [*Laughs and laughs*]

MICHAEL: She was asleep for one hundred years! You've only got thirty-four. You've got sixty-six to go!

CONNIE: Not bad! [*laughing and laughing*]

MICHAEL: Thank God you didn't have to spend those extra years! [Both of us are really laughing now] So here you are now, Connie, and the problems ...

CONNIE: The problem was that when that happened to me, the shock led me all the way down to childbirth which caused me to hate my parents even more.

MICHAEL: Because...

CONNIE: Because [*and getting angry now*] they didn't teach me what I was supposed to know gradually and not hit me with this bomb! Now, it started off with anger at my husband when he died. I was very angry with him when he died. I couldn't begin to tell you how much anger I had when he died. Then my anger from there went to my mother because [*with a spiteful tone*] she didn't allow me to grow as I was supposed to grow. [*Very deliberately*] And that built up even more hatred towards my mother. That was anger, maybe not so much as hatred. I did say a few times that I did hate my mother.

MICHAEL: But she did not prepare you for ...

CONNIE: She did not prepare me for life. That's what I hated her for, not because she was my mother, but because she didn't prepare me for life. This is what I understood when I was hit with all this.

MICHAEL: You were cheated.

CONNIE: I was cheated. That's right! And being cheated makes you angry [*emphasis*] and makes you hate people. Because you can't distinguish one from another, because you weren't taught, you have nothing but hatred inside you and anger and anguish. That's it.

MICHAEL: So when the death happened, you reached inside yourself...

CONNIE: Right down deep, right till I was a little baby.

MICHAEL: But that's the problem; you found out that you went back to babyhood ...

CONNIE: Yes.

MICHAEL: And you didn't have the skills to deal with it.

CONNIE: That's right. I said, "I don't remember growing up. I don't remember anything. I don't remember going through anything. I don't remember being taught or led. All I remember is living day to day, not learning from the world, not understanding what other people go through. I understood that if they had a problem, that was that. What could I do? But, as for me, myself, I did not understand.

MICHAEL: What a shock!

CONNIE: It was a shock! Terrifying!

MICHAEL: What else, today, comes under the umbrella of "these problems" that you referred to earlier, Connie? Now that you're living life for the first time, what do problems look like now?

CONNIE: I think that problems are not that hard. Problems are not that hard *now*. There was the problem: what happened to *me* was the problem; the problem was *me*, trying to see who I was when I never knew who I was to begin with. It was something inside me that I was always fighting all alone, but I never knew what I was fighting. You see, I was always fighting this with Michael.

MICHAEL: What was it? What were you fighting? Do you know now?

CONNIE: Do I know now? Just knowing life. The part that shocked me was the fact that, "This is it? This is what life is all about?" And it really shocked me. I was more or less living in a fantasy until then. I was led into a fantasy world.

MICHAEL: You were unconscious.

CONNIE: Yes, I was unconscious. I wasn't living reality. I never knew that you had to do this in order to get that; you had to go out and work and make your money in order to have what you wanted. I thought everything came on a silver platter, as far as I was concerned! So everything to me was just "peachy"! And it's not. And when that happened to me [*i.e., her awakening*], I said, "It's not peachy! It's not like this at all! What happened to me? What happened to the rose garden that my mother promised me? She didn't tell me that I was going to have wonderful days, bad days. She said that my husband would take care of me and not to worry." And that's all I knew; that's what I was taught. Now, even though everything fell in at once - the problems and the financial part of life and everything - it's still a little fuzzy; it's still a little hard.

MICHAEL: But it's hard because you're learning, not because you're being shocked all the time.

CONNIE: Yes. I'm not getting shocked. The shock is over. The anger has come down now, a huge degree. It has come down so much that there is only a "touch" of it. When I have a little bit of problems that I can't seem to solve, then that anger comes back again. That's when I start blaming Michael because he died and that goes on. But that goes away quickly. It doesn't stay as long as it did for the last seven or eight months. I was on a high level all the time for seven months. For seven months it stayed on a high level: anger, hatred, hating.

MICHAEL: Just constant.

CONNIE: Yes, just constant. It was like ... the pain ... Do you want me to describe pain?

MICHAEL: Yes, go on.

CONNIE: The pain is like - when you burn yourself, the first pain is the crucial pain. It's so hard...

MICHAEL: You almost don't feel it.

CONNIE: You almost don't feel it. That's right. But then, when that *hurting* starts coming in, that's pain! Right? Because first you're numbed. You know how the finger goes numb? And then the hurt comes in because then you know there's pain. Then you have to live with the pain. It's like a long time pain. And then once the pain has died down - you know, when you burn yourself and the cooling sensation is died away, and then you feel that relief in your body that there's no more pain, that it's gone down, but it's gradual - that's how the pain was that I felt with Michael. But the pain: first the numbness, which you don't know if you're breathing, living, or what. That's just numb, total numbness. You don't know anything.

MICHAEL: Never-never-land.

CONNIE: Yes. Never-never-land! Enough to bruise yourself from holding on [emphasis here]. I was holding on to myself. I had four bruises on my legs and I didn't know that I was doing that. It was like hanging on as I felt the whole world just slipped under my feet. I was really hanging on because I had no one to hang on to. I had no one else or anything else to hang on to except my legs. That's what I did. I had marks all the way down my legs from hanging on.

MICHAEL: Down your thighs there.

CONNIE: Yes. Because I felt that I had to hang on, because I thought I was falling off. That's the fear that I had.

MICHAEL: It's an interesting image — "hanging on to yourself."

CONNIE: Hanging on to yourself. Yes. I remember that. That's scary. That's the part that's really scary. Just hanging on to yourself because you've got nothing else to hang on to. I can actually still cry when I ... That pain comes back real quickly. That's the part that you cannot overcome that quickly. That's the pain.

MICHAEL: That's right. I think, Connie, that the pain in "hanging on" is a very "beautiful" pain in one way because it reminds you of the task you have which is to grow up and to be the woman that you are meant to be. Am I on the correct path here with you in understanding you?

CONNIE: Yes.

MICHAEL: In the nine months - which it is tomorrow - you said that it is like giving birth to yourself. If you think about that, there is that inner infant inside you. And it is painful to look back after thirty-four years...

CONNIE: And you always thought that you were a woman and then to think back that you're a scared little girl - this is the painful part, to see yourself as a little girl, but not the woman that you look at every morning in the mirror.

MICHAEL: The thing is, Connie, you're both. You are the woman *and* the little girl. And the joy of watching that little girl grow up, manage feelings, handle situations, seems overwhelming at times.

CONNIE: [*Begins to cry slightly here*] It's so much at once that that's the scary part because it came all at once. And not even having anyone to talk to about it. Even if I did come and talk to you, it's a temporary relief.

MICHAEL: You have to go through it in your own time.

CONNIE: You have to go through it alone. It still doesn't matter even if my mother was there. You are on your own by this time.

MICHAEL: Connie, where's your father in all this? You keep talking about your mother, the fact she let you down, you felt cheated by her.

CONNIE: My mother was the one who bossed everybody. She was the leader of our family. That's why we always said, "My mother, my mother."

MICHAEL: Your father was a wimp?

CONNIE: My father was just a good man who raised five children and listened to my mother. Yes, a wimp! [*Surprises herself by saying this and begins to laugh out loud*]

MICHAEL: That was my definition of a wimp. You just put the words on it. [*Both of us really laughing now!*]

CONNIE: Now that you've described it that way, when I look at him, YES! [*laughs and laughs*]

MICHAEL: We refer to that kind of man as "Little Boy Blue"! He must have been sad a lot of the time.

CONNIE: Yes. My father was not a happy man. He didn't do much with us. [In a serious vein] He was too busy *earning money* [which is what her husband, Michael, was so focussed on as well] to take care of us and have a good life for us, and make sure that he provided for my mother [*begins to sound a "litany" of things he did, but a boring one*] and kept her home; and he had to do the "man's role." Keeping my mother home was a great image for my father! That made him feel that he was *a* man. And he went out and buried himself twenty feet underground so that he could climb down a pipe and get so much money a week so that he could say, "I keep my wife at home."

MICHAEL: So he worked underground? Was that his job?

CONNIE: Pipe layer.

MICHAEL: Pipe layer!

CONNIE: Yes. A very dangerous job. My mother was always a sick woman. So even if my father wanted her to go to work there was no way for her to go to work because she was always sick, or playing sick.

MICHAEL: Playing at being sick.

CONNIE: Yes. Playing at being sick. My mother's the domineering figure in our family. Everything she says "goes"; and if my poor father even wanted to put his two cents worth in, it was all chewed up by my mother. She wouldn't give my dad a chance to even give his say, in any matter, money, or otherwise. This was the opposite of my husband and me. Absolute opposite. I never knew what he did with the money and my father never knew what my mother did with the money; and we all kind of led a closed-in, dark, life.

MICHAEL: Unconscious.

CONNIE: Unconscious. Just like my father. I can see my father now living a dark life.

MICHAEL: He was underground!

CONNIE: Very.

MICHAEL: Even in his job!

CONNIE: Even in his job!

MICHAEL: He physically, literally lived ...

CONNIE: He lived his whole life...

MICHAEL: Underground.

CONNIE: Underground. That's right!

MICHAEL: In psychology, CONNIE, when we say something goes underground, we mean that it goes into the unconscious or it gets repressed. That's what your family ...

CONNIE: That's what my father did.

MICHAEL: You see, Connie, today, the difference between now and nine months ago - you've got perspective; you've got insight; you've got pain; you've got growth; you've got the awareness of all of that. A year ago you didn't have all of that.

CONNIE: No. Heavens! I couldn't even understand my parents. I still had to do as they said. Even they were having problems, we all had to run down there and make sure that they were all right. Now I phone them and ask them if they are all right. As long as they are all right, then there's nothing to run down to.

MICHAEL: They're big people now.

CONNIE: That's right. And now I've got my life and I have to live it in the best way I can. Just the other day I realized something: up until Lisa (*daughter*) was born, I couldn't understand why I had her, as much as I loved her and raised her, with my best abilities, as I understood them, or was taught to raise children. I didn't even know what it was like to raise Lisa.

MICHAEL: How old is she now, Connie?

CONNIE: She's going to be ten. I didn't know what it meant to have a child. I had Lisa, but I didn't understand what it *meant* to have Lisa. I understand *now* what it means to have Lisa.

MICHAEL: Nine months makes a difference, doesn't it?

CONNIE: Yes.

MICHAEL: It's interesting that it is the nine month period that we are doing this interview because again, I keep coming back to the "birth" motif. You're really giving birth to a beautiful future in the sense of yourself.

CONNIE: And now, at least when I look at Lisa, I *look at her*! for who she is, not as a burden. She was a burden for so many years. And I couldn't understand the burden.

MICHAEL: She got in your way.

CONNIE: She was in my way.

MICHAEL: Connie, do you know what she was in the way of? She was in the way of *you* trying to take of your own *inner* child.

CONNIE: Yes, that was myself as a child.

MICHAEL: So, you couldn't take care of her very well because you had ...

CONNIE: Because I was a child myself! That's right!

MICHAEL: It's hard being a parent when you're a child!

CONNIE: That's right. You can't do both.

MICHAEL: The old expression of being a "child bride" could be literally true in your case.

CONNIE: Yes. That's true.

MICHAEL: Connie, what have you learned out of all this?

CONNIE: [*Taking time to ponder and saying the question very deliberately*] What have I learned? [*Then laughs and laughs*] What have I learned?

MICHAEL: What would you tell someone whom you just met visiting ...?

CONNIE: Well, I'll tell you my inner feelings. Problems we solve all the time; so it doesn't feel that I've learned solving the problems. It feels as though I've done this for a long time [*laughs and laughs*]; yet, it's only been nine months that I took over the financial part, but it seems that I've done this forever. I just wasn't aware of it. I probably really did this, but I just did not see what it took to do all this. Right? My inner feeling is that of satisfaction.

MICHAEL: A sense of ...

CONNIE: I did it! I'm the only one who can say I did it and it feels great. There's a sense of satisfaction deep down inside; but you will not feel this until you wake up. You won't. Because if you were to talk to me four months ago, five months ago, six months ago, I would not have this inner feeling. Even though there is still a big confusion between the hurt - there's still hurt losing my husband the way I did, because thirty-seven years is very short, in spite of the fact that we had a troublesome marriage, it's still a shame that he had to lose his life, that his life had to end at thirty-seven - now, that's a big hurt that I'm dealing with. And then the fact that he was the father of my child, and that is a huge part of the hurt. That's a different hurt. And then the fact that I did love him too through all the hustle and the bustle and trying to figure out who am I and what am I, I can actually sit down here, if you were to ask me eight months ago, nine months ago, just before his death, if you were to ask me, "Did you love your husband?" I would have said to you, "I don't know." Because I didn't know whether I loved him. Because of all the confusion of growing up, I didn't know if I loved my husband or not. But now, I look and I see: yes, I did love him. I can actually sit here and say, "Yes," and answer that because even up until after he died, I was still questioning. And I even said that to you, "Did I *ever* love my husband?" I remember saying that to you, "Did I ever love my husband? or, did he love me?" And you know what? I think he loved me too. Only he just didn't know how because he was a little boy, just as I was a little girl.

MICHAEL: Playing house, both of you.

CONNIE: Playing house, yes. He left me [*died*] as a little boy and not as a man. And that's the sad part; that's the hurting part, that it's too bad that ...

MICHAEL: He didn't have a chance to be a man as well.

CONNIE: Yes. And that ... [*she cries now*] ...

MICHAEL: In that sense, Connie, his life has been extremely valuable because of the lesson. I know, Connie, that you have trouble with some of the biblical images, but Jesus pointed out that greater love no person has than to lay down their life for their friend (John 15:13). Michael did that.

CONNIE: That's right.

MICHAEL: Because his life allowed you freedom to grow and to become the ...

CONNIE: I had realized this gift. For four or five months, I was very angry with Michael. I hated him for dying on me. I didn't want him to die. I just hated the fact that he died. I *hated him*! I remember saying, "I hate you for doing this to me! You're rotten! You're terrible! Why did you do this to me? Is this the only way you could get back at me?" I always felt that Michael had to get back at me. He used to always say to me, "You're going to pay for this!"

MICHAEL: You really did!

CONNIE: Yes. That's why I hated him for the longest time. If he hadn't said those heavy words that I used to always hear when we were married... When I used to give him problems, like the separation, he used to say, "You're going to pay for this!" When he died it seemed as though he really had to rub my face right into the ground. In other words, he couldn't hurt me any more than this, so he really had to "get to me."

MICHAEL: Even in death.

CONNIE: Even in death! Yes! "You had to do this to me!" So that's how I felt. But when you overcome the anger and everything, then you come to realize who you are. Little by little you start becoming aware, waking up. Then you remember, then you start think how he was like a little boy, and the sad part is that I didn't get a second chance (to see him grow into a man); and I should've got a second chance because now that I am awake after all this, yes, I'd love to have a second chance with him.

MICHAEL: To put it all into perspective, Connie, you don't have a second chance with Michael, and even if he could see as clearly as you do today, if he were alive, he might not choose to grow the way you have, in which case you still would not have a second chance.

CONNIE: Probably not.

MICHAEL: But, there is a basic principle in life that says that the "seed must die in order that the tree must grow." We have winter in order to have spring. Right now, we are experiencing spring. There is a wonderful life coming out of the ground. In that sense, in the rhythm of the world and the universe, his death is very important. You're alive, and you see today for the first time. You're coming out of the unconscious.

CONNIE: It was only after seven months later that I went up to the cemetery and I said, "You know what, Michael, you know all the times that I hated you for dying, I am kind of happy that you have given me this gift. Now I can see more. It still hurts me to know that you're gone and I would have loved to have shared it with you."

MICHAEL: "I was blind and now I see" (John 9:26).

CONNIE: I was blind and now I see. I know everything now. I see a lot more than I saw then and what you went through wasn't easy either. But you did give me this gift and I am really happy. Deep inside I am happy because I feel that I have a chance. I am not happy that *he* died, but I am happy with *me*, knowing that I've got this chance to see, to re-live my life and *to see it*! Not to live it and not see it!

MICHAEL: That's the tragedy; that's the sadness.

CONNIE: That's right! That's when you're living with frustration, when you have to live it and not see it! But the deep sense of satisfaction, feeling that you have inside you that grow with you, is because you *see* how you're living, and that's the satisfaction. That's the tingling. That's what it is, the tingling feeling. That's what it is, and I have that. And right now, instead of being angry with Michael when I go down to the cemetery, I kiss his picture and thank him and I'm all hugs and kisses. It's not a joy! When I cry, it's a different pain. The only sad part about it is he didn't get to see this. That's the terrible part. Why didn't he? I would like him to share this as well, and I know that's impossible. That's the only thing you're left with. When you say that I'm lonely, yes, the loneliness is that now that I can see I have no one to share it with - at this point, because he died. And you'd want him to see what you're seeing because the feeling is so sensational; that's the hurting part.

MICHAEL: To share.

CONNIE: To share!

MICHAEL: To share the vision.

CONNIE: To share the vision. That's right!

MICHAEL: That's the wonderful thing, Connie, about consciousness and our human journey: when we choose to see, it hurts at times, but the freedom and, as you say, the "tingling sensation" ...

CONNIE: The tingling sensation. Yes. The satisfaction in oneself.

MICHAEL: Then we're living *and* seeing...

CONNIE: *And* seeing!

MICHAEL: Rather than...

CONNIE: Living.

MICHAEL: Just living. Living is putting up.

CONNIE: That's right! Living, we all do that. But to see is a hell of a lot better! [*laughs and laughs*]

MICHAEL: Now, sometimes we don't want to see what we need to see.

CONNIE: That's true. But that's okay as well. That's also life. Before, I didn't like to see what I was seeing. But now that I'm seeing what I am living, it's okay, and I say, "It's all right." I can deal with it, because it's all right.

MICHAEL: What does the future look like for you, Connie?

CONNIE: Super! I love it! [laughs and laughs] Super! In my mind, even though times are still hard, going up and down, but when the good times come up ... I have this image of thinking that my life is going to be super. Like, I'm going to succeed. It might take time because I am all tied up right now and I am not as free as I would like. I would like to go faster than I am going.

MICHAEL: It's called "happy troubles"!

CONNIE: [Laughing] Is that what it's called? Is that "happy troubles"? [*laughs and laughs*] But in my future, deep into my future that I want to see, yes, I think it's going to be fabulous. I think I'm going to succeed in something that I thought I never would. If you were to talk to me ten months ago, I was stupid, dumb; I had all the negative in me. There wasn't *one* thing that was positive. Even when I woke up it wasn't positive. I still don't wake up fabulous, but I know it one day. And if I have that in my life...

MICHAEL: So, today you're experiencing yourself as bright, intelligent, ...

CONNIE: Yes! Today I'm bright, ...

MICHAEL: Can see, can plan, can anticipate, can look forward to.

CONNIE: Yes. All of the above! I can manage. I can do all of those things. I already know that. I can do that.

MICHAEL: You're telling me, Connie, that you have an experience of yourself that you're a competent woman now.

CONNIE: Yes.

MICHAEL: Who also is aware that the little girl inside her is born and is growing and will need tending, but, you're confident now. It's not as though it's a little girl trying to take care of a little girl.

CONNIE: That's right! Now I can do it. Before, I didn't have all those positive things because I was still a child, like running around with her head chopped off. You don't know in which way you're directing yourself, because you don't know in which direction you want to go. But now you know the direction. You can see. So any direction to you is a good direction [laughs] because anything you choose now, you'll be able to tell the difference from one to another if it's right or wrong. Who's to say? Before, people would say, "Well, that's wrong!" Sometimes I used to think, "It isn't *that* wrong." And yet, I would stop myself from doing things because other people would say that whether it was wrong or not. But now I can actually tell you that if it feels good I do it.

MICHAEL: As long as I evaluate it and it fits in...

CONNIE: Fits in to my expectations...

MICHAEL: To your sense of values.

CONNIE: To my sense of values, who I am, then it's right! It may not be right for you, or for anybody else, my *mother* [*laughs here*], or my *father*, but it's right.

MICHAEL: What a wonderful ending to a ...

CONNIE: Very sad story?

MICHAEL: Well, a sad story, but a very life-giving story.

CONNIE: It sounds like a sad story, but it also sounds like a kind of a fairy tale.

MICHAEL: It *is* a fairy tale!

CONNIE: A "once-upon-a-time" story?

MICHAEL: Yes, a "once-upon-a-time" story where ...

CONNIE: And you live happily ever after? [*laughs*] It sounds like that.

MICHAEL: But you only live happily ever after when the prince kisses you and wakes you up. And Michael kissed you when he died.

CONNIE: And woke me up.

MICHAEL: And woke you up.

CONNIE: That's exactly how it went. He did kiss me, and then he died! And I woke up. That's exactly how it happened!

MICHAEL: Now you can look around and see all the things that a lot of other people who have struggled and are walking along have coped with; you can see the dirt on the street; you can see the joy in people's faces; you can see the sorrow in people's eyes at the airport. But, in all of that, you know that life is wonderful and that it has its heights and its depths. But the most important thing I'm hearing you say is, "I exist and I am real and I live and I see!"

CONNIE: I see. That's right.

MICHAEL: Thank you very much, Connie.

"The future is like a corridor into which we can see only by the light coming from behind."

— Edward Weyer (1871-1936)

COMMENTARY

And so we have the beautiful story of Connie, young, 34, widowed. Utterly shocked, utterly thrown back on her own, utterly bashed by life and death.

Her story needs telling because it exemplifies so well the tragedy that parents commit when they do not love each other. When a husband and wife really love each other, this indicates that the true personhood of each is involved.

In Connie's case, there was no true personhood in her parents. This is not to fault them. Like any of us, we do our best. But, as Jung points out, that still does not excuse the consequences. The psyche works with what it has; and little children in a home with parents who are "unconscious" of themselves, of relationships, and the psychological family tree, can pass on tremendous burdens for the children to carry. These parents pass on the "shadow," undeveloped side, of living to their children. The children, the next generation, therefore, have to carry the burden that the parents should have. This is very difficult because each of us has the task or burden of carrying our own psychological and spiritual development, not the parents as well. Parents who refuse, or who cannot look into their souls and do something about themselves so that they are true to themselves leave a terribly shadowy legacy for the children.

Years ago, in the United States, when Michael did weekend retreats in a certain penitentiary, he talked to one of the mothers afterwards. She asked, "What could I have done? I did everything for him!" Michael's only reply was, "What did you do for you? What did you leave undone that was *your* task, your particular responsibility in life?"

Children can always deal with reality; but they cannot deal with shadows. Parents who don't take care of themselves — learn and live their vocation, or work with their own processes of individuation — pass on this tremendous burden for their children to carry on with.

Connie says, "It was unfair!" Of course it is unfair; that's not what children are supposed to carry. Our own personal life is enough of its own, let alone carrying someone else's! Connie says that the net result of growing up in a family environment like this is anger and hatred. Of course. A child learns to hate who she is; she is not loved for who she is and what she can do. She is never given any sense of the way, of her own individual journey, because the parents are too busy caught up with their own personal agendas. That's the tragedy.

So children stay in the shadows — the shadows of their parents' undeveloped selves. Guilt results as well. The biggest tragedy, of course, is that the child, now becoming an adult — at least chronologically — lives life through the eyes of the parents' undeveloped selves and not out of her/his own truth. That's the greatest tragedy. And this state of affairs interferes with the child's own growth and development, necessary for individuation.

To be blocked in life is to feel frustrated; that's a very normal and natural reaction. When children learn to "accept" these blocks early in their development, the resentment and frustration do not go away; they go underground. That's exactly what Connie's father did as well: he spent all his years underground; and her mother was and played at being sick.

No wonder Connie was left "standing in mid-air" when her husband, Michael, died. She's the first to point out that she was "asleep for 34 years," which means that she was unconscious all this time. Her marriage was in title only, certainly not a psychological or spiritual sense. We often get tricked into believing that because we go through the ceremony, or outward sign, of an event filled with potential meaning, such as marriage, that therefore we are in a psychological/spiritual reality called marriage. Not so! The outward event is to signify ideally that the reality has already taken place interiorly. The public manifestation of it is simply a declarative statement, in action, to the collective. This is the ideal. Perhaps many do not have this ideal, but they gradually, as the years go on, live into the reality.

But Connie never even did that so great was her unconsciousness, so much asleep was she! Words didn't make a difference; fights didn't make a difference; threats and actual separations before Michael died didn't make a difference. *Death was the true clarifier!*

Michael's death blew everything apart. Everything unconscious around their relationship collapsed; everything unconscious around her family got exposed; everything unconscious around her feelings and hopes for herself as an individual came to light. In addition to being angry, with feelings of hatred towards Michael and her family, she also faced the deep, dark hole of emptiness that was her legacy from her family. *That was unfair*, as she is quick to point out. She had *nothing* to sustain her in her husband's death, only 10mg. and 20mg. of Valium. She realized for the first time in her life that she was an infant psychologically. How could she possibly even think of raising a child? Lisa was even forgotten for awhile during all this. Then she would wake up a little, and in a panic, want to find Lisa. How can a baby take care of a baby?

In the first interview Connie was indeed "a basket case," as she indicated. She was "all over the place." Except for the automatic needs and drives of her body and mind, nothing else was holding her together. And the deep pain! She was gradually coming to grips with the "dark hole" that was hers, passed on to her by her parents because they could not manage it for themselves. She looked at herself and found *nothing*! It was a very critical time in her life, and she did contemplate suicide. To see oneself and to see nothing is indeed painful. But she did make it through that terrible time. Something in Connie hoped for maturation, for the future. Something, or someone, in her believed in her.

The second interview was nine months later. While Connie was still "wobbly" in many respects -- after all, one does not awake from a 34 year sleep and bounce around automatically! -- she was also a different person. She was finding herself, and she was finding that the real Connie is beautiful, trustworthy, loyal, bright, and very eager to learn. From my point of view, this interview showed her to be extremely "quick" in her sense of humour, of being able to laugh at some of the things that had happened to her. It was she who insisted that she was asleep for 34 years. Now she's learning to see. "I was blind," she says, "but now I can see!" There is true rejoicing in that.

Perhaps the most powerful part of the two interviews was Connie's own realization that Michael's death was really a *gift* to her. We talked about "no greater love hath a man than to lay down his life for his friend." This wasn't being sentimental. In some very incredible way, she intuitively knew and accepted Michael's death as gift. His death opened her eyes. Marjorie, in an earlier chapter (ch. 6), talked about believing and hoping and that there was a reason; we may not know of it at the time, but there *is* a reason. For Marjorie, it was trusting in the Master Plan. For Connie, it was the incredible insight that Michael's death was her gift of life, that in that strange mix of anger, hatred, shouting, screaming, separation, mockery, good times and bad, hope emerged and she found life, rather, she was given life, but through death.

For a person who sees herself as an atheist, she has had a most profound experience of *Life* telling her that the "insides" of Life itself are personal, supportive, loving, trustworthy, and eager for fulfilment. When Michael died, he gave her the gift of individuation. She now has a chance; she now can learn to "grow herself up," first of all, for herself and her individuation task, but secondly, and very important as well, for Lisa, her ten year little girl. This little girl needs a mother who is first and foremost an adult woman. Period. Children need that absolutely. We can't fudge on that one. That's why a man and a woman need to commit themselves to their own individuation journeys first, *then*, they "cleave" to each other. That doesn't mean that they "lean" on each other; they "cleave": they invest in each other's individuation and they can each do that precisely because they are each coming from a position of *individual* strength and integrity. Kahil Gibran, in his book, *The Prophet*, points out that we must be close, but not *too* close! People who get "too" close all the time in relationships feel they need the other person to live. That is what I call "living out of the psychological pocket of the other." It doesn't work. Connie knows that. She tried that for 34 years. It simply doesn't work.

So Lisa, her daughter, now has a chance, and the future for each of them looks open, positive. A new psychological family tree can be created. Connie is still young; she recognizes that. She knows that she can give life another chance. How difficult it must be, as she says, for those people who are older and find themselves in similar circumstances she was in. But she does have another chance.

The first interview was filled with the anger and hostility that Connie failed to let Michael know about in person. According to her, there was so much "unfinished business." He died, shortchanging her, so to speak. I think now,

260 | Widowhood: The Death of a Spouse

when she reflects upon her story, she will find that the "unfinished business" has more to do with herself. She has much work to do on herself; she has many tasks to complete. She must go within to develop herself, at the same as learning to go without to be in the world intelligently and as an adult woman. These two things are all new to her. She knows she wasn't prepared for any of these tasks, but she is willing now to take them up because, even though there is pain, it is a pain that is somehow "beautiful" because it transforms. It transforms one into adulthood, into personhood, and into being a someone with self-identity. I short, a person has a meaning to life.

Death brings us face to face with ourselves. Connie met herself through the gift of Michael's death. She is learning to accept that gift, to face herself, to love Lisa for who she is. Those are the greatest gifts of all in life: love of self, love of children, love of others, and love of *Life*.

"You almost don't feel it. That's right. But then, when that *hurting* starts coming in, that's pain! Right? Because first you're numbed. You know how the finger goes numb? And then the hurt comes in because then you know there's pain. Then you have to live with the pain. It's like a long time pain. And then once the pain has died down - you know, when you burn yourself and the cooling sensation is died away, and then you feel that relief in your body that there's no more pain, that it's gone down, but it's gradual - that's how the pain was that I felt with Michael. But the pain: first the numbness, which you don't know if you're breathing, living, or what. That's just numb, total numbness. You don't know anything."

-- Connie, commenting on her pain and hurting

CHAPTER FOURTEEN

THE DEATH OF A SPOUSE

There is a saying that the unexamined life is not worth living. When someone loses a spouse because of death, this person is thrown into an examination of his/her life. The Temple at Delphi has the words "know thyself," written over it. Its essence is the fundamental message of this chapter: that self-knowledge, and self-awareness are the beginnings of wisdom. As a matter of fact, some philosophers and theologians are now coming to see that what we have traditionally understood as "salvation," is really the climax of self-knowledge, our understanding of ourselves, and what, we have chosen to be in and for ourselves.[1] The case of a man named George points this up as well as he speaks about understanding the death of another: "... prepare people for their own death ..."[2] The message is: take a look at oneself; see who one is; get to know oneself. "One is as one creates oneself in time and relationships."[3]

TWO CHALLENGES

Anyone who seriously[4] searches for the meaning of life will need to come to grips with two significant elements: (1) each of us is the creator of his/her own life in time, and (2) each of us finds him/herself in relationships. These elements signal a profound responsibility. To say that I am the creator of my life in time is not to usurp God's role in creating us. Rather, it is meant to signal the fact that each of us is responsible for him/ herself. Each step along the way in our human journey is a choice we make for who we are and for who we will become. We are creating ourselves in time because we are choosing who we are now, and who will be in time. When I reach a certain age, say 68, you will meet a person who has chosen over the years and over time to be *this* particular person and no other. We have no one to blame; we have chosen ourselves from all the myriad decisions over the years. Of course, the big question looms large: have we chosen ourselves truthfully, honestly, authentically, or are we at age 68 just a lie, to ourselves and to others? Self-creation, therefore, over the years leads to self-definition. That is why it is vital that each of us takes time every now and then to examine our choices, to do some "quality control" on the decisions that go to create us. After all, these decisions are us. A commitment to the examined life and to self-knowledge will give us the means to weed out any "inferior quality" and to reaffirm the in-depth quality of decisions that each of us wants anyway.

We create ourselves by our choices over the years, and at the end of our human journey we have only the result, the fruit, and the conclusion of our choices in self-creation. I think it is much easier at the age of 32, or 46, to examine our lives then, to see what and who our choices have made us, than it is when we know we will be dying shortly. The moment of death — and death is part of our living — is the most dramatic examination of self, the most direct confrontation with the quality and substance of who we are, and what and who over the years we have chosen to be. Perhaps this is why many people are so frightened by death; they have never really pondered the deeper questions of the human journey; perhaps they have not really reflected on the quality of the decisions that they made over the years in deciding to become who they are. Of course, it is never too late, and the task of self-development is really only completed in death. Some would argue that the very opposite takes place, that everything that we've built up over the years is lost. True, from a materialistic or quantitative point of view! But, there is too much evidence, both scientific, philosophic, personal, and theological which argues for just the opposite: more and more the process of living, all life, all human history is moving from the quantitative dimension to the qualitative one. Matter is becoming spirit. The choices that we make to become who we are, are in essence, spiritual choices, and, as such, cannot die or fade away, or rust or burn out. Death, in this viewpoint, is the final liberation from the limitations that held us from total awareness of spirit -- the core of the searcher's quest all through the human journey anyway! Death destroys, but it also liberates; and in terms of our personhood it liberates in us our understanding of ourselves "and what one have chosen to be ... in our selves."[5]

The second significant element that a true searcher for the meaning of life discovers as he/she proceeds on the journey is that identify is found in relationships. In other words, we are "crafted in relationships." Any serious searcher for the meaning of his/her life finds that quality relationships forge insight and development. It's the experience of Martin Buber's I-Thou,[6] that we are not unto ourselves alone, but we are also in relationship with others. It's also interesting to note here that when we talk of God's "grace" — the traditional term — or the "grace of God" — e.g., "There but for the grace of God go I" — we can also translate this word by "relationship."[7] To be out of "grace" with God means not to have a relationship with God, or rather, not to have a positive one, a life-giving one. To be in someone's good graces is to be in someone's favour. The other looks favourably upon us; there is a positive perception. That is relationship.

THE EMERGENCE OF PERSONHOOD

Within relationships, the fabric of our identities is worked out. The interaction forges uniqueness. Sometimes this identity cannot be seen immediately, but if one is faithful to relationship, to the ups and downs, as they say, and each party also chooses authentically (emotionally, physically, spiritually, etc.) for him/herself, a most wonderful creation emerges. It is indeed a celebration, because personhood has emerged. In death this will come to full bloom and all the small fidelities and decisions will come together to focus on the grand celebration of personality that is each of us. In this celebration we will find what we have intuitively known all along on our human journey that God's greatest glory is each of us fully alive as individuals.[8] We will discover that the self we so earnestly sought to create — and which was our task — and the other we longingly wanted to be joined to in relationship, was God's call to us to get to know ourselves and assume responsibility for ourselves as persons in order to meet the Ground of our Being,[9] God, in relationship.

We are crafted in relationship and that is why it is so important that our relationships be healthy. Healthy relationships forge healthy persons; unhealthy relationships forge unhealthy persons. This is partially why, from my experience and research, a widow or widower grieves so deeply: for the wonderful health in the relationship with the deceased that was there, but which is gone now; or, for the obvious and startling absence of health in the relationship and the years of investment — for what? — with the person. This all happens because death forces the questions of quality (below):

DEATH'S QUALITY QUESTIONS

Who are you?
What have you made of yourself?
How are you prepared to die?
Are you prepared to die?
Who will you become now?
What kinds of choices will you make?
What do you want from relationships now?
Who must you be in order to be yourself?

I have said earlier that the mystic is the person who can "peek through the keyhole of reality and see the truth."[10] Each of us is a mystic at one time or another, using this definition as our starting point. We are mystics when we catch deeper insights into the quality of ourselves as searchers and into our relationships. We come to recognize what the great paleontologist, philosopher, and theologian, Pierre Teilhard de Chardin, talked about when he said that "something's afoot in the universe"! We know that we are not only quantitatively alive, that reality is only here and now. Just a cursory reading of subatomic physics shows the illusion of that idea. Reality is as expansive as thought, as insight, as "inner."

Perhaps this is "what" God is, that is, pure insight. St. John, in the New Testament, says God is love.[11] What is it that we crave so much? It is to love and be loved! Could we not say that much of the world's troubles really boil down to the absence of love? Dr. Edgar Jackson[12] points out that there is really nothing quite like "faith" to help the bereaved deal with the impact of life because they begin to see, as we have been trying to show, that it is quality of living that counts and life, in essence, from this perspective, comes to be seen as "transcendent, transpersonal, and spiritual."[13] Transcendence tells us that we are, in our core, essentially spirit, people with a vocation to an unlimited horizon of knowing and loving. "Such concepts can so undergird life that the experience of biological death comes to be perceived as incidental to the rest of life. The life-perception of the God-conscious being far surpasses the biology of the death-event."[13] These insights and strengths can come about when people take time to develop "our own inner kingdom,"[13] or to develop our selves by making decisions whereby we choose who we are and will become and by examining these choices every so often with courage, humility, and openness.

Death makes us talk about the reality of God, either its possibility or its denial. The possibility far outweighs any serious challenges to the contrary. The whole movement of the mind's activity is toward the infinite. "We spontaneously move towards ... a final coherence or complete explanation."[14] Whatever it is, or whoever it is we are so innately driven towards on our human journey — call it Absolute Mystery, if you will — as long as reality raises a question for us, the answer to which can or must explain everything to us to satisfy us — then we also must talk about and affirm the existence of that Mystery. This Mystery is the "point" of final coherence that we strive for; we encounter this Mystery fully in death.[15] One story that highlights this point so poignantly is the following story about a black-American man, a very kind man. He had been the senior janitor in a Baptist Church, and had been a deacon there. The following words were recorded by his pastor who went to visit him one week before he died:

> Pastor, you are being kind to me but you don't need to tell me all these things. The doctor hasn't told me yet but I know I will die in a few days. I am thankful for all the good things the Lord has done for me all of my life. I have never wanted for anything that I rightfully should have had. I love the Lord and I know he loves me. I am not afraid to meet him face to face. He has been so good to me for so long, I know he will keep on being the same way. My wife and my friends have all gone on before me. Now I can go. So, pastor, don't worry about me. I'm only going home and no one is ever unhappy about going home.[16]

His story reminds of the words of the late English poet, John Donne: "Here in this world He bids us come, There in the next He shall bid us welcome."[17] And his story is also reminiscent of what Abraham Lincoln said one time about people: that they are just about as happy as they make up their minds to be.[18] Another very lively and human story also in this regard comes from the following: "But let me tell you — there may not be sex after death, but there sure as hell is sex after sixty-five. And how! It may take a little longer. The heavy breathing may be slightly asthmatic. But you still get there. And it's pretty hot stuff. Maybe even better."[19]

Living life to the fullest, expanding one's personality to the limits, hoping in the potential that is available, envisioning what has not been -- these activities fill the creative spirit; this is what it means to develop a meaning to one's life; this is what is needed to continue, or, in some cases, to begin, now that the death of a spouse has occurred. If death is in the living of life, then reality after the loved one has died must also be full of life. Love life to the fullest; adore it, celebrate it!

Spiritual writers over the centuries have always talked of a particular ingredient necessary to discover essence on the human journey, and that is the reality of solitude, time alone — however it has to be — with oneself. Solitude allows us time to discern, to sort out, if you will, the wheat from the chaff.

Evelyn Underhill, the noted writer on mysticism has said that "to go up alone into the mountain and come back as an ambassador to the world, has been the method of humanity's best friends."[20] With the story of Marjorie we saw how she loved her mountains – a biblical motif if there were ever one! Marjorie loved thinking about and 'going to her mountains.' She loved the mountains and what they stood for. She loved mystery.

In giving counsel to the widowed, we would strongly recommend this "mountain" experience because we firmly believe that while silence confronts us with ourselves, it also heals us. Blaise Pascal said one time, "I have discovered that all human evil comes from this, man's being unable to sit still in a room."[21]

TAKING TIME

Taking time can be a life jacket in the day-to-day goings-on in our lives. It gives us a sense of objectivity, a sense of self, a sense of the relative importance of what we may be facing. Above all, if well done, it can give us a good sense of humour for the humanity of us all. Taking time is that side of us that puts things into perspective, that realizes that so much of what we think and want is really relative when compared to the "big" things in life: death, meaning in life, God, family, love. Taking time helps us to see ourselves for who we are: human beings in a vast universe. We are not the centre of this universe by a long shot! We are unique, but very vulnerable, human beings. We wait upon the graciousness of this universe to give us air, to feed us, to clothe us, and to shelter us. We are given so much; we receive so much.

Taking time reminds us of our relative position in the grand scheme of things. What we see as so important today is gone tomorrow. Yesterday's "absolutes" become today's trivia! We forget so quickly. Taking time gives us our perspective.

A NEW LIFESTYLE

A new lifestyle, therefore, for the widow or widower would do well to embrace some solitary time. This alone time, if properly and wisely invested, will go a long way towards healing the brokenness and loss inside because the person will come to see that a support, far deeper, richer and wider, does uphold him/her and was there all along. For some this support is called God, the life force or love. For others it is the exquisite value of the present moment, the air that is breathed, the smell of the flowers, the flight of a bird. And for still others it will be the purpose that they now have found to their lives, the sense of meaning and of values, the commitment to renewed quality in relationships, and the loving affirmation that all life is to be respected, and that each person must walk with dignity with every moment treasured and lived to its fullest, and every death, however painful, acknowledged as still only relative in the moments of the universe.

Finally, a new lifestyle is to be able to see's own frailty on the human journey, one's own tenuous moments, and yet not to give up. It is to stand tall as a human being, and yes, to walk, living *into*, *through*, and *out of* the reality of death into eternity. It is to believe that life is stronger than death, that the universe is personal, that we are absolutely, and fundamentally, supported by Love as the personal response of our universe, that in spite of all the evil and horrendous tragedy and pain and hurt that we know only so well, we are held in the great loving bosom of Life, of the universe, and of God.

> As I see a dying person moving from day to day toward that ultimate moment, I hope that perhaps I can learn something about how dying is done, something about the arcane mysteries of the magic moment of transition from life to nonlife, something about the components of an ideal death, and even, if the gods are gracious, some guidelines that will teach me how to die well when my own turn comes.[22]

"The question, 'Which is the happiest season of life?' being referred to an aged man, he replied: 'When spring comes, and in the soft air the buds are breaking on the trees, and they are covered with blossoms, I think, How beautiful is Spring! And when the summer comes, and covers the trees with its heavy foliage, and singing birds are among the branches, I think, How beautiful is summer! When autumn loads them with golden fruit, and their leaves bear the gorgeous tint of frost, I think, How beautiful is Autumn! and when it is serene winter, and there is neither foliage nor fruit, then I look up through the leafless branches, as I never could until now, and see the stars shine.' "

— Seneca (Pucius Annaeus Seneca, the Younger (4 BC - AD 65), *Rome's leading intellectual figure in the mid-1st century AD.*

THOUGHTS TO PONDER

1. The examined life is the only life worth living. Death is "examination time."

2. The true searcher on the human journey knows two important facts: (1) the task of self-creation, and (2) the crafting of identity in relationships.

3. The human journey leads one from an emphasis on the quantitative aspects the qualitative ones.

4. Healthy relationships foster healthy persons.

5. Reality is as expansive as thought, as insight, as "inner."

6. At our core we are essentially spirit, people with a vocation to an un-limited horizon of knowing and loving.

7. Death makes us ask a most basic question: where are we heading?

8. Our human journey is moving toward final coherence and explanation.

9. Life must be lived to the fullest, and celebrated!

10. For meaning on the human journey, and for the new lifestyle, now that the death of a loved one has occurred, a certain amount of solitude is necessary.

11. Solitude gives one perspective and gives one back to one's self.

ENDNOTES

Introduction

1. Edwin Shneidman. *Voices of Death. Letters, Diaries and Other Personal Documents for People Facing Death That Provide Comforting Guidance For Each of Us*. New York: Harper and Row, Publishers, 1980, pp. 112, 190-191.

2. Alfred Allan Lewis, Barrie Berns. *Three Out of Four Wives. Widowhood in America*. New York: Macmillan Publishing Co., Inc., 1975, p. 175.

3. Neil Towne and Ronald B. Adler. *Looking Out/Looking In. Interpersonal Communication*. 4th. Edition. Toronto: Holt, Rinehart & Winston, 1984, p. 175.

4. Edwin Shneidman, *op.cit.*, p. 112. See also Thomas Moore. *Dark Nights of the Soul: A Guide to Finding Your Way Through Life's Ordeals*. Gotham Books, 2004, 368 pages. ISBN: 1592400671

5. *Op. cit.*, p. 112. Cf. also Henry A. Murray. *Explorations in Personality*. London & New York: Oxford University Press, 1938; also Karl Rahner, the great German theologian [+1987] says, "... death is just the way life was... Therefore, in a very true sense death is actually anticipated in every moral act in which the higher and more distant goal is preferred to the lower, nearer, and more pleasant one ... death is especially the end from within myself: It is my final act," in *The Practice of Faith. A Handbook of Contemporary Spirituality*. Edited by Karl Lehman and Albert Raffelt. New York: Crossroads, 1984, pp. 295-296.

6. Edwin Shneidman, *op. cit.*, p. 112.

7. John Hinton, "The Influence of Previous Personality on Reactions to Having Terminal Cancer," *Omega*, 1975, Vol. 6, No. 2, pp. 95-111, quoted in Edwin Shneidman, *op. cit.*, p. 113. Also, "For the aged person, the future has come, and all of the accumulation of failures that have made up their part become the resources they have to work with in the present. If the now has never served them well, if they have never been able to enjoy being alive when and where they are, the prospects for retirement are gloomy indeed, for it will inevitably be more of the same. The problems of aging and retirement are not so much external as they are internal. If a person has spent a lifetime developing skills in failure, they will be hard to replace when he is his own boss and must set the course of his own life." From Edgar N. Jackson. *The Many Faces of Grief*. Nashville, Tennessee: The Parthenon Press, 1978, pp. 89-90.

8. Most profoundly said by Jesus of Nazareth, Matt. 6:21 (The New Testament).

9. Edgar Jackson. *Understanding Grief. Its Roots, Dynamics, and Treatment*. Nashville, Tennessee: The Parthenon Press (1957), 1978, p. 27.

Chaper 1

1. Read John Bowles, "The Aristos," quoted in Edwin Shneidman. *Death: Current Perspectives*. Jason Aronson, Inc., published in paperback by Mayfield Publishing Co.,

285 Hamilton Avenue, Palo Alto, California 94301, 1976, pp. 3-7.

2. Edwin Shneidman, *Voices of Death*, op. cit., p. 112.

3. Michael Rock. *Grippings: Trusted Meanings on Our Human Journey*. Oak Publications: Unionville, Ontario, 1987, p. 104. Many thanks are owed to my friend, Kelly Nemeck, OMI, STD who, in 1985, gave me the expression of going *into* death, *through* death and *out of* death. In the Christian understanding of this dying and death process, we go *into*, *through*, and *out of death* into the resurrection, into life eternal. It is a process that *has* to occur in order for our complete personal transformation to occur. This personal transformation is so radical that it transforms us in our very roots existentially.

4. Edwin S. Shneidman, "Death Work and Stages of Dying," in *Death: Current Perspectives*, ibid., p. 444. Shneidman goes on to say that "we must not forget that one of the principal functions of the personality is to protect itself against itself -- against its own ravages, assaults, and threats."

5. In Eric Butterworth. *Spiritual Economics. The Principles and Process of True Prosperity*. Unity Village, Missouri, (1998) 2003, p. 55. ISBN 0-87157-269-X

6. Edgar N. Jackson, *The Many Faces of Grief*, op. cit., p. 148.

7. *Ibid.*, p. 146.

8. Beverley Raphael, MD, "Loss in Adult Life: The Death of a Spouse," in *The Anatomy of Bereavement*. New York: Basic Books Publishers, 1983, p. 177.

9. Karl Rahner, *The Practice of the Faith*, op. cit., p. 296.

10. Jacques Choron. *Death and Western Thought*. New York: 1963, p. 309.

11. *Ibid.*, p. 308.

12. John Bartlett (Ed.). *Familiar Quotations*. 10th. Edition. New York: The Review of Reviews Co., 1916, "Publius Syrus, 42 B.C., p. 897.

13. Jacques Choron, *ibid.*, p. 308.

14. Paul Edwards, "My Death," in *The Encyclopaedia of Philosophy*, Vol. 5. New York: Macmillan Publishing Co., Inc. & The Free Press, 1972, p. 418.

15. Richard Garnett, Leon Vallee, and Alois Brandl (Eds.), "Bacon's Apothegma," *The Universal Anthology*. Vol. 13. New York: Merrill & Baker, 1889, p. 272.

16. Thomas F. O'Meara, "A History of Grace," in Leon J. O'Donovan (Ed.). *A World of Grace*. New York: The Seabury Press (A Crossroad Book), 1980, pp. 78-79.

17. See David Sudnow. *Passing On: The Social Organization of Dying*. Englewood Cliffs, New Jersey: Prentice-Hall, 1967.

18. R. S. Weiss, "The Provisions of Social Relationships," in *Doing Unto Others*. Englewood Cliffs, New Jersey: Prentice-Hall, 1974; cited in Beverley Raphael, MD, "Human Bonds and Death: The Background to Bereavement," article in her

book, *The Anatomy of Bereavement, op. cit.,* p. 4.

19. Jacques Choron, *op. cit.,* p. 309.

Chaper 2

1. Beverley Raphael, MD, "Human Bonds and Death: The Background to Bereavement," in *The Anatomy of Bereavement, op. cit.,* p. 19.

2. R.A. Hinde. *Towards Understanding Relationship.* London: Academic Press, 1978. I am grateful here for this reference to Dr. Beverley Raphael, *ibid.,* p. 20. Also, Arnold Toynbee, in an essay entitled "Various Ways in Which Human Beings Have Sought to Reconcile Themselves to the Fact of Death," outlines nine ways: (1) Hedonism — eat, drink and be merry philosophy (Is. 22:13); cf. also the Latin poet, and Horace's line, "Carpe Diem" (Seize the Moment), in his *Odes,* I, xi, 8; (2) Pessimism - "life is so wretched" (Sophocles, 5th. century B.C.); (3) Attempts to circumvent death by physical countermeasures (e.g., providing food, drink with corpse, e.g., Tutankhamen); (4) Attempts to circumvent death by winning fame (e.g., commemorations, Thucydides); (5) Self-liberation from self-centredness by putting one's treasure in future generations of one's fellow human beings (e.g., Abraham, Gen. 12:2, "I will make of thee a great nation"); (6) Self-liberation from self-centredness by merging oneself in ultimate reality (e.g., the Indian quest); (7) The belief in the personal immortality of human souls (e.g., Pythagoras, Orphics, Judaeo-Christian belief, etc.); (8) The belief in the

resurrection of human bodies (Jesus, St. Paul, Acts 17:32); and (9) The hope of heaven and the fear of hell.

3. T. Parsons, "Death in American Society: A Brief Working Paper," *American Behavioral Scientist,* Vol. 6, 1963, pp. 61-65. I am grateful here also to Dr. Beverley Raphael, *op. cit.,* p. 20, for this reference.

4. As quoted in Dr. Beverley Raphael, *op. cit.,* p. 20. "Seeking an answer to death is perhaps the greatest wild-goose chase of human existence," in Gil Elliott. *The Twentieth Century Book of The Dead.* New York: Ballantine Books (a Division of Random House, Inc. and Penguin Books, Ltd.), 1972, p. 130. Cf. also the article, "Agents of Death," in Edwin Shneidman. *Death: Current Perspectives.* Jason Aronson, Inc., published in paperback by Mayfield Publishing Co., 285 Hamilton Avenue, Palo Alto, California 94301, 1976, pp. 110-133, where the author shows that in the 20th. century, 110 million people were killed!

5. G. Gorer, "The Pornography of Death," in *Modern Writings,* ed. by W. Phillips & P. Rahy. New York: McGraw-Hill, 1959; also, *Death, Grief and Mourning.* New York: Doubleday & Co., Inc., 1965; cf. also the words of Edgar Herzog, "... the 'excess of death' has produced a tendency in man and woman to shut themselves off from this aspect of life by putting aside all thought of death. This leads to the inhibition of real becoming, and creates in its place an appearance of security which is, in fact, continually threatened by unconscious anxieties giving rise to neuroses ... understand neurosis in this existential way ... a failure of the psyche to

come to grips with 'the basic condition of human existence' ... One of the most important of these basic conditions is death," in *Psyche and Death. Death-Demons in Folklore, Myths and Modern Dreams.* Dallas, Texas: Spring Publications, 1983, p. 10.

6. E.S. Schneiderman, "On the Deroman-ticization of Death," *American Journal of Psychotherapy*, Volume 25, No. 1, 1971, pp. 4-7.

7. W.G. Warren and P.N. Chopra, "An Australian Survey of Attitudes to Death," *Australian Journal of Social Issues*, Vol. 14, 1979, pp. 140-152; D.J. Templer, "The Construction and Validation of a Death Anxiety Scale," *Journal of General Psychology*, Vol. 82, 1980, pp. 165-177; L.D. Nelson, C.C. Nelson, "A Factor Analytic Inquiry into the Multidimensionality of Death Anxiety," *Omega*, Vol. 6, 1975, 171-178. These references are cited in Dr. Beverley Raphael, *op. cit.*, p. 21. Also, our North American culture is addicted to the "youth" image. There is a multi-billion dollar industry alive telling women, for instance, that beauty is what counts. Thus, men and women don't age gracefully in our culture. "Wrinkles are out; softness is in!" We have even taken this attitude into the death environment. For many centuries, especially with Catholics, it was forbidden to have cremation because, in the Middle Ages, because people were denying or voicing suspicions about the resurrection of the body. The Catholic Church, to counteract that, said only a 'natural' burial was admissible for Catholics, not a cremated one! An earlier historical example is the technology of mummification carried over from ancient

Egypt. This practice was an indication of people's 'reluctance' to say that death had actually occurred. It also implied, of course, that the 'dead person' was now on a new voyage, a new journey. Even today we say, in "viewing" a body in the funeral parlour, "My, she looks good!" or, "He looks as though he's only asleep!" The illusion of well-being, compliments of the mortician's artwork! The comment has been made that many people fare better *after* they die - in the impersonal care of their deteriorating body by the funeral parlours - than in real life (Cf. Barbara G. Walker. *The Crone. Woman of Age, Wisdom, and Power*. San Francisco: Harper & Row, 1985, p. 34.) Who, then, before dying, listened to their feelings and their emotional needs? Bruce's story in a later chapter is a beautiful example of a man who did choose to listen to his wife when she was dying, and who sees the importance of the listening activity for the remaining spouse. The widowed spouse needs to be listened to now that his/her spouse has died.

8. Beverley Raphael, MD, *op. cit.*, p. 21. The myth of the *Epic of Gilgamesh* "may be the oldest recorded tale of a superhuman search for a lost Eden in which man could not die," in Edwin Shneidman. *Death: Current Perspectives, op. cit.*, p. 56. Later, this was to be refined into the alchemist's search for the elixir, "... the basic substance that would, ingested or otherwise taken, assure man of eternal life on earth" (*ibid.*, p. 56). This quest for immortality "... is as nearly universal as anything we know pertaining to the inner wishes inherent in man for the indefinite perpetuation of the self," in N. Cousins. *The Celebration of Life: A Dialogue on Immortality and Infinity*. New York: Harper & Row, 1974, p. 4 (quoted in

Edwin Shneidman, *op. cit.*, p. 57). "Certainly the keys to eternal youth or life that men sought reveal a deep spiritual hunger" (Shneidman, *op. cit.*, p. 57). Ponce de Leon never did find his fountain of Life (Ps. 36) in the early 1500's, but "in his search he discovered Florida where the aged still go hoping to regain their vigor," in O. Segerberg, Jr. *The Immortality Factor.* New York: E.P. Dutton & Co., 1974 (quoted in Edwin Shneidman, *op. cit.*, p. 58).

9. Voltaire said one time, "The human species is the only one which knows it will die, and it knows this through experience" (*Dictionnaire Philosophique*, in Robert C. Olson, "Death," *The Encyclopaedia of Philosophy*, Volume I. New York: Macmillan Publishing Co., Inc., and The Free Press, 1972, p. 307.

10. Milton Gatch, "The Biblical Tradition," in *Death: Meaning and Morality in Christian Thought and Contemporary Culture.* New York: The Seabury Press, 1969, quoted in Edwin Shneidman. *Death: Current Perspectives*, *op. cit.*, p. 45.

11. Milton Gatch, *ibid.*, p. 46.

12. Gen. 25:1-11.

13. Milton Gatch, *op. cit.*, p. 47.

14. Gen. 25:8.

15. Milton Gatch, *op. cit.*, p. 48.

16. *Ibid.*, p. 49.

17. Dan. 12:2-3.

18. Milton Gatch, *op. cit.*, p. 50.

19. Mark 12:28-34.

20. Milton Gatch, *op. cit.*, quoted in Edwin Shneidman, *op. cit.*, p. 53.

21. 1 Cor. 15:12-22.

22. This question of "eternal life" has been with students of philosophy and life since people began to reflect. Marcus Tullius Cicero, the Roman philosopher, wrote, "There is, I know not how, in the minds of men, a certain presage, as it were, of a future existence; and this takes the deepest root, and is most discoverable in the greatest geniuses and most exalted souls," in Carrol E. Simcox (Ed.). *A Treasury of Quotations on Christian Themes.* New York: The Seabury Press, A Crossroad Book, 1975, p. 231; also, John Donne, the English poet, wrote, "Here in this world He bids us come, there in the next He bids us welcome," *ibid.*, p. 231; cf. also, Ps. 22:26; Matt. 10:28; John 11:25-26.

23. 3 Kings 17:8-15; 4 Kings 4:1-7.

24. Is. 54:4; Ruth. 1:13.24.

25. Gen. 38:11; Lev. 22:13; Ruth 1:8.

26. Ex. 22:21-23; Is. 1:17, 23; Job 22:9; 31:16; Ps. 93 (94):6; Zach. 7:10.

27. Mal. 3:5; Deut. 14:29; 16:11, 14.

28. O.J. Baab, "Widow," *The Interpreter's Dictionary of the Bible.* Volume 4. New York: Abingdon Press, 1962, p. 842.

29. O.J. Baab, *op. cit.*, p. 842.

30. H. Jamieson, "Widow," in Merrill C. Tenney (Ed.). *The Zondervan Pictorial Encyclopaedia of the Bible*. Volume 5. Grand Rapids, Mich.: Zondervan Publishing House, 1977, p. 928.

31. John L. McKenzie, "Widow," *Dictionary of the Bible*. Milwaukee: The Bruce Publishing Company, 1965, p. 927.

32. *Ibid.*, p. 927.

33. H. Jamieson, *op. cit.*, p. 928.

34. Job 24:21; 29:13; Ps. 94:6; Is. 1:23; Mal. 3:5.

35. George B. Eager, "Widow," in James Orr [John L. Nuelsen, Edgar Y. Mullins], (Ed.). *The International Standard Bible Encyclopaedia*, Volume V. Grand Rapids, Michigan: Wm. B. Erdmans Publishing Company, 1978, p. 3084.

36. Lewis N. Dembitz, "Widow," in Isidore Singer. *The Jewish Encyclopaedia*. Volume 12. New York: Funk and Wagnalls Company, 1912, p. 514.

37. Mark 12:40; Luke 20:47.

38. Acts 9:36-41; 1 Tim. 5:13-16.

39. Mircea Eliade. *A History of Religious Ideas*. Volume I. *From the Stone Age to the Eleusinian Mysteries*. Chicago: University of Chicago Press, 1978, p. 51.

40. A. Closs, "Death (Primitive Concepts Of)," *New Catholic Encyclopaedia*. Volume 14. Toronto: McGraw-Hill Book Co., 1967, p. 686.

41. Mircea Eliade, "Mythologies of Death: An Introduction," *Occultism, Witchcraft, and Cultural Fashions*. Chicago: University of Chicago Press, 1976, p. 33.

42. Mircea Eliade, *op. cit.*, pp. 33ff. For example, the stories from Africa, "Two Messengers" and "The Message that Failed" both show that "God sent the chameleon to the ancestors with the message that they would be immortal and sent the lizard with the message that they would die. But the chameleon paused along the way, and the lizard arrived first. After she had delivered her message, death entered the world (cf. also, Hane Abrahamsson. *The Origin of Death: Studies in African Mythology*. Uppsala, 1951). Again, another myth, a Melanesian one, shows death as a stupid action of mythic ancestors, and says that as the first men advanced in life, they "cast their skins like snakes and came out with their youth renewed. But once an old woman, coming home rejuvenated, was not recognized by her child. In order to pacify the child, she put her old skin on again, and from that time on men became mortal" (Mircea Eliade, *op. cit.*, p. 34; cf. also, R.H. Codrington. *The Melanesians*. Oxford, 1895). From an Indonesian myth we read, "In the beginning, the sky was very near to the earth, and the Creator used to let down his gifts to men at the end of a rope. One day he lowered a stone. But the ancestors would have none of it, and called out to their Maker: 'What have we to do with this stone? Give us something else.' God complied; some time later God let down a banana, which they joyfully accepted. Then the ancestors heard a voice from heaven saying: 'Because ye have chosen the banana, your life shall be like its life. When the banana-tree has offspring, the

parent stem dies; so shall ye die and your children shall step into your place. Had ye chosen the stone, your life would have been like the life of the stone, changeless and immortal" (Mircea Eliade, ibid., p. 34; cf. also, J.G. Frazer. *The Belief in Immortality*. 3 Vols. Volume I. London, 1913, 74-75). Eliade goes on to say that the meaning of the Indonesian myth shows the mysterious interplay of life and death. The stone is both indestructibility *and* inertia, whereas life is both creative and free. Ultimately this meant spiritual creativity and freedom; therefore, death became part of the human condition. A person's specific destiny could now be fulfilled because of the awareness the person had of his/ her mortality.

43. "Mythologies of Death: An Introduction," *op. cit.*, p. 35.

44. *Ibid.*, p. 36.

45. *Ibid.*, p. 38. "... as is well known, any initiation consists essentially of a symbolic death followed by a rebirth or resurrection". In another place, Eliade says, "... since man's life is like the life of cereals, strength and perenniality become accessible *through death*" (*A History of Religious Ideas*. Volume I, *op. cit.*, p. 91).

46. Mircea Eliade, "Mythologies of Death: An Introduction," *ibid.*, p. 40.

47. *Ibid.*, p. 40. Some interesting contemporary stories are told in this regard concerning the killing of death to bring in spring: "The most widespread custom in Europe is this: children make a guy from straw and branches and carry it out of the village saying: 'We are carrying Death to the water', ... Then they throw it into a lake or well, or else burn it. In Austria, all the audience fight around Death's funeral pyre to get hold of a bit of the effigy. There we see the fertilizing power of Death - a power attaching to all the symbols of vegetation, and to the ashes of the wood burnt during all the various festivals of the regeneration of nature and the beginning of the New Year. As soon as Death has been driven out or killed, Spring is brought in," in Mircea Eliade. *Patterns in Comparative Religion*. New York: Sheed & Ward, 1958, p. 317; cf. also Eliade's comments on the meaning of death: "Nevertheless, in many archaic cultures, as the myth of the Stone and the Banana so gracefully suggests, death is considered a necessary complement of life. Essentially, this means that death changes man's ontological status. The separation of the soul from the body brings about a new modality of being. From this point on, man is reduced to a spiritual existence; he becomes a ghost, a 'spirit' ("Mythologies of Death: An Introduction," *op. cit.*, p. 35).

48. Mircea Eliade. *A History of Religious Ideas*. Vol. I, *op. cit.*, p. 99.

49. Mircea Eliade. *Shamanism. Archaic Techniques of Ecstasy*. Bollingen Series LXXVI. Princeton, New Jersey: Princeton University Press, 1964, p. 356.

50. C.S. Lewis. *A Grief Observed*. New York: The Seabury Press, 1961, p. 1. I am thankful for this reference to Ira O. Glick, Robert S. Parkes and C. Murray. *The First Year of Bereavement*. Toronto: John Wiley & Sons, 1974, p. 286.

51. Anne Munley, Ph.D. *The Hospice Alternative. A New Context for Death and Dying*. New York: Basic Books, Inc., Publishers, 1983, p. 113.

52. Carrol E. Simcox (Ed.), "Death," in *A Treasury of Quotations on Christian Themes*. New York: The Seabury Press, A Crossroad Book, 1975, pp. 225-226.

53. Karl Rahner, "Death," *Sacramentum Mundi. An Encyclopaedia of Theology*. Volume II. New York: Herder & Herder, 1968, p. 58.

54. *Op cit.*, p. 59; cf. Luke 16:26; John 9:4; 2 Cor. 5:10; Gal. 6:10.

55. *Ibid.*, p. 61.

56. Alfred Allan Lewis and Barrie Berns. *Three Out of Four Wives. Widowhood in America*. New York: Macmillan Publishing Co., Inc., 1975, pp. 39-40.

57. Anne Munley, *op. cit.*, p. 13.

58. "Death and Social Structure," in *Death and Identity*, ed. Robert Fulton, Bowie, Md.: Charles Press, 1976, p. 44; quoted in Anne Munley, *ibid.*, p. 15.

59. Derek Gill. *Quest: The Life of Elizabeth Kubler-Ross*. New York: Harper & Row, 1980, p. 144. A new contribution in re-envisioning medicine is found *Humane Medicine: A Journal of the Art and Science of Medicine*, c/o Toronto Western Hospital, 399 Bathurst Street, Toronto, Ontario M5T 2S8, (416) 364-9974. I am very grateful to the Executive Director, John O. Godden, MD, for giving me my first copy (November 1987, Vol. 3, No. 2).

60. Robert Blauner, *op. cit.*, p. 44; quoted in Anne Munley, *op. cit.*, p. 15.

61. Phyllis R. Silverman, Dorothy MacKenzie, Mary Pettipas and Elizabeth Wilson (Eds.). *Helping Each Other In Widowhood*. New York, New York: Health Sciences Publishing Corp., 1974, p. 144.

62. Anne Munley, *op.* cit., p. 13.

63. *Ibid.*, p. 13.

64. *Ibid.*, pp. 5-6.

65. Anne Munley, *op. cit.*, p. 12.

66. *Op. cit.*, p. 18.66.

67. New York: Basic Books, Inc., Publishers, 1983, 349 pages.

68. *Ibid.*, p. 5.

69. Anne Munley, *op. cit.*, p. 19, a reference Munley has located in the *American Journal of Nursing* Volume 70, February 1970, p. 336.

70. "In the history of the Christian life and also in the history of the life of mankind as a whole there can be found obviously varying styles of dying. The method and custom of a particular society presents to its individual members a definite style of dying, to be preferred as right and proper, at least for the 'normal' case. In Christendom, too, there are such 'rules for dying' and they have not always simply remained the same. In particular a certain style of dying was expected from those holding important positions in the Church, a style in which their rank, their

responsibility for others, their Christian faith, could be presented as an example. Formerly, a Christian died within his family circle, said goodbye there, blessed them, had a few last words to say, asserted his orthodox faith and his Christian hope, etc. It is very different today, when, as a result of thrusting the sick into the impersonal atmosphere of public hospitals, dying has largely become styleless," Karl Rahner, *The Practice of Faith, op. cit.,* p. 294.

Chapter 3

1. Edwin Shneidman. *Voices of Death: Letters, Diaries and Other Personal Documents For People Facing Death That Provide Comforting Guidance For Each Of Us.* New York: Harper & Row, Publishers, 1980, p. 144.

2. Beverley Raphael, M.D. *The Anatomy of Bereavement.* New York: Basic Books Publishers, 1983, p. 402. George Romanes says it very beautifully in describing his reaction to the death of his friend, Charles Darwin: "Half the interest of my life seems to have gone when I cannot look forward any more to his dear voice of welcome or to the letters which were my greatest happiness. For now there is no one to venerate, no one to work for, or to think about while working. I always knew that I was leaning on these feelings too much, but I could not try to prevent them; and so at last I am left with a loneliness that can never be filled," in Carrol E. Simcox (Ed.). *A Treasury of Quotations on Christian Themes.* New York: The Seabury Press, A Crossroad Book, 1975, p. 223; or, Dr. Jackson talking about the most painful form of loneliness, "... that which comes with the death of one who has been so

dearly loved and been so close to the centre of life that it seems life will never be the same without him. The loneliness that accompanies acute grief is an assault on the meaning of life itself. It is a threat to the inner security system of an individual. It is a devastating loss of some of the essential nature of the self," in *The Many Faces of Grief.* Nashville, Tennessee: Parthenon Press, 1978, p. 33.

3. Jane Burgess Kohn and Willard K. Kohn. *The Widower. What He Faces, What He Feels, What He Needs.* Boston: Beacon Press, 1978, p. 25-26.

4. Ira O. Glick, Robert S. Weiss, C. Murray Parkes, *op. cit.,* p. 300.

5. *Ibid.,* p. 67; also, from another author, "I began to realize that the only cure for loneliness lay deep inside oneself and that if that vast expanse of help could be found and tapped, there would also be a way to leave loneliness altogether," Lynn Caine. *Lifelines.* Garden City, New York: Doubleday & Company, Inc., 1978, p. 66.

6. Edgar N. Jackson. *Understanding Grief. Its Roots, Dynamics, and Treatment.* Nashville, Tennessee: The Parthenon Press (1957), 1978, p. 26.

7. Ira O. Glick, *op. cit.,* p. viii.

8. While this is my model, I do wish to acknowledge my indebtedness in clarifying the concepts and for the on-going discussion of bereavement to Dr. Beverley Raphael, M.D., *op. cit.,* pp. 33-73.

9. Carrol E. Simcox (Ed.), *op. cit.,* p. 109.

10. Quoted in Lynn Caine, *op. cit.*, pp. 67-68.

11. Silverman et al., *op. cit.*, p. 4-10. Also, only after the spouse's death does grief truly begin," Ira O. Glick, *et al., op. cit.*, p. 295.

12. *Op. cit.*, p. 10.

13. Sigmund Freud, "Mourning and Melancholia," (1917) *Collected Papers.* New York: Basic Books, 1959, Volume 4, pp. 152-170.

14. Ira O. Glick, *et al., op. cit.*, p. 6; also, we can say that grief is "... the emotional and related reactions that occur at the time and following the loss by death of an important person in the emotional life of an individual who has reached the state of development where he has the capacity for object love. Grief is the emotion that is involved in the work of mourning, whereby a person seeks to disengage himself from the demanding relationship that has existed and to reinvest his emotional capital in new and productive directions for the health and welfare of his future life in society," Edgar N. Jackson. *Understanding Grief: Its Roots, Dynamics, and Treatment.* Nashville, Tennessee: Parthenon Press (19157), p. 18.

15. Edgar N. Jackson. *The Many Faces of Grief.* Nashville, Tennessee: Then Parthenon Press, 1978, p. 11.

16. *Ibid.*, p. 118.

17. Edgar N. Jackson. *Understanding Grief, op. cit.*, p. 147.

18. Act I, Scene 2; Scene 7. I am indebted for these references to Edgar N. Jackson. *Understanding Grief, op. cit.*, p. 162.

19. *Ibid.*, p. 162. Some of the recognizable symptoms of abnormal grief are the following: (1) overactivity and pretending that one is very 'together'; (2) coming down with the symptoms of the deceased's last illness; (3) psychosomatic disorders and diseases, e.g., ulcerative colitis; (4) behaving quite differently with friends and relatives; (5) intense hostility against specific persons; (6) acting out life, rather than really feeling it and living it; (7) general listlessness and a disintegration of social relationships; (8) going overboard (i.e., unreasonable generosity) such that this behaviour damages one's social and economic stability, and (9) agitated moods of depression (*ibid.*, p. 168).

20. Judy Talelbaum. *The Courage To Grieve.* New York: Lippincott & Crowell, Publishers, 1980, p. 9.

21. Beverley Raphael, MD, "The Experience of Bereavement: Separation and Mourning," in *The Anatomy of Bereavement, op. cit.*, p. 33.

22. Judy Tatelbaum. *The Courage To Grieve.* New York: Lipincott & Crowell, Publishers, 1980, p. 28.

23. Alfred Allan Lewis, Barrie Berns, *op. cit.*, p. 30.

24. Beverley Raphael, M.D., "The Experience of Bereavement: Separation and Mourning," in *The Anatomy of Bereavement, op. cit.*, p. 33.

25. St. Paul, in the New Testament, says that we can't even imagine the quality and uniqueness of this afterlife for those, as he put it, who love God: "No eye has seen, no ear has heard, no mind has conceived what God has prepared for those who love him" (1 Cor. 2:9); cf. also, Isaiah 64:3-4; Jer. 3:16. Translation from: *The Holy Bible. New International Version*. Containing The Old Testament and The New Testament. Grand Rapids, Michigan: Zondervan Bible Publishers, 1984, p. 1194.

26. Beverley Raphael, M.D., "The Experience of Bereavement: Separation and Mourning," in *The Anatomy of Bereavement*, *op. cit.*, p. 39.

27. Sigmund Freud, "Mourning and Melancholia," (1917), *op. cit.*, reference found in Beverley Raphael, M.D., *ibid.*, p. 44.

28. R.C. Bak, "Being in Love and Object Loss," *International Journal of Psychoanalysis*, Vol. 54, 1973, pp. 1-8, reference found in Beverley Raphael, M.D., *ibid.*, p. 44.

29. D.C. Madison and W.L. Walker, "Factors Affecting the Outcome of Conjugal Bereavement," *British Journal of Psychiatry*, Vol. 113, 1967, pp. 1057-1067, reference cited in Beverley Raphael, M.D., *ibid.*, p. 48.

Chapter 4

1. Carol D. Harvey and Howard M. Bahr, "Widowhood Morale, and Affiliation," *Journal of Marriage and the Family*, February 1974, p. 97. The authors also say, "Widowhood is also felt by the society as a whole. Widows tend to be economically poor... the negative impact sometimes attributed to widowhood derives not from widowhood status but rather from socioeconomic status... they are much poorer than the married," pp. 97, 106.

2. Dr. Helena Lopata, "The Widow In America: A Study of the Older Widow," cassette tape, Seneca College, Leslie Campus, Tape #0565694, North York, Ontario, Canada. The authors mention the average age in their study as 56; also, "The median age of women at the beginning of their widowhood is fifty-two" (Alfred Allan Lewis and Barrie, Berns, *op. cit.*, p. 9).

3. Alfred Allan Lewis and Barrie Berns, *op. cit.*, p. 12.

4. Judy Tatelbaum, *op. cit.*, p. 83, 87.

5. Alfred Allan Lewis and Barrier Berns, *op. cit.*, p. 6. Bequaert describes society's ranking as such: 1) married women - superior; 2) widows — pitiable; and divorcees — deviants (Lucia H. Bequaert. *Single Women: Alone and Together*. Boston: Beacon Press, 1976, pp. 43ff).

6. Jane Burgess Kohn and Willard K. Kohn. *The Widower. What He Faces, What He Feels, What He Needs*. Boston: Beacon Press, 1978, p. 87.

7. Kohn and Kohn refer to this as the "fifth wheel syndrome" *op. cit.*, p. 82.

8. *Ibid.*, p. 84.

9. Ira O. Glick *et al.*, *op. cit.*, p. 263.

10. Obviously the research presented here is dependent upon these socio-cultural patterns. It will be interesting to read about widowed spouses in 30-50 years from now given that we have many two-income earners and often a significant difference in the marital roles.

11. Ira O. Glick *et al.*, op. cit., p. 272.

12. *Ibid.*, p. 273.

13. *Ibid.*, p. 125ff.

14. An interesting aside here is that "a number of widows felt that their brothers-in-law to some extent continued the life or character of their husbands," Glick *et al.*, *ibid.*, p. 90. Also, "the husband's brother might be given his best suits and coats, not only because the brother was often about the same size, but also because he was felt to be the closest and the most deserving recipient," *ibid.*, p. 154.

15. Beverley Raphael, M.D., "Loss in Adult Life: The Death of a Spouse," in *The Anatomy of Bereavement, op. cit.*, p. 181.

16. *Ibid.*, p. 188.

17. *Ibid.*, p. 190.

18. *Ibid.*, p. 194.

19. Found in Alfred Allan Lewis and Barrier Berns, *op. cit.*, pp. 31-32.

Chapter 6

1. Gale D. Webbe. *The Night and Nothing*. New York: Seabury Press, 1964, p. 109. I am indebted here to M. Scott Peck, M.D. *People of the Lie: The Hope for Healing Human Evil.* New York: Simon & Schuster, Inc. (A Touchstone Book), 1983, p. 269.

2. Francis Kelly Nemeck. *Receptivity*. New York: Vantage Press, 1985, p. 100.

Chapter 7

1. John Gillespie Magee, Jr., "High Flight," *New Horizons: An Anthology of Short Poems for Senior Students*. Ed. by Bert Case Diltz. Toronto: McClelland & Stewart Limited Publishers, 1954, p. 216. This is the famous poem, quoted by the late President Ronald Regan, on the death of the astronauts, and contains such precious lines as: "Oh, I have slipped the surly bonds of earth and danced the skies on laughter-silvered wings," and ends with "put out my hand and touched the face of God."

Chapter 14

1. "Salvation means precisely the ultimate validity of our real self-understanding and free self-realization before God. It is the confirmation of our way of understanding ourselves and what we have chosen to be ... in ourselves," Anne E. Carr, "Starting With the Human," in Leo J. O'Donovan (Ed.). *A World of Grace*. New York: Seabury Press (A Crossroad Book), 1980, p. 26.

2. Jane Burgess Kohn and Willard K. Kohn, *op. cit.*, p. 86.

3. Anne E. Carr, *op. cit.*, p. 24; also, "The person who from early years has felt emotionally secure is able to meet the most disconcerting experiences with a measure

of inner adequacy that serves him well," in Edgar N. Jackson. *Understanding Grief. Its Roots, Dynamics, and Treatment*, *op. cit.*, p. 37; and again, "Emotional maturity is the best assurance for meeting stress with competence," *ibid.*, p. 43. Finally, "... our capacity for being present to ourselves [is] ... that basic characteristic which makes human existence spiritual existence," in William V. Dych, "Theology in a New Key," in Leo J. O'Donovan (Ed.), *op. cit.*, p. 5.

4. Even though every human being is a radical questioner, not everyone takes this inner calling to search in an in-depth way. From a modern existentialist, process, and theological point of view, we are the result of the decisions in our life. *I am* the sum total of my choices. However, we are also aware of the key Jungian insight of the self-realization of the unconscious that Dr. Anthony Stevens, the noted British medical researcher has outlined in his book *Archetypes. A Natural History of the Self*. New York: Quill (Wm. Morrow & Co., Inc.), 1982, p. 141. Dr. Carl Jung, in his *Memories, Dreams, Reflections* (recorded and edited by Aniela Jaffe. London: Collins and Routledge & Kegan Paul, 1963, p. 3) said that "everything in the unconscious seeks outward manifestation, and the personality too desires to evolve out of its unconscious conditions to experience itself as a whole." In another place, Jung writes that "the Self, like the unconscious is an *a priori* existent out of which the ego evolves. It is ... an unconscious prefiguration of the ego. *It is not I who create myself, rather I happen to myself*" -- *Collected Works*. Vol. 11. Bollingen Series XX. 3rd Printing. Princeton, New Jersey: Princeton University Press, 1975, par. 391, *italics mine*.

Dr. Stevens (above) points out that Jung, with this last statement in particular, put traditional psychology on its head! Jung proposed a Copernican revolution for psychology. This is an exceedingly important point, in view of what I write in the chapter about one creating oneself. The true reality is that the inner Self is the *Centre*, and the ego is the *satellite*. The centre of the personality is the Self, not the ego or conscious personality. The ego is often under the illusion that it thinks *it* is the centre! The ego is the "executive assistant" to the inner Self. From "out here" — the external world — it looks *as though* I am creating myself by myself. However, on a deep soul level, *I am being created* by the deepest interiority of my personality: by the Self, or by God. We are co-creators. T h i s insight about life is also congruent with what we have been saying about death all along: as we undergo life, we also undergo death; as life happens to us, so death happens to us; as we happen most especially to ourselves (to quote Jung) in life, so we happen to ourselves in death.

5. Anne E. Carr, *op. cit.*, p. 26.

6. Martin Buber. *I and Thou*. Tr. by Walter Kaufman. New York: Charles Scribner Sons, 1970.

7. The word "grace" has specific theological meanings if one reads theological treatises (cf. Leon-Dufour, Xavier. *Dictionary of Biblical Theology*. New York: Desclée, 1967, pp. 191ff.), but I believe it does not violate theological thought to see God's grace as God's relationship, first in the Godhead, and then within each of us; cf. also Juan Luis Secundo. *Grace and the Human Condition*. Vol. II. *A Theology for Artisans of*

a New Humanity Series. New York: Maryknoll, 1973.

8. The original quote was from St. Iranaeus, the early church Father, "God's glory is man fully alive"!

9. Paul Tillich, the late, but noted, Protestant theologian's expression; cf. *Systematic Theology.* Vol. I. Chicago: University of Chicago Press, pp. 112, 116-117, 155-158.

10. Edgar N. Jackson. *The Many Faces of Grief, op. cit.,* p. 148. Dr. Jackson is here making a reference to Henry Margenau, the Yale physicist. See page 2 of this book.

11. 1 John 4:8.

12. *Op. cit.,* p. 146.

13. Anne E. Carr, *op. cit.,* p. 20; also, "The world imitates God, and it does so because human beings find it finally insufficient to answer their questions... The drive of the mind is the anticipatory experience of God, because the drive of the mind is for a coherence that 'makes sense' out of everything... the mind moves toward reality and finds that it is finally and radically mystery," Michael J. Buckley, *op. cit.,* p. 34, 35.

14. Michael J. Buckley, "Within the Holy Mystery," in Leo J. O'Donovan (Ed.), *op. cit.,* p. 37; also, "Our experience of the finite world opens us to a horizon which ever recedes as we move through the finite; there is always a 'more' to be known and to be loved and to be lived. We are aware of it, but can never reach it; it is there, but it ever exceeds our grasp... This transcendence brings us not to a content of knowledge which we grasp, but to an absolute question." in William V. Dych, "A Theology in a New Key," in Leo J. O'Donovan (Ed.), *op. cit.,* p. 9.

15. Thomas Merton, the late Trappist monk [+1968], has these beautiful words to say from a talk he gave, "A Life Free From Care," when he moved into his hermitage: "Life is this simple ... It is care," in Jim Forest, "Various Identities: Review of *The Seven Mountains of Thomas Merton* by Michael Mott," *The Merton Seasonal of Bellarmine College,* Vol. 10, No. 1, Winter 1985, p. 18; see also Appendix B, "Care of the Bereaved." In another place Merton wrote the following lines as well (*The Way of Chuang Tzu.* New York: New Directions, 1965, p. 57): "The Master came at his right time ... Here is how the ancients said all this in four words: 'God cuts the thread'."

16. *Op. cit.,* p. 236.

17. Quoted in Carrol E. Simcox (Ed.), *op. cit.,* p. 231.

18. Jane Burgess Kohn and Willard K. Kohn, *op. cit.,* p. 96.

19. Alfred Allan Lewis and Barrie Berns, *op. cit.,* p. 49.

20. Carroll E. Simcox (Ed.), *op. cit.,* p. 108.

21. No. 139 of his *Pensees* of 1670. Jean de la Bryere wrote also, "All men's misfortunes spring from their hatred of being alone," quoted in Carroll E. Simcox (Ed.), *ibid.,* p. 108.

22. Edwin Shneidman, Ph.D. *Death: Current Perspectives, op. cit.,* pp. 449-450.

BIBLIOGRAPHY

Abrams, Ruth. *Not Alone With Cancer*. Springfield, llinois: Charles C. Thomas, 1974.

Abrahamsson, Hane. *The Origin of Death: Studies in African Mythology*. Uppsala, 1957.

Aries, Phillipe. *The Hour of Our Death*. New York: Alfred A. Knopf, 1981.

_____. *Western Attitudes Toward Death*. Baltimore, Md.: John Hopkins University Press, 1974.

Athearn, Louise Montague. *What Every Formerly Married Woman Should Know: Answers to the Most Intimate Questions Formerly Married Women Ask*. New York: D. McKay Co., 1973.

Averill, J., "Grief: Its Nature and Significance," *Psychological Bulletin*, Vol. 70, 1968, pp. 721-48.

Baab, O.J., "Widow," *The Interpreter's Dictionary of the Bible*, Vol. 4. New York: Abingdon Press, 1962, pp. 842-843.

Bak, R.C., "Being in Love and Object Loss," *International Journal of Psychoanalysis*, Vol. 54, 1973, pp. 1-8.

Bankoff, Elizabeth A., "Effects of Friendship Support on the Psychological Well-Being of Widows," *Research in the Interweave of Social Roles*, Vol. 2, 1981, pp. 109-139.

Barrett, C.J., "The Effectiveness of Widow's Groups in Facilitating Change," *Journal of Consulting and Clinical Psychology*, Vol. 46, No. 1, 1978, pp. 20-31.

Barrett, Carol J. and Karen M. Schneweiss, "An Empirical Search for Stages of Widowhood," *Omega: Journal of Death & Dying*, Vol. 11, No. 2, 1980-81, pp. 97-104.

Bartlett, John (Ed.). *Familiar Quotations*. 10th. Edition. New York: The Review of Reviews Co., 1916, "Publius Syrus, 42 B.P.," pp. 894-900.

Becker, Ernest. *The Denial of Death*. New York: Free Press, 1973.

Benton, Richard G. *Death and Dying. Principles and Practices in Patient Care*. Toronto: Van Nostrand Reinhold Company, 1978.

Bequaert, Lucia H. *Single Women: Alone and Together*. Boston: Beacon Press, 1976.

Bernardo, Felix M., "Widowhood Status in the United States: Perspectives on a Neglected Aspect of the Family's Life-Cycle," *The Family Coordinator*, Vol. 17, 1968, pp. 191-203.

Blau, David, "On Widowhood: Discussion," *Journal of Geriatric Psychiatry*, Vol. 8, No. 1, 1975, pp. 29-40.

Blauner Robert, "Death and Social Structure," in *Death and Identity*, ed. Robert Fulton. Bowie, Md.: Charles Press, 1976.

Bornstein, Philipp W., et al., "The Depression of Widowhood After Thirteen Months," *British Journal of Psychiatry*, Vol. 122, No. 570, 1973, pp. 561-566.

Boros, L. *The Mystery of Death*. New York: Herder and Herder, 1965.

Boulding, Elise. *The Underside of History*. Boulder: Westview Press, 1976.

Bowlby, J., *Loss: Sadness and Depression*. Vol. 3 in Attachment and Loss. London: Hogarth Press, 1980.

Boyar, J.I. *The Construction and Partial Validation of a Scale for the Measurement of the Fear of Death*. Rochester, New York: University of Rochester, 1964.

Brain, Robert. *Friends and Lovers*. New York: Basic Books, 1976.

Buber, Martin. *I and Thou*. Tr. by Walter Kaufman. New York: Charles Scribners Sons, 1970.

Buckley, Michael J., "Within the Holy Mystery," in Leo J. O'Donovan (Ed.). *A World of Grace*. New York: The Seabury Press (A Crossroad Book), 1980, pp. 31-49.

Butterworth, Eric. *Spiritual Economics. The Principles and Process of True Prosperity*. Unity Village, Missouri, (1998) 2003.

Caine, Lynn. *Lifelines*. Garden City, New York: Doubleday & Co., Inc., 1978.

_____. *Widow*. New York: Harper & Row, 1975.

Caplan, G. *Principles of Preventive Psychiatry*. New York: Basic Books, 1964.

Carey, Raymond G., "Weathering Widowhood: Problems and Adjustment of the Widowed During the First Year," *Omega: Journal of Death & Dying*, Vol. 10, No. 2, 1979-80, pp. 163-174.

Carr, Anne E., "Starting with the Human," in Leo J. O'Donovan (Ed.). *A World of Grace*. New York: The Seabury Press (A Crossroad Book), 1980, pp. 17-30.

Charmaz, Kathy. *The Social Reality of Death*. Reading, Mass.: Addison-Wesley, 1980.

Choron, Jacques. *Death and Western Thought*. New York: Macmillan, 1970.

Church, Dawson and Dr. Alan Sherr (Eds). *The Heart of the Healer*. New York, New York: Aslan Publishing, 1987.

Clayton, Paula J., "The Clinical Morbidity of the First Year of Bereavement: A Review," *Comprehensive Psychiatry*, Vol. 14, No. 2, 1973, pp. 151-157.

_____, "The Depression of Widowhood," *British Journal of Psychiatry*, Vol. 121, 1972, pp. 71-78.

Clayton, Paula J., James A. Halikas, William L. Maurice and Eli Robins, "Anticipatory Grief and Widowhood," *British Journal of Psychiatry*, Vol. 122, No. 566, 1973, pp. 47-51.

Clayton, Paula J., J.A. Halikas and W.L. Maurice, "The Bereavement of the Widowed," *Diseases of the Nervous System*, Vol. 32, No. 9, 1971, pp. 592-604.

Closs, A., "Death (Primitive Concepts of)," *New Catholic Encyclopaedia*, Volume 14. Toronto: McGraw-Hill Book Co., 1967, pp. 686-687.

Codrington, R.H. *The Melanesians*, London: Oxford, 1895.

Collet, L.J. and D. Lester, "The Fear of Death and the Fear of Dying," *Journal of Psychology*, Vol. 72, 1969, pp. 179-181.

Conroy, Richard C., "Widows and Widowhood," *New York State Journal of Medicine*, Vol. 77, No. 3, 1977, pp. 357-360.

Cousins, N. *The Celebration of Life: A Dialogue on Immortality and Infinity.* New York: Harper & Row, 1974.

Darwin, Charles. *The Expression of Emotion in Men and Animals.* London: Murray, 1872.

Dean, S., "Metapsychiatry: The Confluence of Psychiatry and Mysticism," in S. Dean (Ed.). *Psychiatry and Mysticism.* Chicago: Nelson-Hall, 1975, pp. 3-18.

Dembitz, Lewis N., "Widow," in Isadore Singer, PhD. *The Jewish Encyclopaedia.* Volume 12. New York: Funk and Wagnalls Company, 1912, pp. 514-515.

Des Pres, Terrence. *The Survivor.* New York: Pocket Books, 1977.

Dessonville, Connie L., "The Role of Anticipatory Bereavement in the Adjustment to Widowhood in Older Women," *Dissertation Abstracts International,* Vol. 43, No. 12-B, 1983, p. 4139.

Dickstein, L.S., "Death Concern: Measurement and Correlates," *Psychological Reports,* Vol. 30, 1972, pp. 563-571.

Dych, William V., "Theology in a New Key," in Leo J. O'Donovan (Ed.). *A World of Grace.* New York: The Seabury Press (A Crossroad Book), 1980, pp. 1-16.

Eager, Geo. B., "Widow," in James Orr, John L. Nuelsen, Edgar Y. Mullins (Eds.). *The International Standard Bible Enclyclopaedia.* Vol. V. Grand Rapids, Michigan: Wm. B. Eerdmans Publishing Co., 1978, 3084.

Eddy, James and Wesley Alles. *Death Education.* St. Louis: C.V. Mosby, 1983.

Edwards, Paul, "My Death," *The Encyclopaedia of Philosophy.* Volume 5. New York: Macmillan Publishing Co., Inc., and The Free Press, 1972, 416-419.

Eliade, Mircea. *A History of Religious Ideas.* Volume I. *From the Stone Age to the Eleusinian Mysteries.* Chicago: University of Chicago Press, 1978.

_____, "Mythologies of Death: An Introduction," *Occultism, Witchcraft, and Cultural Fashions.* Chicago: University of Chicago Press, 1976, pp. 32-46.

_____. *Patterns in Comparative Religion.* New York: Sheed and Ward, 1958.

_____. *Shamanism. Archaic Techniques of Ecstasy.* Bollingen Series LXXV. Princeton, New Jersey: Princeton University Press, 1964.

Elliot, Gil. *The Twentieth Century Book of the Dead.* New York: Ballantine Books (a Division of Random House, Inc. and Penguin Books, Ltd.), 1972.

Engel, G.L., "Is Grief a Disease?" *Psychosomatic Medicine,* Vol. 23, 1961, pp. 18-22.

Ewens, James Patricia Herrington. *Hospice.* Santa Fe, New Mexico: Beer & Co., 1982.

Farrrell James J. *Inventing the American Way of Death, 1830-1920.* Philadelphia, Pennsylvania: Temple University Press, 1980.

Feifel, Herman. *New Means of Death.* New York: McGraw-Hill, 1977.

Feifel, Herman (Ed.). *The Meaning of Death.* New York: McGraw-Hill, 1959.

Forest, Jim, "Various Identities: Review of The Seven Mountains of Thomas Merton by Michael Mott," *The Merton Seasonal of Bellarmine College*, Vol. 10, No. 1, Winter 1985, pp. 16-18.

Fowler, James, "Stages of Faith," *Psychology Today*, Vol. 17, No. 11, November 1983, pp. 56-62.

Fox, Matthew, "Hospice: Denying the Denial of Death," *Creation*, Vol. 2, No. 3, July/August 1986, pp. 26-28.

Frazer, J.G. *The Belief in Immortality*. 3 Vols. London, 1913, Vol. I, pp. 74-75.

Freud, Sigmund, "Mourning and Melancholia," (1917) *Collected Papers*. New York: Basic Books, 1959, Vol. 4, pp. 152-170.

Fulton, Robert, Eric Markusen, Greg Owen and James L. Scheiber. *Death and Dying: Challenge and Change*. San Francisco: Boyd & Fraser, 1981.

Gallagher, Dolores E., "Psychological Factors Affection Adaptation to Bereavement in the Elderly," *International Journal of Aging & Human Development*, Vol. 14, No. 2, 1981-82, pp. 79-95.

Garnett, Richard, Leon Vallee and Alois Brandle (Eds.), "Bacon's Apothegms," *The Universal Anthology*. Vol. 13. New York: Merrill & Baker, 1889, pp. 263-277.

Gatch, Milton, "The Biblical Tradition," in *Death: Meaning and Morality in Christian Thought and Contemporary Culture*. New York: The Seabury Press, 1969, pp. 45-58.

Gennep, Arnold Van. *The Rites of Passage*. Chicago: University of Chicago Press, 1960.

Gill, Derek. *Quest: The Life of Elizabeth Kübler-Ross*. New York: Harper & Row, 1980.

Glaser, Barney and Anselm Strauss. *Awareness of Dying*. Chicago: Aldine, 1965.

Glick, Ira O., Robert S. Weiss, and C. Murray Parkes. *The First Year of Bereavement*. Toronto: John Wiley Sons, 1974.

Gorer, G. *Death, Grief and Mourning*. New York: Doubleday & Co., Inc., 1965.

_____, "The Pornography of Death," in W. Phillips, P. Rahv (Eds.). *Modern Writings*. New York: McGraw-Hill, 1959.

Greenblatt, M., "The Grieving Spouse," *American Journal of Psychiatry*, Vol. 135, 1978, pp. 43-46.

Handel, P.J., "The Relationship Between Subjective Expectancy, Death Anxiety and General Anxiety," *Journal of Clinical Psychology*, Vol. 25, 1969, pp. 39-42.

Harvey, Carol D. and Howard M. Bahr, "Widowhood, Morale, and Affiliation," *Journal of Marriage and the Family*, February 1974, pp. 97-106.

Hauser, Marilyn J., "Bereavement Outcome for Widows," *Journal of Psychosocial Nursing and Mental Health Services*, Vol. 21, No. 9, 1983, pp. 22-31.

_____, "Profiles of Widowhood: Characteristics of Widows Related to Bereavement Outcome Scores," *Dissertation Abstracts International*, Vol. 43, No. 12-B, 1983, p. 4147.

Held, M.L., "Widow, (In the Bible)," *New Catholic Encyclopaedia*, Volume 14. Toronto: McGraw-Hill Book Co., 1967, pp. 903-904.

Herzog, Edgar. *Psyche and Death. Death-Demons in Folklore, Myths and Modern Dreams*. Dallas, Texas: Spring Publications, 1983.

_____, "The Horror of Death," in *Psyche and Death. Death-Demons in Folklore, Myths and Modern Dreams*. Dallas, Texas: Spring Publications, 1983, pp. 21-27.

Heyman, Dorothy K. and Daniel T. Gianturco, "Long-Term Adaptation by the Elderly to Bereavement," *Journal of Gerontology*, Vol. 28, No. 3, 1973, pp. 359-362.

Hinde, R.A. *Towards Understanding Relationships*. London: Academic Press, 1978.

Hinton, John. *Dying*. London: Penguin Books (Pelican Original 1967), 1967.

_____, "The Influences of Previous Personality on Reactions to Having Terminal Cancer," *Omega: Journal of Death & Dying*, Vol. 6, No. 2, 1975, pp. 95-111.

Humane Medicine. A Journal of the Art and Science of Medicine. c/o Toronto Western Hospital, 399 Bathurst Street, Toronto, Ontario M5T 2S8 Canada, (416) 364-9974.

Illich, Ivan. *Medical Nemesis*. New York: Bantam Books, 1976.

Jackson, Edgar N. *The Many Faces of Grief*. Nashville, Tennessee: The Parthenon Press, 1978.

_____. *Understanding Grief: Its Roots, Dynamics, and Treatment*. Nashville, Tennessee: Parthenon Press (1957), 1978.

Jamieson, H., "Widow," in Merrill C. Tenney (Ed.). *The Zondervan Pictorial Encyclopaedia of the Bible*. Volume V. Grand Rapids, Michigan: Zondervan Publishing House, 1977, pp. 928-929.

Joyce, Christopher, "A Time for Grieving," *Psychology Today*, Vol. 18, No. 11, November 1984, pp. 42-46.

Jung, Carl. *Collected Works*. Vol. 11. Bollingen Series XX. 3rd. Printing. Princeton, New Jersey: Princeton University Press, 1975, par. 391.

_____. *Memories, Dreams, Reflections*. Recorded and edited by Aniela Jaffe. London: Collins and Routledge & Kegan Paul, 1963.

Kahana, Ralph J., 'On Widowhood: Introduction," *Journal of Geriatric Psychiatry*, Vol. 8, No. 1, 19175, pp. 5-8.

Kastenbaum, Robert J. *Death, Society and Human Experience*. St. Louis: C.V. Mosby, 1977, pp. 209-213.

Kastenbaum, Robert J. and Ruth Aisenberg. *The Psychology of Death*. New York: Springer, 1972.

Klerman, G.L., J.E. Izen, "The Effects of Bereavement and Grief on Physical Health and General Well Being," *Advances in Psychosomatic Medicine*, Vol. 9, 1977, pp. 63-68.

Kohn, Jane Burgess and Willard K. Kohn. *The Widower. What He Faces, What He Feels, What He Needs*. Boston: Beacon Press, 1978.

Kostenbaum, Peter. *Is There an Answer to Death?* Englewood Cliffs, New Jersey: Prentice-Hall, 1976.

K?bler-Ross, Elizabeth. *On Death and Dying*. New York: Macmillan, 1969.

Léon-Dufour, Xavier. *Dictionary of Biblical Theology*. New York: Desclée Co., 1967.

Lester, D., "Experimental and Correlational Studies of the Fear of Death," *Psychological Bulletin*, Vol. 67, 1967, pp. 27-36.

Levin, Sidney, "On Widowhood: Discussion," *Journal of Geriatric Psychiatry*, Vol. 8, No. 1, 1975, pp. 57-59.

Levinson, Jay I., "An Investigation of Existential Vacuum in Grief Via Widowhood," *Dissertation Abstracts International*, Vol. 41, No. 2-B, 1980, p. 694.

Levy-Bruhl, Lucien. *Primitive Mentality*. Tr. Lilian A. Clare. London, 1923.

Lewis, C.S. *A Grief Observed*. New York: The Seabury Press, 1961.

Lewis, Alfred Allan and Barrie Berns. *Three Out of Four Wives. Widowhood in America*. New York: Macmillan Publishing Co., Inc., 1975.

Lifton, R.J. and E. Olson, "The Human Meaning of Total Disaster: The Buffalo Creek Experience," *Psychiatry*, Vol. 39, 1976, pp. 1-18.

_____. *Living and Dying*. New York: Bantam, 1974.

Lindemann, E., "Symptomology and Management of Acute Grief," *American Journal of Psychiatry*, Vol. 101, 1944, pp. 141-148.

Loflan, Lyn H. *The Craft of Dying*. Beverly Hills, California: Sage, 1978.

Lopata, Helena Z., "Living Through Widowhood," *Psychology Today*, Vol. 7, No. 2, 1973, pp. 87-92.

_____, "On Widowhood: Discussion," *Journal of Geriatric Psychiatry*, Vol. 8, No. 1, 1975, pp. 57-59.

_____, "The Widow in America: A Study of the Older Widow," cassette tape #0565694, Seneca College [Leslie Campus], North York, Ontario, Canada.

_____. *Widowhood in an American City*. Cambridge, Mass.: Schenkman, 1973.

Lopata, Helena Z., Heinemann, Gloria D. and Joanne Baum, , "Loneliness: Antecedents and Coping Strategies in the Lives of Widows," in Letitia Anne Peplau, Daniel Perlman (Eds.). *Loneliness: A Sourcebook of Current Research and Therapy*. Toronto: John Wiley and Sons (A Wiley-Interscience Publication), 1982, pp. 310-326.

Madison, D.C. and A. Viola, "The Health of Widows in the Year Following Bereavement," *Journal of Psychosomatic Research*, Vol. 12, 1968, pp. 297-306.

Madison, D.C. and W.L. Walker, "Factors Affecting the Outcome of Conjugal Bereavement," *British Journal of Psychiatry*, Vol. 113, 1967, pp. 1057-1067.

Magee, John Gillespie, Jr., "High Flight," in *New Horisons: An Anthology of Short Poems for Senior Students*, ed. by Bert Case Diltz. Toronto: McClelland & Steward Limited Publishers, 1954.

Mandelbaum, David G., "Social Uses of Funeral Rites," in Herman Feifel (Ed.). *The Meaning of Death*. New York: McGraw-Hill, 1959.

Marris, Peter. *Loss and Change*. London: Routledge & Kegan Paul, 1974.

_____. *Widows and Their Families*. London: Routledge & Kegan Paul, 1958.

Martin, W., "Waiting for the End," *The Atlantic Monthly*, June 1982, pp. 31-37.

McDermott, Brian O., "The Bonds of Freedom," in Leo J. O'Donovan (Ed.). *A World of Grace*. New York: The Seabury Press (A Crossroad Book), 1980, pp. 50-63.

McDermott, N. and S. Cobb, "A Psychiatric Survey of 50 Cases of Bronchial Asthma," *Psychosomatic Medicine*, Vol. 1, 1939, pp. 201-204.

McKenzie, John L., "Widow," *Dictionary of The Bible*. Milwaukee: The Bruce Publishing Co., 1965, p. 927.

Merton, Thomas. *Spiritual Direction and Meditation*. Collegeville, Minn.: Liturgical Press, 1960.

Mitford, Jessica. *The American Way of Death*. Greenwich, Conn.: Fawcett, 1979.

Munley, Anne. *The Hospice Alternative. A New Context for Death and Dying*. New York: Basic Books, Inc., Publishers, 1983.

Murray, Henry A. *Explorations in Personality*. London & New York: Oxford University Press, 1938.

Nelson, L.D. and C.C. Nelson, "A Factor Analytic Inquiry into the Multi-dimensionality of Death Anxiety," *Omega: Journal of Death & Dying*, Vol. 6, 1975, pp. 171-178.

Nemeck, Francis Kelly. *Receptivity*. New York: Vantage Press, 1985.

Nemeck, Francis Kelly and Marie Theresa Coombs. *The Way of Spiritual Direction*. Wilmington, Delaware: Michael Glazier, 1985.

O'Donovan, Leo J. (Ed.). *A World of Grace*. New York: The Seabury Press (A Crossroad Book), 1980.

O'Meara, Thomas F., "A History of Grace," in Leo J. O'Donovan. *A World of Grace*. New York: The Seabury Press (A Crossroad Book), pp. 76-91.

Olson, Robert C., "Death," *The Encyclopaedia of Theology*, Vol. I. New York: Macmillan Publishing Co., Inc. and The Free Press, 1972, pp. 307-309.

Parkes, C.M. *Bereavement: Studies of Grief in Adult Life*. London: Tavistock, 1972.

_____, "Psychological Aspects," *The Management of Terminal Disease*. London: Edward Arnold, 1978.

_____, "Psychosocial Transitions: A Field for Study," *Social Science and Medicine*, Vol. 5, 1971, pp. 101-115.

Parkes, C.M., B. Benjamin and R.G. Fitzgerald, "Broken Heart: A Statistical Study of Increased Mortality Among Widowers," *British Medical Journal*, Vol. 1, 1969, pp. 740-743.

Parrinder, E.G., "God in African Mythology," in Joseph M. Kitagawa, Charles H. Long (Eds.). *Myths and Symbols. Studies in Honor of Mircea Eliade*. Chicago: The University of Chicago Press, 1971, pp. 111-125.

Parrish-Harra, C.A. *A New Age Handbook on Death and Dying*. Marina del Rey, California: De Vorss, 1982.

Parsons, T., "Death in American Society: A Brief Working Paper," *American Behavioral Scientist*, Vol. 6, 1963, pp. 61-65.

Pascal, Blaise. *Les Pensées*. 1670. No. 139.

Peplau, Letitia Anne and Daniel Perlman, (Eds.). *Loneliness: A Sourcebook of Current Research and Therapy*. Toronto: John Wiley & Sons (A Wiley-Interscience Publication), 1982.

Pincus, L. *Death in the Family*. New York: Random House, 1974.

Powell, John. *Fully Human. Fully Alive*. Allen, Texas: Argus Communications, 1976.

Rahner, Karl, "Death," Sacramentum Mundi. *An Encyclopaedia of Theology*. Volume II. New York: Herder & Herder, 1968, pp. 58-62.

_____. *The Practice of Faith*. A Handbook of Contemporary Spirituality. New York: Crossroad, 1984.

Raphael, Beverley, "Human Bonds and Death: The Background to Bereavement," in *The Anatomy of Bereavement*. New York: Basic Books Publishers, 1983, pp. 3-32.

_____, "Loss in Adult Life: The Death of a Spouse," in *The Anatomy of Bereavement*. New York: Basic Books Publishers, 1983, pp. 177-228.

_____, "Personal Disaster," *Australian and New Zealand Journal of Psychiatry*, Vol. 15, 1981, pp. 183-198.

_____. *The Anatomy of Bereavement*. New York: Basic Books Publishers, 1983.

_____, "The Experience of Bereavement: Separation and Mourning," in *The Anatomy of Bereavement*. New York: Basic Books Publishers, 1983, pp. 33-73.

Reid, Janice, "A Time to Live, a Time to Grieve: Patterns and Processes of Mourning Among the Yolngu of Australia," *Cultural Medical Psychiatry*, Vol. 3, No. 4, 1979, pp. 319-346.

Ring, Kenneth. *Heading Toward Omega. In Search of the Meaning of the Near-Death Experience*. New York: William Morrow & Co., Inc., 1984.

Rock, Michael E. *Grippings: Reflections on the Human Journey*. Unionville, Ontario: Oak Publications, 1987. Out of print.

_____. *Reflections: The Human Journey*. Unionville, Ontario: Oak Publications, 1985. Out of print.

Rosenblatt, P.C., R.P. Walsh and D.A. Jackson. *Grief and Mourning in Cross-Cultural Perspective*. New Haven: HRAF Press, 1976.

Ross, C.W. *Death Concerns and Responses to Dying Patients' Statements*. University of Missouri and Columbia Doctoral Dissertation. Xerox available from Xerox University Microfilms, Ann Arbor, Michigan, 1976.

Sarnoff, I. And S.E. Corwin, "Castration Anxiety and the Fear of Death," *Journal of Personality*, Vol. 27, 1959, pp. 374-385.

Schlaffer, Edit and Cheryl Bernard, "The Survivors: Some Hypotheses on the Significance for Older Women of the Loss of Spouse," *Zeitschrift für Gerontologie*, Vol. 11, No. 1, 1978, pp. 90-97. [in German]

Schlesinger, B., "The Widow and Widower and Remarriage: Selected Findings," *Omega: Journal of Death & Dying*, Vol. 2, 1971, pp. 10-18.

Schneiderman, E.S., "On the Deromanticization of Death," *American Journal of Psychotherapy*, Vol. 25, No. 1, 1971, pp. 4-7.

Schulz, Richard and David Aderman, "Clinical Research and the Stages of Dying," *Omega: Journal of Death & Dying*, Vol. 5, 1974, pp. 137-144.

Scot, Reginald. *Discoveries of Witchcraft*. Yorkshire, U.K.: Rowmand & Littlefield, 1973.

Secundo, Juan Luis. *Grace and the Human Condition*. Vol. II. *A Theology for Artisans of a New Humanity*. New York: Maryknoll, 1973.

Shneidman, Edwin. *Death: Current Perspectives*. Jason Aronson, Inc. Published in paperback by Mayfield Publishing Co., 285 Hamilton Avenue, Palo Alto, California 94301, 1976.

_____, "Death Work and Stages of Dying," in *Death: Current Perspectives*. Jason Aronson, Inc. Published in paperback by Mayfield Publishing Co., 285 Hamilton Avenue, Palo Alto, California 94301, 1976, 443-451.

_____, "Postvention and the Survivor-Victim," in *Deaths of Man*. New York: Quadrangle/The New York Times Book Co., 1973, reprinted in *Death: Current Perspectives*. Jason Aronson, Inc. Published in paperback by Mayfield Publishing Co., 285 Hamilton Avenue, Palo Alto, California 94301, 1976,pp. 343-355.

_____ *Voices of Death. Letters, Diaries and Other Personal Documents From People Facing Death That Provide Comforting Guidance for Each of Us*. New York: Harper & Row, Publishers, 1980.

Silverman, Phyllis R., "Widowhood and Preventive Intervention," *Family Co-ordinator*, Vol. 21, 1972, pp. 95-102.

Silverman, Phyllis R. and Adele Cooperband, "On Widowhood: Mutual Help and the Elderly Widow," *Journal of Geriatric Psychiatry*, Vol. 8, No. 1, 1975, pp. 9-27.

Silverman, Phyllis R., Dorothy MacKenzie, Mary Pettipas and Elizabeth Wilson (Eds.). *Helping Each Other In Widowhood*. New York, New York: Health Sciences Publishing Corp., 1974.

Simcox, Carrol E. (Ed.). *A Treasury of Quotations on Christian Themes*. New York: The Seabury Press (A Crossroad Book), 1975.

Singer, Cynthia M., "Correlates of Grief in Widowhood," *Dissertation Abstracts International*, Vol. 43, No. 4-B, 1982, pp. 1268-1269.

Standard, David E., "The Puritan Way of Death," in Fulton, Robert, Eric Markusen, Greg Owen and James L. Scheiber. *Death and Dying: Challenge and Change*. San Francisco: Boyd & Fraser, 1981.

Scheiber, Jane L. *Death and Dying: Challenge and Change*. San Francisco: Boyd & Frazer, 1981.

Steele, R.L., "Dying, Death and Bereavement Among the Maya Indians of Mesoamerica," *American Psychologist*, Vol. 32, Vol. 12, 1977, pp. 1060-1068.

Stevens, Anthony. *Archetypes. A Natural History of the Self*. New York: Quill (Wm. Morrow & Co., Inc.), 1982.

Sudnow, David. *Passing On: The Social Organization of Dying*. Englewood Cliffs, New Jersey: Prentice-Hall, 1967.

Sunder, Das, S., "Grief and the Immanent Threat of Non-Being," *British Journal of Psychiatry*, Vol. 118, 1971, pp. 545-568.

Tatelbaum, Judy. *The Courage To Grieve*. New York: Lippincott & Crowell, Publishers, 1980.

Taylor, Jeremy. *The Rule and Exercise of Holy Dying*. New York: Arno Press, 1972.

Templer, D.I., "The Construction and Validation of a Death Anxiety Scale," *Journal of General Psychology*, Vol. 82, 1970, pp. 165-177.

The International Standard Bible Encyclopaedia. Edited by James Orr, et al. Grand Rapids, Michigan: Wm. B. Eerdmans Publishers Co., (1929), 1978, Vol. I-V.

Tillich, Paul. *Systematic Theology*. Vol. I. Chicago: University of Chicago Press, 1951.

Tolar, A. Unpublished Data, 1966. Cited in P.J. Handel, "The Relationship Between Subjective Expectancy, Death Anxiety and General Anxiety," *Journal of Clinical Psychology*, Vol. 25, 1969, pp. 39-42.

Towne, Neil and Ronald B. Adler. Looking Out/Looking In. 4th. Edition. Toronto: Holt, Rinehart, 1984.

Trombley, Eugene, "A Psychiatrist's Response to a Life-Threatening Illness," *Life-Threatening Behavior*, Vol. 2, No. 1, 1972, pp. 26-34.

Vachon, Mary S., "Identity Change Over the First Two Years of Bereavement: Social Relationships and Social Support in Widowhood," *Dissertation Abstracts International*, Vol. 40, No. 9-A, 1980, pp. 5205-5207.

Vachon, M., W. Lyall, J. Rogers, J., K. Freedman-Letofsky, K. and S. Freedman, "A Controlled Study of Self-Help Intervention for Widows," *American Journal of Psychiatry*, Vol. 137, 1980, pp. 1380-84.

Walker, Barbara G. *The Crone. Woman of Age, Wisdom, and Power*. San Francisco: Harper & Row, 1985.

Walls, Nanetta and Andrew W. Meyers, "Outcome in Group Treatments for Bereavement: Experimental Results and Recommendations for Clinical Practice," *International Journal of Mental Health*, Vol. 13, No. 3-4, 1984-85, pp. 126-147.

Warren, W.G. and P.N. Chopra, "An Australian Survey of Attitudes to Death," *Australian Journal of Social Issues*, Vol. 14, 1979, pp. 140-152.

Wass, Hannelore. *Dying: Facing the Facts*. Washington, D.C.: Hemisphere, 1976.

Weiss, Edwardo. *Principles of Psychodynamics*. New York: Grune & Stratton, Inc., 1950.

Weiss, R.S., "The Provisions of Social Relationships," in *Doing Unto Others*. Englewood Cliffs, New Jersey: Prentice-Hall, 1974.

"Widow, The," (Filmstrip). 2 rolls, colour, 35 mm. & 2 cassettes (2-track, 31 min. each). Irvine, California: Concept Media, 1979.

Williamson, John B., et al. *Aging and Society*. NY: Rinehart & Winston, 1980, pp. 333-35.

Woodfield, Robert L. and Linda L. Viney, "A Personal Construct Approach to the Conjugally Bereaved Woman," *Omega: Journal of Death & Dying*, Vol. 15, No. 1, 1984-85, pp. 1-13.

WYLIE, Betty Jane. *Beginnings: A Book for Widows*. Toronto: McClelland and Stewart Ltd., 1977.

"We become what we behold. We shape our tools and then our tools shape us."

— Marshall McLuhan (1911-1980)

WEBSITES: ADDITIONAL KEY RESOURCES

This page is not an endorsement of these websites,
simply a notational itemization for further follow-up to this book

1. "Widowhood and Starting Again": Personal Reflections by a Widow
    (http://www.wholefamily.com/about60plus/widowhood/)

2. "Widowhood": Dealing with the Loss and Grief of the Terminally Ill
    (http://relationshipdirectory.com/widowhood.html)

3. "Share Your Stories": The First Year After the Loss of a Partner
    (http://laurieannweis.com/)

4. "Expanding Your Horizons - Widowed Persons Service" (U.S.)
    (http://www.senioranswers.org/Pages/widowhood.htm)

5. "Eldercare, Critical Care, Death and Dying" (Canada)
    (http://www.thefuneraldirectory.com/links.html)

6. "How to Cope With Being Widowed"
    (http://seniors-site.com/widowm/coping.html)

7. "Widowhood: Consequences on Income for Senior Women" (Canada)
    (http://www.statcan.ca/english/research/11-621-MIE/11-621-MIE2004015.htm)

8. "Death of a Spouse: Financial Steps You Should Take" (U.S.)
    (http://www.gofso.com/Premium/LE/19_le_lo/fg/fg-Death_Spouse.html)

9. "Coping Resources - Death of a Spouse" (U.S.)
    (http://dying.about.com/od/deathofaspouse/)

10. "Share Grief Online"
    (http://www.sharegrief.com/phorum/read.php?f=1&i=709&t=696)

11. "Funeral Issues" (Canada)
    (http://www.everestofthunderbay.com/funeral_issues.html)
    (http://www.chapelridgefh.com/english/resources.htm)

12. "Funeral Issues" (U.S.)
    (http://endoflifecare.tripod.com/Caregiving/id92.html)

13. "Seniors Canada Online"
(http://www.seniors.gc.ca/scolPortSearchAZ.jsp?&font=0&lang=en&geo=0&keyword=Widowhood)

14. "Death, Dying and the Afterlife in Religion and Mythology"
(http://dying.about.com/od/deathinreligionandmyth/)

15. "Spirituality & Alternative Healing Articles"
(http://www.skdesigns.com/internet/articles/)

16. "Spiritual Care Resources"
(http://www.spcare.org/resources/)

17. "Death Related Weblinks"
(http://www.stolaf.edu/people/leming/death.html)

18. "Free Inspirational Resources"
(http://www.stolaf.edu/people/leming/death.html)

19. "Losing a Spouse: What Hurts and What Helps"
(http://mentalhealth.about.com/library/sci/1102/blspouse1102.htm)

20. "Free Mental Health Help" (U.S.)
(http://matthewleskobooks.com/grants_loans/MentalHealthHelp.htm)

21. "Self-Help Clearinghouses Across the World" (U.S., Canada, International)
(http://mentalhelp.net/selfhelp/selfhelp.php?id=859)

22. "What happens after death? The Ultimate Guide to Forensic Entomology"
(http://folk.uio.no/mostarke/forens_ent/afterdeath.shtml)

23. "Death: The Last Taboo"
(http://deathonline.net/what_happens/index.cfm)

24. "Death and Dying: Stages and Issues"
(http://www.drugs.com/CG/DEATH_AND_DYING.html)

25. "Resources for Widows"
(http://www.ability.org.uk/widows.html)

26. "Resources on Death, Dying, and Grief"
(http://www.rowinsky.com/ResourcesOnDeathDyingGrief.htm)

27. "Widowhood and Myths: Articles"
    (http://widows-and-widowers.com/library/Articles/articles07.htm)

28. "Hospice Foundation of America" (U.S.)
    (http://www.hospicefoundation.org/)

29. "The Canadian Hospice Palliative Care Association" (Canada)
    (http://www.chpca.net/)

30. "Young Widows and Widowers"
    (http://www.youngwidowsandwidowers.com/RelatedLinks.htm)

31. "Juorney of Hearts: Articles on Grief"
    (http://www.journeyofhearts.org/jofh)

32. "Hospice Care Ring"
    (http://www.ringsurf.com/netring?ring=hospicecare;action=list)

33. "This Old Lawyer: Talks on Widowhood"
    (http://www.thisoldlawyer.com/frontpage.asp?subject=6)

INDEX

pocket, psychological, 28
pornography of death, 13
position, personal, 59
positive, thinking, 13; ferret out, 201
posterity, 24; of tribe, 14
potency, psychological, 29; potential, 266
poverty, 39
power, 152; base, 163; transformative, 230
practical realm, 120
praise, 90
Presbyterians, 84
presence, 77, 80. 101, 115; God's, 24, 79, 81
pressure, 218
primitives, 18
prince, 255
priorities, 162
privacy, 89, 121
privileged person, 17
problems, 239, 241, 242, 247, 248; emotional,
214; solvers, 21; social, 22
process, grieving, 118; 119
productivity, 21
projection, 11; self, xvi; psychological, 7;
recollection of, 8
prosperity, 203
protection, 38
Psalm, 23rd, 87
psyche, 33, 67, 256; psychic, 138; defense, 1;
isolation, 21
psychological, feet, 32, 35; pocket, xv, 28; of
other, 259; potency, 29; psychologist, 213;
behavioural, 145; soul, 145
Publicius Syrus, 4
punishment for sin, 16
purpose, x, 66, 163
PWP, 147

Q

quality, control, 262; existence, 27; in
relationships, 267; of life, x, 10, 16; of living,
15, 24; of relationships, 22; questions, xiii,
85, 264; and depth, 62

R

Rahner, Karl, 20
randomness, 126
rapaciousness, 66
rationalism, 21
RCMP, 46
reaction, pathological, 36
real doll, 237
reality 33, 34, 36, 40, 66, 68, 84, 115, 142, 161,
186, 230, 256, 264, 266; of death, 13, 24, 34;
foothills of, 131; living, 118; ugly, 117;
ultimate, 2
realization, 162, 258
realness, 8
reap what we sow, 96
reason, 259
reassurance, xiv, 6
recognition, 90
recoil phase, 31
recollection of projections, 8, 9, 11
recovery, emotional, 39; social, 39
refinement, 14
reflection, 157, 158
Reflections: The Human Journey, 53, 201
regression, xvi,
reincarnation, 18
relationship, 6, 7, 11, 24, 27, 35, 36, 50, 54,
100, 130, 132, 202, 219; dynamics, 145;
people, 6; relatedness, 6, 131; social, 34,
179;
relatives, 100
relief, 183
religion, 17, 18, 67, 197; act of, 24; sign of, 24
remembering, 234
remission, 138
remorse, and guilt, 33
reputation, 85
research, communications, 121
resentment, 144, 146, 162
resilience, 35
resources, 51; personal, 80
responsibility, 75, 117, 147, 256, 261

ISBN 141202452-8

9 781412 024525